Keeping the Republic

AMERICAN POLITICAL THOUGHT

Jeremy D. Bailey and Susan McWilliams Barndt
Series Editors

Wilson Carey McWilliams and Lance Banning
Founding Editors

Keeping the Republic

A DEFENSE OF AMERICAN CONSTITUTIONALISM

Dennis Hale and Marc Landy

University Press of Kansas

© 2024 by the University Press of Kansas
All rights reserved

Published by the University Press of Kansas (Lawrence, Kansas 66045),
which was organized by the Kansas Board of Regents and is operated
and funded by Emporia State University, Fort Hays State University,
Kansas State University, Pittsburg State University, the University of
Kansas, and Wichita State University.

Library of Congress Cataloging-in-Publication Data is available.

Names: Hale, Dennis, author. | Landy, Marc, author.
Title: Keeping the Republic : a defense of American constitutionalism /
  Dennis Hale and Marc Landy.
Description: Lawrence: University Press of Kansas, 2024. | Includes
  bibliographical references and index.
Identifiers: LCCN 2023019865 (print) | LCCN 2023019866 (ebook)
  ISBN 9780700636235 (cloth)
  ISBN 9780700636242 (ebook)
Subjects: LCSH: United States. Constitution. | Constitutional law—
UniteStates. | Law reform—United States.
Classification: LCC KF4550 .H3435 2024 (print) | LCC KF4550
(ebook) | DDC 342.73—dc23/eng/20231016
LC record available at https://lccn.loc.gov/2023019865.
LC ebook record available at https://lccn.loc.gov/2023019866.

British Library Cataloguing-in-Publication Data is available.

Printed in the United States of America

The paper used in this publication is acid free and meets the minimum
requirements of the American National Standard for Permanence of
Paper for Printed Library Materials Z39.48–1992.

Of course, all this was a long time ago in a land far, far away. Perhaps the people of our own times have become wise enough that they do not need to hear these things. I personally think the younger generation in particular needs to hear such things. That is because these young people must now try to pick up the pieces left over from a Baby Boom generation that thought itself very wise indeed.

—*Hugh Heclo, "Thinking Institutionally," address at Boston College, April 5, 2013*

Our Constitution is . . . intended as a protection against those who consider themselves wise enough to disregard it; and to protect ourselves against the impulse to credit their wisdom—to which error we are particularly prone in times of anxiety.

—*David Mamet,* National Review, *July 6, 2020*

Because Roman civilization died following the barbarian invasions, we are perhaps too much inclined to believe that civilization cannot die in any other way.

—*Alexis de Tocqueville,* Democracy in America, *vol. 2, ch. 10*

Contents

Acknowledgments

We are especially grateful to our Boston College colleagues Shep Melnick, Peter Skerry, Robert Faulkner, and Christopher Bruell for their encouragement, tough love, and discerning criticism. Our dear friend Steve Thomas provided sage advice and steadfast support. We would also like to thank our Kansas editor, David Congdon, and our series editors, Jeremy Bailey and Susan McWilliams Barndt, for their encouragement and their incisive criticisms.

Keeping the Republic

Introduction

"The Constitution Is Broken and Should Not Be Reclaimed." This headline from a *New York Times* editorial, written by two law professors (from Harvard and Yale), is simply a more hyperbolic expression of a point of view that has become increasingly prominent in the writings of law professors, journalists, political scientists, and politicians who deem the Constitution to be not only "broken," but also "paralyzing," "undemocratic," and "obsolete."[1] Even more prevalent are arguments for abolishing or radically changing key aspects of the document: the Electoral College, the Senate, the amendment process, the presidential veto, and the lifetime appointment of Supreme Court justices.

Keeping the Republic is a defense of the American constitutional order, and a response to its critics, including those who are estranged from the very idea of a fixed constitution.[2] The central argument of the book is that the Constitution provides for a free government because it places effective limits on the exercise of power. This is an essential ingredient of any good government—even one that aims to be a popular government. That the people should rule is a given among republicans; that the people can do anything they want is a proposition that no sane person could believe. Thus, the limits that the Constitution places on American political life are not a problem, but a solution to a problem. That problem we define more precisely as the difficulty (even the danger) of popular government in a *massive modern state* (the focus of chapter 1). The United States was the first nation to attempt this.

The way in which a people can live, including the way they can hope to be governed, is determined by several things: the natural and social environment; the country's size; the bellicosity of its neighbors. For example, do the people live in a verdant, crop-friendly environment, or do they live in a desert?[3] It is impossible to imagine the way of life of the English people transposed to Arabia. Is the social environment congenial to widespread participation? Alexis de Tocqueville argued that the availability of land in North America, and the absence of a "landed aristocracy" whose political privileges were tied to their property holdings, made America a profoundly different place, socially as well as politically, from Europe—the first truly *democratic* society, the first nation where it could be said that an "equality of condition" prevailed among the citizens.[4] Another important variable is what the public thinks a "good" government looks like. How the citizens define "good" will set the parameters within which founders—constitution writers—must work. In revolutionary America, the only government that the public would accept as good was a popular government—one that rested on the broad consent of citizens, who would be given the responsibility of choosing their representatives at both the national, state, and local levels.

This understanding of a "good" government was almost unique in the eighteenth century—and there was no nation as large as the United States where it could be found. (Switzerland, for example, had the freest government in Europe in 1787, but it was only one-third the size of Virginia.) This American understanding was the product of many generations of de facto self-government, by a largely English-speaking people huddled on the coast of a largely unknown continent. They had a wealth of experience built up over these generations in such practical matters as how to elect a legislature, how to govern a town, how to choose and then place limits on their governors, and how to tax themselves for their own good.[5] They were accustomed to living in freedom—and they were accustomed to the kind of equality that is possible when there are no lords or bishops in the neighborhood to tell them what to do, and no arbitrary restrictions on either movement from place to place, the ownership of land, or the selection of a profession or occupation.

When it came time to reconstruct the political order after the defeat of the British, the relevant models were therefore close to hand. That they did not work perfectly during the years of the Articles of Confederation—a time of interstate as well as intrastate conflict—required a second effort: the Constitutional Convention that met from mid-May to mid-September 1787. That convention created a national government much different from the one under the Articles, and a new relationship between that government and the much older governments of the former colonies, now states. It this particular ordering of American political life that this book will attempt to explain and defend.

First, however, it is important to note the significant obstacles to stable popular government that are presented by any modern state—even its American version. It is important to notice also that *modernity itself*, as a way of thinking and being in the world, is the original source of these difficulties.[6] It will be our contention that not only did the constitutional framework embody a measured and wise response to the problems of the time, it also remains the best framework for coping with the problems modernity poses for Americans today.[7] We treat the Framers as men who understood many of the problems that modernity brings with it, and who thought very carefully about how to deal with those problems—how to embrace modernity without *simply* embracing it, but in order to tame it.

THE BIRTH OF MODERN POLITICS

To best appreciate the superiority of the American constitutional order it is first necessary to look at the profound transformations, both philosophical and practical, that lie at the heart of modernity, and then enumerate the politically relevant challenges that modernity presents to all governments. Modernity is above all a way of thinking about the relationship between the individual and the community, and it is difficult sometimes to appreciate the novelty of what, for so many generations, we have simply taken for granted as true: that human beings are created equal, that they have "natural rights" that governments are obliged to protect, and that the test of a good government is whether or not it makes possible the "pursuit of happiness" for the maximum number of citizens. These ideas were not taken seriously, or even contemplated by the mass of citizen/subjects anywhere in the world, until roughly the seventeenth century. Where did they come from?

Although he did not initiate every aspect of that theoretical transformation, the first writer to promulgate it systematically was Thomas Hobbes.[8] Hobbes did nothing less than revolutionize the understanding of human nature. In Hobbes's teaching, humans have no souls; they are simply the sum of their passions. He preaches a thorough-going materialism, in which all natural and human things are reduced to objects in motion. This required a cautious demotion of Christianity, as the moral foundation of the state, and a less cautious demotion of the churches ("the outworks of the enemy") as competitors for the loyalty of the kingdom's subjects. But it also required a critique of the ancient philosophers, most importantly Aristotle, who argued that humans are by nature "political animals," who have a propensity to engage with others to achieve common purposes not realizable on one's own. Humans, Aristotle taught, are not by nature solitary. They also have the power of speech about "good and evil . . . just and unjust," and they seek both to rule, and to be ruled, in ways that strike them as good.[9] By nature, they accept legitimate authority but also seek to influence how that authority is exercised. They are also inclined—at least some of them—to seek the highest goods the city has to offer, which tend to be *virtues* rather than *things*: for example, prudence, greatness of soul (magnanimity), justice, and the honor that the possession of such virtues conveys. Citizens are not simply good or bad. Rather, they are varying amounts of each—although some are wiser, more courageous, or more magnanimous than others. Humans are passionate, acquisitive, cowardly, short-sighted, self-interested, and willful, even as they are brave, reasonable, sociable, discerning, and virtuous. And the same individual might display any of these virtues, or any of these vices, at different times or under different circumstances.

Hobbes did not so much reject Aristotle and the other philosophers of antiquity as he sought to supplant them—to improve on their understanding of politics. Hobbes insisted that the individual is not essentially social or political, but private and alone.[10] There is no innate human propensity to engage in political life. People only join a political community in order to obtain and safeguard the private ends that they cannot fulfill on their own. Unfortunately, left to their own devices, people will succumb to their passions, giving rise to conflict and war and the violent deaths that ensue. Therefore, humans must escape from their natural state in order to satisfy their passions for peace and security.[11] They must leave the "state of nature" and grant the power to suppress the conflicts that passions engender to a sovereign, who Hobbes calls *Leviathan*.[12] This is their "natural right," and it leads to the idea of establishing a form of rule capable of protecting the subjects' lives. Hobbes also praises the quest for "commodious living," by which he means the desire for the comforts made possible by a more vigorous commerce. Although that pursuit must remain subordinate to the quest for security, Hobbes perceives no moral constraint on the natural passion to indulge in the pleasures that only prosperity can bring ("such things as are necessary to commodious living").[13]

Hobbes conceives the world in exclusively material terms. The state can be ruled by reason because it is nothing other than matter in motion and therefore requires no resort to divine intervention. Any effort to explain things with reference to miracles and other forms of revelation Hobbes refers to as "superstition."[14]

The two most dangerous threats to the peaceful regime that Hobbes imagines are posed by religion and the quest for honor and glory: that is, the churches and the aristocracy. Hobbes was all too aware of the deadly impact of religious strife, given the terrible destruction that religious war had already brought to Europe and was now bringing to England. How could people refrain from slaughtering one another when their very souls and their path to the afterlife were at stake? Hobbes sought to redirect human attention away from such "superstitions" to *worldly* matters, especially the quest for peace and prosperity. He could not prove that revelation was a hoax, since the very idea of revelation lay outside his materialist/rationalist model of the universe. (And even *hinting* that it might be a hoax was dangerous.) Rather, by establishing a regime in which subjects would be secure and materially well-off, subjects could be weaned away from a focus on the divine and enticed into concentrating on material concerns. In this way (and perhaps only in this way), the kingdom could be made peaceful—so long as the sovereign was powerful enough to keep the peace.

Honor and glory are natural passions, and so they could not simply be eradicated. The English nobility had made their own contribution to the violent conflicts that had troubled the kingdom for generations. But suppression of these passions would require a weaning process and arguments carefully crafted to appeal to the subjects' fears and desires. The quality of life in a regime dedicated to self-preservation would cause people, gradually, to focus on their material wants, and thus to become less interested in the dangerous passions of honor and glory and more concerned with the safety and comforts made possible by a regime of peace and prosperity. To that end, Hobbes's depiction of the state of nature—life without the Leviathan—was made as gruesome as possible, in order to sober up people who were prone to becoming intoxicated by the quest for power and the honors that accompanied it—by showing just how dreadful life would be in the absence of peace and security.

Power is crucial for Hobbes because it is the means for satisfying passions in the short term, and providing the wherewithal to satisfy them in the future. Power is also relative. If passions clash, one's ability to satisfy them rests on one's power relative to one's competitors. And, since desires and the competition to satisfy them are ongoing, one can never have too much power. This will make subjects ever anxious, and anxiety about the future makes them ever more restless in the present. Happiness therefore requires continual striving. Gaining power is thus a natural human activity, even as the quest for honor and glory represent perversions of that necessary human attribute. This restlessness requires a government powerful enough to keep human striving out of the danger zones (religion, the love of glory) and confined to the zones of private pleasures and enchantments.

Because Hobbes appears to make the Leviathan all powerful, he could be misunderstood to be an advocate of totalitarianism. But this is not the case. First of all, Hobbes introduces the most basic of all liberal ideas, *consent*. People leave the state of nature voluntarily, willingly exchanging control over their own actions in order to achieve peace and security. In this sense the mass of people exerts a power they did not have under any previous regime.[15] For example, in the ancient city, even under a "democratic" constitution, only a very small percentage of the city's residents actually took part in its governing.[16] Second, although the means available to the Leviathan were in principle unconstrained, its ends were limited. It had no other goal than to provide peace and security. Such narrow ends place severe restraints on the sovereign because the sovereign had no right to do things that were not geared toward those ends. Thus, there is no justification for the all-encompassing government implied by the word "totalitarian" or even the highly ambitious, intrusive governments found in modern nation-states. Hobbes is thus the inventor of limited government.[17]

The Leviathan, ironically, turns out to be something of a sheep in wolf's clothing. It is not going to declare war on its great enemies—religion, honor, and glory—but rather, as discussed above, it will rely on weaning people away from such desires by substituting new ones: safety and prosperity. Coming as it did at the very end of the English civil wars (conventionally dated from 1642 to 1651), this argument could not have failed to make an impression, given that those wars had killed roughly 2 percent of the entire population of the kingdom.[18]

We have called Hobbes's teaching "transformative" because it established crucial differences between premodern and modern thinking. A strict materialism is now fundamental, not only to scientific thinking but also to political thinking, as if politics had an affinity with physics. Ever since Hobbes, subjects and citizens are usually conceived not as political animals (as Aristotle taught) but as private individuals who view politics not as an essential part of their natures but rather as a means for obtaining the power necessary to satisfy their desires.

The doctrine of "natural rights" has also undergone a transformation. The most important fact about "human nature" is the fear of death and the desire to live a life of comfort and security. Politics is not a way to seek the rich variety of goods that a well-governed community makes possible, since the competition for such goods is likely to lead to the kinds of civil conflict that only the

Leviathan can suppress. Accepting the Leviathan is the price to be paid for peace and quiet.

And, as Hobbes taught, there is no end to the satisfaction of desires, because satisfying a current desire simply leads to an urge to fulfill future desires. To pursue this quest requires a continued need for ever greater power, which means that life will be full of anxiety and stress. The modern market economy is premised on this principle of supply and demand, the former defined by resources and the latter by desires. In the Christian era, religion once sought to tame material desires, but the post-Reformation religious wars undoubtedly created a receptive audience for Hobbes's argument for subordinating church to state in the interest of peace. Religion would continue to exist, but it would no longer constitute a fundamental claim to the sovereign's right to rule. Indeed, a very large proportion of the citizens of the typical modern state do not worship, even if they do not fully define themselves as atheists.[19]

As Hobbes foresaw, the quest for honor and glory has not disappeared, but it is of no small significance that those seeking to satisfy such passions often pretend not to be doing so. Politicians claim to be merely servants of the people. Overt striving for glory is mostly confined to worlds outside of politics, for example, in the worlds of sports and entertainment, and also of course in the military. Politicians, no matter how ambitious, are understood to be "public servants" rather than "rulers." As we will discuss later, modern principles have not entirely displaced premodern concerns for courage, loyalty, duty, magnanimity, contemplation, and religious piety—but the modern principles have largely pushed the older notions to the periphery.

This fact deprives a modern regime of crucial advantages enjoyed by its premodern predecessors. Since modern citizens do not think of themselves as political animals, they have no natural inclination to form political communities and to undertake the duties and obligations that such communities engender. They are naturally individualist, private, and self-interested.[20] Without an established church, rulers can no longer bathe in the aura of the supernatural, claiming God as the source of their legitimacy. Because citizens are continually restless and dissatisfied as they discover an infinitely expanding set of desires, the ruler will never rule over a placid and contented populace. The people demand liberty and equality, but how is the ruler to provide both of these demands, which are naturally at war with one another?[21]

But if Hobbes hoped to guide both sovereign and subjects in ways that could establish a more peaceful kingdom, he failed. English politics in the generation following the publication of *Leviathan* (in 1651) was hardly peaceful. The monarchy was abolished by the forces responsible for the arrest and execution of Charles I in 1649, and during the next decade the United Kingdom was briefly a republic under the rule of the Protector, Oliver Cromwell (and after Oliver's death, his son Richard). The monarchy was restored in 1660, ending Britain's first and only experiment in republican government.

But a generation after Hobbes, another effort was made to put politics on a new and more peaceful footing—even as English politics was about to enter another period of strife. John Locke's attempt to solve the political problem is found in *The First and Second Treatises of Government*, published in 1689—in the midst of the so-called Glorious Revolution, the political events that are generally considered to have been the origin of the constitutionally constrained monarchy that begins the modern period of English political history.[22]

John Locke and Thomas Hobbes are both paired as "social contract" theorists, although this pairing at first encounter seems puzzling. Where Hobbes seems grim—without the establishment of a commonwealth, life is "nasty, brutish, and short"—Locke appears to be hopeful: the "commonwealth" is the result of a rational decision on the part of free individuals to engage in a social contract, in order to better their chances for a peaceful and prosperous life. Hobbes argues that the people create the sovereign in order to avoid anarchy and civil war, because, as he argued, the greatest fear is the "fear of violent death."[23] Subjects really have no choice but to allow the sovereign whatever powers it needs in order to achieve a lasting civil peace—because this is the reason they created the sovereign in the first place.[24] The message of *The First and Second Treatises* is that individuals, in the natural state, lived without the need for government, until the development of commerce made their lives more comfortable, but also more complicated.[25] This makes Locke's argument seem more benign than Hobbes's argument, but this difference should not mislead us. *In both versions, the political association did not exist until people created it for their own private reasons.* The difference is that in Locke's telling of this tale, it is not simply, or even primarily, the fear of violent death that pushes men into the commonwealth; rather, it is the desire for comforts, prosperity, and the liberty to acquire and manage property.

But first Locke poses this question, in *The Second Treatise*: Since God gave the world to all mankind in common, how is it (some people wonder) that some have use of certain pieces of property that others are not allowed to use?[26] That is, where does *private* property come from? And what are we to make of the obvious inequality of possessions found everywhere?

Locke argued that humans were not, in their "natural state," political beings whose natures impelled them to owe allegiance or form political communities. We know this because reason tells us it is so, but scripture agrees. The Bible tells us, after all, that God created male and female, and gave them dominion over the animals and plants that God has provided for their use. Humans lived in this natural state, without laws to bind them, other than the "natural law," which gives to each individual the right to control what is his own: that is, his labor, and what his labor produces. "To understand political power right, and derive it from its original, we must consider, what state all men are naturally in, and that is, a state of perfect freedom to order their actions, and dispose of their possessions and persons, as they think fit, within the bounds of the law of nature, without asking leave, or depending upon the will of any other man."[27] In the beginning, this rule put a simple limit on private property—whatever could be taken from the common stock for private use, provided that "there was enough and as good left over for others." What we mix our labor with—by catching the rabbit, or growing the grain—is rightfully ours.

We could expect very little difficulty in this natural state, since there was an abundance of food and a scarcity of people.[28] Admittedly, there might be some individuals who would seek to "engross" more than their fair share, but most of what they gathered would spoil before they could consume it. Reason—in this case, the desire not to waste time gathering food that would only spoil—would solve this problem automatically. Some might turn violent, of course, but we could easily kill anyone who threated our life.

The change in this simple arrangement came with the discovery of a substance that had no intrinsic use but that did not spoil, and therefore could "stand for" a haunch of deer or a bushel of apples: gold ("some piece of metal, pleased with its color").[29] Discovering how this otherwise useless metal could be used to "stand for" actual commodities is the beginning of a process of invention and discovery that will have important consequences:

1. Now it *will* be possible to "hoard" more than can be immediately used, since the gold, which can be exchanged for actual produce, will never spoil. More importantly, money makes a *market* possible. Instead of lugging deer legs hither and yon to trade for potatoes, we could stroll

over to the market with coins in our pocket and trade them for the things we need but have not labored over ourselves.

2. Inequality of possessions now becomes inevitable, as some men will be better at subduing the land and producing a surplus.

3. The surplus will actually be a blessing, however, rather than a source of conflict, since more food will make it possible for the population to grow; and

4. Protecting what is ours becomes more difficult, because what we own might be spread over a great expanse of territory, and conflicts over who has the right to which piece of land will become more frequent and more dangerous.

So, men being reasonable (most of them anyway), we discover the need for rules, and therefore for some way of enforcing those rules, and judging legitimate disputes between those who have reasonable claims to the same bits of what "God has given to all mankind in common."

To the obvious question—When was the world really like this?—Locke has a simple answer. "Government is everywhere antecedent to records."[30] We cannot know that this is how the modern world really began, but what we can agree on is that the conflict over property, whenever it first occurred, would have suggested a rational solution. Men would have agreed to form a civil association (a "commonwealth") in order to supply what the natural state lacked: a body to make laws, an executive to enforce the laws, and judges to resolve disputes.

What is missing from this simple story? Everything an English reader would have expected from a "treatise on government." There is no mention of a king, or a parliament, or an established religion[31]—and there could not have been many books published in Locke's lifetime that did not mention these familiar institutions. Locke has simply changed the entire story: nothing in *The Second Treatise* brings up any of the questions and conflicts that had determined the day-to-day lives of Englishmen for the past century. Even more successfully than Hobbes, perhaps, Locke profoundly changed the way in which English readers (and many others) thought, not only about governing, but about the political association itself: where it came from, why it is essential, how it should be governed.

Most importantly, Locke explains that "free and equal" individuals would only have agreed to leave the natural state and "put on the bonds of society" in order to better secure the rights they had by nature but that they could no longer secure properly in the absence of government. Locke defined these rights as "life, liberty, and estate."[32] Only a government that could reliably protect these rights could have a legitimate claim on the citizens' loyalty. This argument, of course, explicitly rejects the traditional English understanding of loyalty, which is that loyalty is owed by those below to those above: to knights, kings, and bishops. But the knights, kings, and bishops have been swept from the board; what remain are the individual members of society (the pawns?), who will owe no allegiance to anyone or anything to which they have not given their consent, either directly (at the moment the commonwealth is created) or indirectly—by accepting the benefits of a peaceful civil commonwealth, without which they would be back in the state of nature, chasing deer and picking acorns, like their long-ago and long-forgotten (and perhaps imaginary) ancestors.

THE AGE OF NATURAL RIGHTS

The philosophers of the eighteenth century made important additions to the "natural rights" doctrines so important to the English, both at home and in their North American colonies. This period has come to be known as "the Age of Enlightenment." Its central element, as promulgated by its most important progenitors, among whom were the French philosophes, was *reason*. Truth and human improvement depended on the human mind to logically and analytically think through the conditions of existence without resort to preexisting prejudices. As we have seen, this idea is already present in Hobbes, but he saw the decline of unreason as a weaning process. In particular, subjects would be "weaned" of their various religious enthusiasms by an appreciation of what the commonwealth is designed to provide. Locke referred to this great benefit as "peace, quiet, and property."[33] French followers of the philosophes had a significantly different goal in mind: "liberty, equality, fraternity," all of which would need to be imposed on political life immediately, even if that meant bloody suppression of the "unreasonables."

The fundamentality of reason implied universality. As Gertrude Himmelfarb explains, "The function of reason was to produce universal principles independent of historical circumstance and national spirit."[34] Thus, through the rigorous application of reason, social, economic, and political truths could be ascertained, and those truths would enable all peoples to first fully understand their true natures (and their "true natures," of course, would all be identical) and then live and govern themselves in accord with those universal principles.

Reason also implied a commitment to science, understood as "empiricism." To be accepted as valid, propositions had to be subject to empirical verification. If they could not be proved false after being subjected to the most rigorous testing, then and only then could they be considered to be true. This commitment to science had two major effects. It greatly accelerated technological change, which increasingly involved the application of scientific principles as opposed to mere trial and error. And, most profoundly, it undermined religion, since faith was, by definition, not subject to empirical verification—or at least, not in the here and now.

The *political* manifestation of modernity, the modern nation-state, is not simply the product of individualism, natural rights, or the Enlightenment. Nor is it entirely modern. In fact, the particularism implied by the nation—by "nationalism"—is to some degree at odds with the modern principle of universality, yet it has shown remarkable strength—witness Brexit and the Ukrainian resistance to a Russian takeover. And, quite obviously, abstract reason does not dominate political decision making, despite the dreams of the philosophes. Yet one should not underestimate the importance of reason, materialism, individualism, science, technology, and the selective impact of universality as embodied in the concept of natural rights, to the modern project. As stated earlier, most modern governments are secular, with no official link between ruling and religious faith.[35] They claim to rely on the consent of the governed. Modern states acknowledge (or pretend to), and try to secure, the universal principles of human and civil rights. They claim to base themselves on reasoned political ideas and gain legitimacy from doing so. Their geographic, economic, and demographic contours would be impossible if not for the revolutions in transportation, manufacture, food production, and communications that the practical application of science and the unleashing of human appetites has brought about. And, at least for the many millions, including many who profess religion, the power of secularism and modern science brings with it a preoccupation with things of this world.

The Framers were deeply influenced by Hobbes and the great liberal philosophers who came after him, especially Locke, Montesquieu, and Hume. *The Federalist* more frequently quotes Hume and Montesquieu, but the incorporation of seminal ideas such as natural rights, consent, the primacy of security for life, liberty, and estate displays their great debt to John Locke as well. The

Framers prided themselves on being enlightened and on freeing America from the shackles of feudalism and of founding "a new political science." Later we shall highlight their premodern commitments and understandings, but it is also necessary to keep in mind the degree to which their thought bore the marks of a long tradition of political philosophy.

MODERN POLITICS

Regardless of their specific roots, and because they have multiple roots, the following are the most politically relevant attributes of modernity. In a modern state no person can, without fear of ridicule, claim to be better than another as a matter of birth. Equality is the rule. In the public sphere, rank does *not* have its privileges. Claims of superiority are only considered valid if they are based on a rational principle, merit. Of course, equality and merit are often honored in the breach. But such hypocrisy does not undermine the compelling nature of such claims.

The modern state is enormous in scale. It is true that there are also some small states, but those exist at the sufferance of the large ones that could easily conquer them if they chose to. The United States is not Switzerland—but then neither is France, England, Russia, Japan, or any of the important modern states that have smaller populations than the United States. Before the modern period, large political entities were empires rather than nations, and they lacked the level of political integration, stable borders, and administrative control that modern states enjoy.[36] Self-government is not possible in an empire.

Scale means not just acreage, but people—and large populations are more important than large territories, as Locke pointed out.[37] It is inevitable that the vast populations of modern states will bring diversity with them. Modern states therefore typically encompass many different ethnic, cultural, racial, and religious groups. Sometimes these diverse elements are separated into different regions and locales, but often they are intermingled—and not always harmoniously. Nations as different from one another as Canada, Nigeria, the United States, and India have experienced conflict, sometimes violent, between groups of citizens whose differences of ethnicity, religion, or language were stronger than their commitment to a common national home. Among the large modern states only Japan is ethnically, culturally, and racially homogeneous.

When polities were small, as they were in the ancient republics and in the American colonies, direct rule by the people was at least possible. All the citizens of Athens or of a New England town could gather in one place and deliberate among themselves as to how to address issues of common concern. Because their number was small, citizens had the chance to speak and be heard. Yet because the modern state numbers in the tens or hundreds of millions, direct participation is impossible except for a small fraction, counting both office holders and an activist fringe. Each citizen comes to compose an infinitesimal fraction of the whole. Not only does this place practical limits on direct participation, but it also makes it very difficult to resist the conclusion that any one individual is simply too insignificant to matter politically and, therefore, one may readily become passive. Because all modern states claim to rule in the name of the people, those who belong to it are called *citizens*, not *subjects*, as they would be called in a monarchy. And yet, arithmetic reality threatens to turn them into subjects, in fact if not in name. Thus, the claim of "popular sovereignty" does not, per se, protect against autocratic rule.

In modern states populations are not only large and diverse; they are also highly mobile. Indeed, states like Brazil, India, Pakistan, and Nigeria, which lack many attributes of modernity but have experienced vast improvements in transportation and public health, have also experienced high rates of movement from rural areas to major cities. And these and other poor countries have also contributed to high rates of *global* mobility by migrating in large numbers to the more fully modern states of Western Europe, as well as to Britain, Canada, and the United States. As a result of both international and internal migration, whole new communities and neighborhoods have arisen, but their inhabitants have not yet put down strong roots and continue to live among strangers. The long human era when most people lived and died not very far from where they and their ancestors were born is now coming to an end.

To ensure peace and security, modern states must command and mobilize huge militaries—the twentieth century became the most violent and destructive in human history as a result. But even if a state is peace loving, it still must protect itself from other states that may not share its peaceful outlook, as Britain and France discovered, to their sorrow, in the 1940s. To do so, it must match the military might of the most aggressive and powerful state that might threaten it. Lacking enormous military muscle, it will either be conquered or rendered subservient by a foreign power.[38] And unlike premodern armies, which were helter-skelter affairs, mobilized in haste and demobilized in peacetime, modern armed forces are professionals who remain permanently mobilized. Not only does this strain organizational capacity, but it imposes an enormous recurrent tax burden on the citizenry. Modern states require a level of routine coercive capacity unknown and unavailable to their premodern counterparts.

The government that is strong enough to protect the people is strong enough to tyrannize them as well. Modern history is replete with examples of leaders using their armies and national police forces to terrorize the population or punish their opponents, and of generals ordering their troops to turn their guns on elected governments and to replace those governments with a military dictatorship. Napoleon and Mao were generals before becoming tyrants. Hitler and Stalin established powerful armies and apparatuses of civilian control capable of creating vast empires, repressing dissent, and indulging in the mass murder of millions of their own people as well as millions of those they conquered. What this sad history reveals is that, in addition to the other challenges posed by modernity, modern states can be *dangerous*.

The quest for material well-being and longer lives ensured that the fruits of modern science and technology would be aimed at providing prosperity, longevity, and physical well-being, as well as military capability. As a result, the vast majority of people in a modern state will be wealthier than human beings have ever been, except for the tiniest minority. And in some places even middle-class citizens will enjoy a material abundance unknown even to the premodern aristocracy. Unfortunately, as Hobbes foresaw, well-being does not breed contentment. As citizens' more immediate wants are satisfied, new desires emerge that they seek to fulfill. As productive capacity increases, citizens become less content with their current levels of consumption. When Samuel Gompers, the first president of the American Federation of Labor, was asked what the American worker wanted, he had a simple answer: "more."[39] He was right: modern citizens do not want merely "enough"; they expect the pie to grow larger forever, and for their own shares to grow as well. Thus, the more government accomplishes in providing for people's wants, the more the people pressure it to do even better. The ever-expanding demand to provide for human welfare complements the need for security to make government ever more powerful and intrusive. And, as advances are made in nutrition, sanitation, and medical science, people in modern states live much longer and infant and child mortality decline. Populations will therefore grow, contributing to the problems caused by size.

FRANCE

To better appreciate the Framers' achievement in both acknowledging and constraining the political impact of modernity, it is useful to compare it to the fruits of the other great eighteenth-century revolution, the French, which reached its apotheosis during the Reign of Terror. The French revolutionaries fully embraced modernity, especially reason and its derivative, universality. Reason was both the acid disintegrating the existing barriers to human flourishing—custom, habit, feudalism, religion—and the fundament upon which future flourishing would rest. The rule of reason took many forms. All formal claims to superiority were abolished. There would be no more nobility— nobles lost not only their titles and property, but often their lives as well. Persons would no longer address each other as "sir" or "madam" but simply as "citizen."[40] Because the existing division of the country into provinces embodied noble claims and ancient customs, the old map of France was thrown away. The new map eliminated the provinces and instead carved up the country into *departments* whose borders purposefully ignored existing provincial divisions, and claimed to be based instead on rational geographic principles. The departments had no independent claims to governing authority; their authority derived entirely from their status as administrative units of the central government in Paris.

Time and dates were likewise detached from their irrational designations. Clocks were redesigned to designate hundred-minute hours and ten-hour days. The calendar was decimalized. Weeks were divided into ten days whose names were replaced by numbers. Although there would still be twelve months, each month would now consist of three ten-day weeks, whose traditional names would be replaced by names from nature—for example, Frimaire ("frost"), and Thermidor ("heat"). Historical time was no longer separated into before and after Christ's birth. Instead, history was dated from the first year of the revolution, and new holidays were created to replace the old. There would be no more "irrational" units of weights and measures. These would now be decimalized—100 centimeters to the meter, 1,000 grams to the kilogram, and so on.

The tragedy, and, sadly, the recurring impact, of the French Revolution was that it could not rest content with salutary and/or modest efforts to govern according to reason. It sought nothing less than the full-fledged imposition of life according to fixed, rational principles. This required the fundamental reorientation of the human psyche. Himmelfarb quotes Robespierre as taking on the task of "changing human nature . . . transforming each individual . . . bringing about a complete regeneration . . . and . . . of creating a new people." The French Revolution sought to "change human nature."[41]

Because most people were so steeped in habit, custom, religion, and conventional understandings of how to think and behave, the necessary transformation could not be achieved incrementally, or even peacefully. It required nothing less than a Reign of Terror. Historical estimates vary, but even those at the lower end place the official executions at 17,000. Deaths resulting from the mob violence the revolution provoked, and those who died in prison, elevate that number to 40,000 or more. This amounted to the death of at least one out of every seven hundred residents of France.[42] Regardless of what they were accused of, these victims, and the many more who had their property confiscated and/or who were incarcerated, had no benefit of habeas corpus or trial by a jury of their peers. The guillotine was the chosen method of official execution because of the speed and efficiency with which it could be deployed. For the duration of the Terror the Catholic Church was effectively put out of business, priests were subject to abuse, and church lands were confiscated. Although lip service was paid to liberty, the Terror rendered liberty null and void.

Since they were crafting a constitution for what was clearly a modern state, the American Framers gave great credence to reason, science, and universality. They abolished all feudal remnants[43] and, as Lincoln stressed, they considered the "self-evident" rights enunciated in the Declaration of Independence as the unstated premise upon which the Constitution itself was based. Their path diverged from the French because they did not aspire to *transform* human beings or human nature itself. They accepted human nature as it was, because they understood that human nature cannot be changed. However, they diverged from Hobbes by not claiming that human nature consisted of nothing but the interplay of passions. They sought to devise a form of government that both relied on a premodern understanding of human virtue and sought to compensate for, rather than extirpate, human failings. In *Federalist* 51, for example, Publius recognizes that "If men were angels, no government would be necessary. If angels were to govern men, neither external nor internal controls on government would be necessary."[44] But men were not angels and could not be made to be so. They were passionate, self-interested, and prone to forming factions. They desired power.

They were also virtuous, thoughtful, and public spirited—but not reliably so. To succeed, government would have to adapt to this ambivalent reality. As we shall show later on, the Framers built upon human virtues and sought to check human foibles. They allowed premodern qualities of human life to coexist with modern ones. Humans could aspire to knowledge and progress even as they clung to religion, custom, and other "nonrational" beliefs and practices.

OUTLINE OF THE BOOK

Chapter 1 amplifies the central argument of the book: the need that the Constitutional Framers understood to both adapt to modernity and, at the same time, to discipline modernity to make it compatible with republican government and human nature. It provides a deeper look at modernity and the political challenges posed by the effort to establish a large modern state that is also a republic. We examine the key modern challenges—size, diversity, expertise, administration, dynamism—as well as the perennial threats to republics posed by external and internal security threats, the decline of civic virtue, and the ever-present possibility of despotism. We go beyond conventional, overly mechanistic descriptions of the key constitutional elements to provide a more nuanced understanding of such key components as federalism, representation, and the separation of powers.

The heart of this book is a defense of the Constitution against its long line of influential critics. Chapter 2 provides a "natural history" of constitutional criticism in order to fully appreciate the depth and strength of the most important of those critiques, and to show how they anticipate and undergird contemporary constitutional criticism. It begins with the Anti-Federalists and proceeds chronologically in order to trace the development of anticonstitutional thought as well as the insightful defense of the Constitution by Frederick Douglass. Among the critical voices we consider are Henry David Thoreau, William Lloyd Garrison, Edward Bellamy, Herbert Croly, Theodore Roosevelt, Woodrow Wilson, Franklin Roosevelt and his "Braintrust," and the New Left thinkers who emerged in the 1960s. Chapter 2 ends with a look at the modern political science critique of the Constitution as exemplified by Robert Dahl and by several contemporary legal scholars.

Chapter 3 mirrors chapter 2: it responds to the major criticisms of the Constitution in the generations since its adoption, pointing out how the original constitutional framework, supplemented by crucial amendments abolishing slavery and expanding voting rights, remains the best framework for sustaining a stable popular government.

Critics of the Constitution target several of its provisions, but as chapter 2 demonstrates, underlying these complaints is a deeper critique of the *spirit* of the Constitution, and of the massive republic that it founded. That spirit—indeed, America itself—is said to be inherently undemocratic, fostering excessive individualism, greed, inequality, and corruption. Because the nation's founders indulged the institution of slavery, the Constitution itself is often said to be an instrument of exploitation. It is insufficiently protective of rights, and because it is so difficult to amend, it forces the living to be governed by the dead. Chapter 3 considers each of these underlying critiques, offering a defense of those specific provisions that the critics claim are most undemocratic. These provisions include the Electoral College, the Senate, federalism, state control of election law, and the authority of the Supreme Court. We counter each of these specific objections by explaining the critical mitigating function performed by each of these allegedly "undemocratic" elements of our political and constitutional order.

But before making these counter arguments we address the central error of the critics: their mistaken supposition that America should be a *majoritarian* democracy rather than the *mitigated* democracy created by the Constitution. Critics imply that if all the obstacles to majority rule the Constitution establishes were removed, the American people would be freer and better governed. But the Constitution mitigates, not because it wishes to oppose popular rule, but because it seeks to discipline popular rule by restraining public action. It erects hurdles, not barriers, and it constrains democracy in order to discourage *impulsive* democracy, the notion that majorities should obtain their goals in real time.

The problems with impulsive democracy are perhaps easier to grasp if one considers how one thinks and behaves in one's own private life. No one is immune from feelings of anger, desire, jealousy, and resentment that would prove destructive if acted upon in the moment. Impulse control is a pervasive aspect of daily life. We each find ways to control those impulses. Some avoid walking down the frozen food aisle at the supermarket because they know that if they do they will buy ice cream and eat the whole quart when they bring it home. If impulse control is so critical regarding private matters, why would it not prove equally important with respect to public matters?

In daily life, we frequently change our mind. To avoid mistakes, we refrain from acting until we have the time to revisit the question and think again. We may take the time to talk with friends and colleagues, and, based on those conversations, we may even adopt a different course. In a similar way, the constitutional impediments to immediacy enable such reasoned consideration with respect to public decisions. Because they encourage public officials to act *deliberately*—that is, calmly and slowly—they have the opportunity to think, to engage in prolonged discussion with others, to listen, and to learn. Deliberation is even more important in public than in private life. Whereas the impact of a private decision may be limited to ourselves and those close to us, a public decision affects a much wider circle with a wider diversity of interests and outlooks. Therefore, collective decision making is about far more than finding the "right answer" to a problem. Critically, it involves efforts to talk the problem through in the hopes of reconciling differences, or, at least, of making compromises in an effort to minimize the sense of loss on the part of those in the minority. Because interests and outlooks do inevitably diverge, especially in a large society, it is rarely possible to make political decisions that satisfy everybody. The inevitably of conflict heightens the importance of deliberation because it is only through extensive, reasoned discussion that decisions can be reached that do the best job of keeping the social fabric intact.[45] Thus, the Constitution's checks on democracy are not intended to obstruct the popular will, but to restrain it.

Fortunately, the difficulties inherent in taming impulsive democracy were mitigated by a crucial extra-constitutional development: the advent of political parties, and more particularly the two-party system. The Constitution does not mention political parties; indeed, the Framers were opposed to them because of their capacity to foster divisiveness, or what we would now refer to as "polarization."[46] But in attempting to discourage partisanship, the Framers did not fully account for the *political* character of human beings. In a popular government the people will insist on playing a major role in the choice of *all* their national leaders—not only the members of the House of Representative, but also the nation's chief executive. This is precisely what the Constitution enables. But choosing their leaders from among a collection of (sometimes) ambitious men, not known to the voters personally, presents a challenge that the Framers did not anticipate: how to tell the sheep from the goats. Choosing a national legislature—or even a state legislature—will not be like choosing town officials, whose character and abilities are likely to be known to the people in town. In a large country parties are therefore inevitable because they provide a (usually) rational principle for sorting candidates, based on each party's general understanding of how government should be conducted. Luckily the Constitutional acknowledgment of state-focused governance, the encouragement that the Twelfth Amendment gives to a presidential/vice-presidential ticket, and the imposition of state control over elections actually encouraged the formation of the decentralized two-party system that at least until recently has been a crucial reinforcement of mitigated, deliberative democracy.[47]

However, the future may be far worse than the past or even the present. The title of this book comes from a quote attributed to Benjamin Franklin, who was stopped on the street in Philadelphia after the Constitutional Convention and asked this question: "What kind of government have you given us, Dr. Franklin?" To which Franklin replied: "A republic, madam, if you can keep it."[48] As the title of this book suggests, the problem of "keeping the republic" persists, and the fact that political parties are increasingly unable to perform their historic role is one of the most profound threats to sustaining republican rule.

This moment in our nation's history has produced more than the usual amount of complaints about the Constitution. Democrats object to the fact that in two recent elections, the Republican candidate won the White House with a majority of the Electoral College votes but a minority of the popular vote. George W. Bush defeated Al Gore in 2000 by winning Florida (Gore had lost his own state of Tennessee)—while getting roughly a half-million fewer votes than Gore nationwide. Donald Trump defeated Hillary Clinton in 2016 by winning the Electoral College while losing the popular vote by almost three million votes. Democrats are also angry at the Supreme Court, for a number of reasons: "giving" the 2000 election to Bush; challenging President Obama's signature health-care law by finding an essential part of it to be unconstitutional; refusing to intervene in a controversial Texas law sharply restricting access to abortions; and, most recently, overturning the 1965 *Roe v. Wade* decision, thus sending decisions about abortion laws back to the states. Democrats have also attempted, so far without success, to replace state authority over election laws with a single federal statute, ostensibly to prevent the "suppression of minority voter turnout."[49]

We will have a lot more to say, of course, about the Constitution and its critics. But the original motivation for writing this book was the growing sense of anger at the Constitution and mounting impatience with the restrictions it places on the gratification of immediate political impulses and demands—all of which were noticeable even before the controversies engendered by the COVID-19 pandemic.

But this defense naturally raises an important question: If the political order the Constitution provides for is so excellent, why has confidence in the constitutional design declined in modern times? And does this decline have something to do with the drastic decline in the level of trust that citizens accord to their government? To further complicate the issue, the low level of trust, which has descended into the teens, coexists with strong public support for the notion that the federal government should do *even more* to improve the lives of the people, often in the form of "programmatic rights" that only the government can secure.[50] As James Q. Wilson astutely observed, the traditional *legitimacy* barrier has been broken in modern times. The citizenry and its elected representatives no long ask two questions about a proposed policy: is it a good idea, and is it constitutional? They are content to ask only the former.[51] Nor do they limit rights claims to those included in the Bill of Rights, which places the most important constraints on government. Rather they claim a right to such diverse *things* as health care, a safe and clean environment, and a guaranteed income that only the apparently untrustworthy government can provide—and only if it is given even more power than it already has.

In Chapter 4 we address these bedeviling questions. To find the answers, we revisit the most critical periods of twentieth-century policy transformation: the New Deal and the Great Society, where we find important examples that remain *in the constitutional grain* but also key examples where legislation has run counter to the grain in obvious and destructive ways. By the term "constitutional grain" we do not mean what a lawyer might mean when using the term "constitutional." We are purposely choosing a metaphor from outside of politics, borrowing instead from another practical art: carpentry. Working *with* the grain rather than *against* it is a way to make the end result more durable and even more attractive. In constitutional terms, working with the grain of the Constitution is a way to deal with the problems of modern life that comports with our deepest political principles, and with the way in which the constitutional regime was meant to operate.

It's also a way to profit from an important lesson from the Founding era: when contemplating the pursuit of valuable public ends, it makes a great difference precisely how those ends are accomplished. The Constitution established a granular structure designed to promote deliberation, consensus, and public participation, without surrendering the values of stability, energy, and legitimacy—conceding, by the way, that such a government might sometimes be slow to act. Additionally, the Constitution supposes that there are some things a national government can do well, and some things that it cannot do well—and therefore should not attempt at all. Some things, that is, are best left to levels of government closer to the problems at hand. To use the simplest example of what the Framers meant, the federal government is demonstrably better at sending a man to the moon than it has been at improving math and reading scores in a local grade school.

It is well to remember as well that the government can and must remain energetic, but it can and should do so without undermining those constitutional arrangements that have made popular, representative government possible in the world's largest democracy. The difficulty develops when judicial and bureaucratic excesses and congressional inattention cause problems to be attacked with methods that distort constitutional forms and principles. Not only do those distortions threaten our liberty, but they are often ineffective as well, and therefore sap government of its energy (and tax revenue), as well as the public confidence it needs in order to govern legitimately.

Chapter 4 concludes with an examination of public policy-making since the late 1960s, in order to solve the mystery of how robust progressive policy expansion continued even in the absence of progressive majorities in Congress or among the voters. Public policy continues to frequently go against the constitutional grain even though the Democratic Party dominance that undergirded the New Deal and the Great Society has waned. From 1968 to 2020 Republicans held the presidency for more years than the Democrats, and divided government has dominated the Congress, yet no serious retrenchment has taken place.

The key to solving the mystery is to recognize how two key aspects of modern policy-making work to hide the true costs and the practical import of what the government is actually doing. Contemporary American government is unusually opaque, conducted largely out of sight, and driven by legislation that is more often than not exceedingly long, excessively detailed, and therefore increasingly difficult for even the most well-informed citizen to understand. To take one perhaps extreme comparison: the Wagner Act of 1936, which aimed to transform American labor relations, was only eight pages long; the Affordable Care Act of 2009, which aimed to transform health insurance, was 906 pages long.[52]

As Chris DeMuth has argued, the real price tag of expansionary American public policy is greatly understated by two forms of "taxation evasion"—regulation and deficit spending.[53] Because the public does not see the true cost of ever-more-expensive federal programs, it is all the more willing to ignore the breakdown of the legitimacy barrier. This is especially true for the many citizens whose incomes do not generate any federal income tax obligations.[54] In addition, federal regulation hides the true costs of programs by shifting the burden from the federal budget, and hence from the taxpayer, to the private sector and to state and local governments. Congress has been unwilling to increase taxes since the late 1960s but has pursued several ambitious and expensive goals via regulation instead: to improve the environment, make workplaces safer, increase handicapped access, and myriad other policy ambitions. However, since the private sector can for the most part pass along the costs of compliance to consumers, the public pays—but does not know how much it is paying, or even that it is paying at all.

Deficit spending has the same obfuscating effect. The public has the mistaken impression that government expansion is coming free of charge because the government does not pay for it in real time by raising everyone's taxes, but defers payment to the future through the mechanism of debt finance. It borrows money by selling bonds, taking advantage of the fact that global investors (e.g., China) consider the United States to be a solid credit risk. But eventually these bonds will have to be redeemed, which means that Americans are trading current pain for pain imposed on their children and grandchildren. As of 2020 the federal debt was the highest in the nation's history, and not only in peacetime. It has now surpassed the debt incurred to pay for the Second World War—and yet congressional Democrats are currently hoping (as we write) to spend $3.5 trillion more on "physical and social infrastructure."[55]

The other crucial means of hiding what the government is doing is what Shep Melnick calls "leapfrogging." Leapfrogging occurs when either a court or an agency takes an initiative; the other branch then adds to the regulation and sends it back to the first, which in turn makes the regulation a bit more demanding.[56] Originally devised as a means to prevent the Nixon administration from retreating from Great Society goals, leapfrogging soon outgrew its initial partisan purpose. It has now become standard operating procedure during Democratic as well as Republican administrations, as agency officials have come to treasure it as a means for implementing policies that might well prove unpopular if they had to pass Congress and be exposed to the glare of publicity. Thus taxation evasion stealthiness is exacerbated by these successful efforts to avoid public scrutiny. Chapter 4 provides many examples of leap-frogging at work in diverse policy areas including civil rights, environment, higher education, and special education.

Of course, the public supports racial and gender equality, better schools, environmental quality, and aid for the physically and mentally disabled—but due to the opaque interactions of courts and bureaucrats it has no clear window into how these policies are actually implemented, or even what the policies actually are. So it falls to Congress to bring the "invisible government" into the light of day and curb it. Yet Congress has abdicated its duty as statutory guardian, ignoring the persistent habit of leapfrogging that circumvents the letter of the law. Its members have become so enamored of proclaiming their partisan proclivities that they have neglected the hard work of framing statutes, debating their merits, curbing the courts, and overseeing policy implementation.

The United States has many of the attributes of a modern state. It will inevitably take on a wide variety of tasks, and those charged with performing those tasks will just as inevitably seek to maximize their discretion in doing so. And now the bureaucrats have acquired a powerful ally in the judiciary. Mindful of the possibility that federal officials might be less than faithful to their assigned roles, the Framers created a key countervailing power—the Congress—hoping that the ambition of its members would drive them to fight against executive and judicial aggrandizement. The future of the republic rests on the willingness of Congress to reassert that noble ambition.[57]

In Chapter 5 we argue that the Framers had a theory about American citizenship, one that was consistent with the constitutional order they brought into being. It seeks to explain how the constitutional order encourages the citizen to think and act politically. The elbow room that federalism gives to local government enables the citizen to fulfill a variety of responsibilities, serving in important local roles—managing schools, libraries, conservation and other committees that supplement the activities of elected local officials, and most especially, serving on juries. What the creation of a powerful national government requires is that citizens acquire a novel political discipline, combining loyalty to the nation with loyalty to, and affection for, their local states and communities. Above the local level, citizens cannot play as robust a role. The nature of representative government requires them to function primarily as choosers. They choose the state and national executives and representatives who will govern them. When citizens shift gears from exercising the civic office locally to *choosing* their government nationally, they will have acquired the ability to recognize in others the deliberative qualities that they have taught themselves. They will then be capable of making what Publius referred to as an "honorable determination"[58]—that is, a sound choice about who will exercise the kind of political responsibilities that citizens will not be able, because of the huge scale of the country, to exercise directly. They will have learned to understand politics well enough to choose those with the qualities they understand to be necessary, and to reject those who lack those qualities. In this way, local politics is meant to be a kind of school where Americans will continue to practice the civic habits and skills that made it possible to establish a great republic in the first place.

What is true of the citizens is also true of those they choose to serve them. Members of Congress, for example, are also meant to be "honorable determiners" who would put aside the urge to "virtue signal," or to demonize their opponents. Instead they would do their duty by crafting constitutionally responsible statutes, revisiting those laws when they produce unanticipated negative consequences, and strictly overseeing their implementation.

The book ends with a consideration of the greatest challenges to constitutional government that must be faced by both representatives and the citizens who choose them. We remind the reader of the primary goals the constitutional order is expected to accomplish: liberty, equality, justice, security, prosperity, and civic comity—and how the constitutional order enables those goals to be sustained.

CAVEATS

This book traces one consistent pattern of threats to the constitutional order, those posed by majoritarian critics of the Constitution. We do not purport to thoroughly investigate every manner of threat to that order that has arisen. Of greatest contemporary significance, we acknowledge the threat posed by the demagoguery of Donald Trump. His refusal to accept the results of the 2020 election posed a direct threat to constitutional stability. He compounded the damage by egging on the demonstration that then turned into an assault on the Capitol. During the bulk of his term, his anticonstitutional bark was worse than his bite, in part because (as Miles Taylor recounts in his memoir of his service in the administration) Trump's worst instincts were countermanded or subverted by his underlings.[59] But in his myriad "tweets," he consistently overstated the true extent of his powers. Even though in most cases Trump did not follow through with his threats, he nonetheless set a dangerous example. As Landy and Milkis argue in *Presidential Greatness*, the president is the civic educator in chief. It is his duty to instruct the public and its representatives about how to remain in what we will later describe as the "constitutional grain."[60] Constitutional miseducation by the president is therefore seriously destructive. But Trump did not operate in a vacuum. There has been a disturbing trend of doubting the legitimacy of election outcomes, which began with Al Gore's complaints about the outcome of the 2000 election. Hillary Clinton made unsubstantiated claims about a Trump/Russia conspiracy to influence the 2016 election—claims that the Mueller Report did not confirm.

Although the advocates of unbridled majoritarianism are not directly responsible for Trump's behavior, surely their denigration of critical institutional checks on demagoguery—such as an insulated Supreme Court, a partially undemocratic Senate, and presidential selection by leadership-dominated party conventions—fostered the conditions in which a candidate like Donald Trump could come to power. Nor are his predecessors free of responsibility. Starting with Franklin Delano Roosevelt, many of them have contributed to the rise of what Arthur Schlesinger Jr. dubbed "the imperial presidency," a presidency that increasingly escapes from constitutionally prescribed and extra-constitutional checks on his authority.[61]

When FDR ran for a third and then fourth term he did not violate the letter of the Constitution. However, George Washington originated the tradition of presidents limiting themselves to two terms, and that norm served as a crucial check on subsequent presidents treating the office as their personal property. Perhaps FDR's third-term candidacy can be defended based on the critical need to successfully mobilize to fight the Axis. But his fourth-term candidacy embodied just the sort of presidential narcissism Washington's precedent sought to prevent. In 1944 the war was virtually won and FDR's health was failing. Indeed, he died after only three months in office. Surely the republic would have been better served had Roosevelt declined a fourth-term campaign. He did not even deign to prepare Vice President Harry Truman to assume the office in the event of his death, and Truman was not expected to be the one to succeed him in 1948. Although Truman vastly exceeded expectations, he too contributed to the imperial presidency by embarking on the Korean War without seeking or obtaining a declaration of war from Congress. In chapter 3 we discuss President Lyndon Baines Johnson's subversion of the color-blind intent of the 1964 Civil Rights Act by issuing an executive order mandating racial quotas in hiring.

The imperial presidential expansion is bipartisan. Nixon tried to evade congressional scrutiny of the Watergate crime and coverups, although in this case the Supreme Court and Congress rose to the task of thwarting him. In the Iran-Contra scandal, the Reagan administration clandestinely evaded the dictate of Congress. George W. Bush's signing of statements indicating an intention to ignore portions of statutes pertaining to the War on Terror, and Barack Obama's executive orders granting working papers to illegal immigrants, are the most recent pre-Trump examples of the imperial presidency at work. Thus, Trump's usurpations were facilitated by the aggrandizements perpetrated by influential predecessors and by the majoritarian constitutional critics (ironically, since they are by no means supporters of Donald Trump) whose vilifications of the spirit and letter of the Constitution are the failures with which this book contends.

Nor do we ignore the stain of racism, dating back to the arrival of the first slaves in the colonies in 1619. We pay particular attention to one of the most profound analysts of racism, the Constitution, and of American society— Frederick Douglass. We do not pretend that the original, unamended Constitution inhibited slavery. However, we view 1619 as only one of the seminal dates in preconstitutional history. Besides the Declaration of Independence, which speaks a language of universal rights, not rights for "white people," we would include such crucial moments as John Winthrop's speech aboard the *Arabella* ("A Model of Christian Charity"), and the Northwest Ordinance, passed under the Articles of Confederation, which banned slavery in what would later become Ohio, Michigan, and Indiana. Nor, as we discuss in chapter 2, do we accept the 1619 Project's assertation that "Our founding ideals of liberty and equality were false when they were written. . . . The framers carefully constructed a document that preserved and protected slavery without ever using the word. In the texts in which they were making the case for freedom to the world, they did not want to explicitly enshrine their hypocrisy, so they sought to hide it."[62]

"Enshrining and "hiding" fail to convey the full complexity of the Constitutional Convention's consideration of slavery and the profound importance of keeping the words "slave" and "slavery" out of the document (see chapter 2). We acknowledge the deep disparities in life chances between whites and Blacks.[63] Nonetheless we will argue that the current constitutional framework, buttressed by the 1964 and 1965 civil rights laws, no longer impedes serious efforts to diminish those disparities. The problem is not the Constitution but rather the failure to abide by it. As James Madison recognized, in order to maintain fidelity to the Constitution it is important that it become an object of veneration, an imperative that the majoritarian critics we consider fail to recognize.[64]

CHAPTER 1

America as a Modern State

WHAT IS MODERNITY?

The word "modern" has a seductive but contradictory appeal. Who doesn't love "modern medicine" or "modern technology," both of which have immeasurably improved the conditions of human life? On the other hand, who cannot be moved by the horrors of "modern warfare" or "modern tyranny"? Yet it is undoubtedly the case that all of us are drawn, often unconsciously, to the view that "modernity" has so transformed life that anything "premodern" can have no more than an antiquarian appeal.

This view, prefigured in the writings of Hobbes and his successors, as we discussed in the previous chapter, would *seem* to be especially the case in politics, where the reality of the modern state, resting in large part on Hobbesian premises, presents a stark contrast with everything that came before it—even the empires of Rome and Byzantium. Products of the centralizing monarchies of the fifteenth to eighteenth centuries, the modern state is enormous, covering vast territories and home to populations larger than any of the ancient city-states, or any of the fiefdoms and city-states of the Holy Roman Empire.[1] Built by a combination of military conquest and shrewd political management, states like France, Prussia, and the United Kingdom generated new forms of rule, built enormous armies, acquired colonies, and imposed an increasingly centralized rule over their peoples—with more or less success in different kingdoms. Populations grew, economies matured, armies became more effective, and "national" cultures began to spread to the farthest corners of the realm. In the process, the modern state also gave birth to modern revolutions—and, paradoxically, to modern democracy in all of its varied forms.

These enormous states were also more heterogeneous than any of the ancient cities, or than the municipal republics such as Venice and Geneva. Their great size made such diversity inevitable. Consolidating many smaller provinces and cities into a single nation-state meant putting under the same roof populations with diverse languages, customs, and—especially after the Reformation splintered Christendom—religious loyalties.[2] Step one in the process of consolidation was often the task of imposing a single "national" language on the nation—a process that was often resisted, and that (in Europe) was never entirely successful.[3]

Thus, the temptation to ignore the past: if modern states are so different from anything that came before, why pay *attention* to anything that came before? This is a dangerous mistake. For one thing, it encourages us to ignore ancient wisdom, believing it to be, necessarily, irrelevant to our current condition or our current aspirations. Why read Plato and Aristotle when you can read John Rawls and Noam Chomsky? Why bother to study premodern politics when the modern state has so transcended the forms of political community it long ago replaced? But paying close attention to premodern discussions of politics can armor us against the modern conceit that there is nothing to be learned from the distant past—and against the most dangerous of all modern conceits, namely, that *there is no such thing as human nature.* After all, if everything has changed, why should that not also include humanity itself?

POLITICS AND HUMAN NATURE

The Framers of the American Constitution operated with an understanding of human nature that mixed three traditions, in complicated ways: ancient political science, Christianity, and the liberal political science associated with John Locke, among many others.[4] The most trenchant of the Constitution's critics, by contrast, in keeping with much of modern philosophy, reject the idea of a fixed human nature. That view takes its inspiration not from the American Revolution but from the French Revolution. Human beings are products of their environment, the French revolutionaries believed; change the environment, and you change the human. There are no "natural" needs or propensities beyond what is necessary for physical survival; everything else is a product of education and environment.

This chapter describes how the Framers of the Constitution accepted modernity, but at the same time sought to discipline modernity to make it compatible with republican government and human nature. In contrast to the Jacobin tendencies and longings described in this book's introduction, the Framers were at once ambitious and realistic. They accepted human beings as they were and sought to construct a political framework for a modern republic grounded in human nature, considering both its strengths and weaknesses—paying special attention to the *particular* strengths and weaknesses of Americans.[5] The best guide to understanding this complex undertaking is provided by *The Federalist*, the collection of essays by James Madison, Alexander Hamilton, and John Jay written to explain the Constitution to the members of the state ratifying conventions and the voters who would elect them.

MODERNITY AND THE FRAMERS

The Framers were not cynics. Though greatly influenced by previous liberal thinking, they did not fully accept as low a view of humankind as propagated by Hobbes and only somewhat sugar-coated in Locke. But neither did they share the utopian delusion that humans could be perfected, or that the human species could be remade from scratch—a view that separated them from their revolutionary counterparts in France, who never doubted that humanity could be made again—an aspiration shared by their ideological descendants in the revolutions of the twentieth century. Under the spell of this idea, the French revolutionaries created a series of regimes that alternated between civil war, tyranny, and weakness, failing to achieve *any* of the aims of the revolution—liberty, equality, fraternity—and failing also to provide the minimum requirements of stability, order, and justice.[6]

Many modern reformers, like their intellectual ancestors, reject the idea of a fixed human nature. In this view, there are no "natural" needs or propensities beyond what is necessary for physical survival; everything else is a product of education and environment. Thus, the enthusiasm for the idea of remaking humanity from scratch.[7] This is where the weakness of so many critiques of the Constitution is most obvious. Because of their dismissal of the need to accommodate human nature, those critics fail to notice *what problem the Constitution was attempting to solve*, and they fail to understand *how* the Constitution proposed to solve it.

As Aristotle taught, man is a political animal. Humans are not by nature solitary. They also have the power of speech about "good and evil . . . just and unjust," and they seek both to rule and to be ruled in ways that strike them as good.[8] By nature they accept legitimate authority but also seek to influence how that authority is exercised. They are not simply good or bad, but varying amounts of each. They are passionate, acquisitive, cowardly, short-sighted, self-interested, and willful, even as they are brave, reasonable, sociable, discerning, and virtuous. And the same individual might display any of these virtues, or any of these vices, at different times or under different circumstances.

As *The Federalist* recognized, man's political nature is not reducible to mere self-interest. It includes also a "proud determination" to *rule* rather than simply *be* ruled, no matter how well.[9] In defending modern improvements in the science of politics, *The Federalist* attempts to preserve republican political life while modifying its practice so as to make it compatible with other human aims. A person can be both a private citizen generally absorbed in his own individual pursuits, spared the vexing and perhaps risky task of continually making political decisions, and at other times a political partisan, entitled to have his opinions taken seriously because each citizen has an equal share in the authority of a republican regime.

The capacity to reason is innate but, *pace* the Jacobins, disembodied reason does not rule us. We are also creatures of our senses and emotions, tied to particular people, places, and things. It is pleasing to say we love humankind, but we do not, and cannot. We love our spouses, children, lovers, friends. We live *somewhere*, not *everywhere*, and if we live somewhere long enough we develop strong ties to a particular place. The origin of the word "patriotism" is the Greek word "pater," father. Our loyalty to a place is akin to a family loyalty. We did not make a reasoned choice about what family to be born into, and in many cases our location is likewise accidental, and yet we normally have strong attachments to both.[10]

Particularity breeds enmity as well as affection. To love the Red Sox is to hate the Yankees. Families and communities may become overbearing. The Constitution responds to both the positive and negative aspects of emotive attachment. It makes only limited intrusions into the private world of neighborhoods, families, and friends, enabling them to flourish. But it also guards against giving those aspects an excessive hold over us. It creates a large republic in which citizens enjoy the ability to move from place to place, to escape bonds of family and place—to leave Boston, for example, so they can root for the Yankees in peace.

The Federalists were not Jacobins, attempting to clear all obstacles in the path of virtue; but neither were they strict disciples of Hobbes and Locke. The social contract considers humans purely in their private capacity. The reason for leaving the "state of nature" is to secure our natural rights—above all, the rights to personal security and property, or (as in Hobbes's more severe version) to preserve life itself. As long as life, liberty, and property are protected, Locke implies, the form that a government takes is irrelevant.[11] But the political aspect of human nature, if it is not to be repressed by despotism, requires a specific form of government, a *republican* form. Properly constructed, a republic not only secures life, liberty, and property; it allows humans to satisfy their intrinsic urge to engage politically.[12] Unlike classical republicans, however, the Framers did not think that this political aspect was reducible to the love of virtue. Virtue played its role, most notably in the love of fame, "the ruling passion of the noblest minds."[13] But as David Epstein argues, the political aspect also has a selfish dimension. People seek to *assert themselves* politically, an urge that is not reducible either to pursuing private interest *or* to pursuing the common good.[14]

Thus, even as they praised England's mixed regime for its capacity to protect life and property, the authors of *The Federalist* criticized that regime for not fully supporting *self-assertiveness*, a task that required a fully republican form of government.[15] Epstein's study probes "why and how *The Federalist* proposes to combine liberalism with a 'strictly republican' form of government."[16] As we shall examine further, the constitutional framework succeeds in allowing these multivariate dimensions of human nature to coexist. Republican government as the Constitution constructs it enables citizens to express both their private and political selves. For example, they can be largely absorbed in the pursuit private goods, or indulge in private pleasures, while being enabled also to dive into the political realm to express their opinions and take public action.[17]

EQUALITY OF CONDITIONS

In constructing a government that was both liberal *and* republican, and that acknowledged the exigencies of modernity, the Framers could count upon a number of attributes that made America better suited to this challenge than other countries. In crucial respects it was already a modern country. It was unique in its lack of a hereditary, landed aristocracy, displaying what Tocqueville referred to as an "equality of conditions."[18] In Europe, the aristocracy owned most of the arable land. Those who actually farmed were mere tenants who had little prospect of ever owning their own farms. By contrast, all Americans citizens were, in principle, equal in status.[19] Obviously, this did not mean that they were equally rich or powerful or famous. None of them had to kowtow to a lord or lady. All could own land, which they could freely buy and sell. Property-holding was widespread. Most Americans were farmers, and thus owning their own farms and being free to sell their crops instilled in them a feeling of independence and self-worth that their land-renting counterparts in Europe could not enjoy.

It is no coincidence that a synonym for "farmer" is "cultivator," implying that enormous care, art, and patience are required to grow things well. It is unlikely that those who are mere tenants, who might well be turned out, and whose children will not inherit, will be as determined, patient, and successful cultivators as their land-owning American brethren. American farmers developed a deeper involvement and attachment to their land and, by extension, to their localities. It was precisely this experience of freedom for the many, with access to land and the possibility of prosperity, that underlay the enormous power of the Declaration's proposition that "all men are created equal, and are endowed by their Creator" with the unalienable rights to "life, liberty, and the pursuit of happiness." As we will see, this meeting of experience and idea—so obviously incompatible with the institution of slavery—meant that one or the other, either equality or slavery, would have to be extinguished.

Although not all Americans supported the revolution,[20] for the most part Americans fought the British and not each other. By contrast, the French Revolution was rooted in class warfare. French aristocrats fought bitterly to retain their privileged position and then their very lives. They lost, but the mass executions and property confiscation the aristocracy suffered nurtured a profound and continuing hatred of and condescension toward the "unwashed" uncultured masses who had defeated them. More damaging still, those masses transposed their hatred of aristocracy into hatred and suspicion of their "betters," whoever they might imagine them to be.[21]

Britain did not suffer from armed class warfare—aristocratic privilege declined gradually during the nineteenth and early twentieth centuries, although it did not disappear entirely, and neither did the aristocratic class itself. Nonetheless, the bitterness bred of class divisions bedeviled British life as well.[22] In America, the lack of a landed aristocracy kept the poison of class warfare from inflaming the population. Although Progressive historians would later claim that the Constitution was written for the benefit of the upper class, this was not the perception of the majority of Americans. They would never have voted to ratify a document designed to harm them, and since most of them were property owners themselves, the protection that the Constitution offered to the rights of property was welcomed, not resented.

And it helps to be lucky. Although the 1780s witnessed a good deal of chaos and the potential for insurrection provided by Shays' Rebellion,[23] on the whole the Framers still bathed in the afterglow of the American Revolution. Partisanship, an inherent fact of human relations in a free country, had yet to take root and grow to its full potential. Americans were still, for the most part, the children of the Declaration of Independence and open to endorsing a political framework that embodied the revolution's great promise of life, liberty, and the pursuit of happiness—a promise that the Federalist faction argued, convincingly, could not be kept without a new and better frame of government. Bitter partisanship would come in time, but only after the Constitution was in place and George Washington's first term had built sufficient support for it that it could survive intact the bitter battles between Federalists and Republicans that would follow immediately.[24] Such luck cannot be replicated. One has only to think about how contemporary partisan and factional feuds would permeate a new constitutional convention to see just how fortunate was the timing of the original one.

Most importantly, as it went about the task of constituting itself as a powerful yet free government, America benefited from the high level of political experience and sophistication to be found among its people. By the time of the writing of the Constitution, the American colonies had been largely self-governing for more than 150 years—the equivalent of six or seven generations. Unlike any of their contemporaries, except the Swiss, Americans were habituated to self-rule. They had actual experience in coping with the complex circumstances that human nature poses and modernity imposes.[25]

For the most part, Britain had chosen not to intervene in the day-to-day matters that dominated colonial political life. After all, most colonists were English and identified strongly with the mother country, so why spend the time and effort to tell the colonists how to live? So long as the colonists promised to govern themselves in ways that were "consistent with the laws of this our realm of England," the monarch was content to leave them alone. In any case, the British were, for much of the time, engaged in a series of desperate conflicts: a regicide, the abolition of the monarchy and the establishment of a "Commonwealth" under Oliver Cromwell, a religious civil war, and finally a restoration of the monarchy and its "taming" during the Glorious Revolution. They had little time or energy for the close supervision of their colonies.

This laissez-faire attitude changed abruptly in the 1760s in the wake of the French and Indian War.[26] Winning that war had been very costly. The British government felt strongly that the colonists should pay their fair share of those costs, especially since in the minds of the British government, a prime purpose of the war had been to protect the colonies from French armies and their tribal allies living along what was then the American frontier. When the colonies balked at paying taxes they had not voted for, the British exerted much harsher and coercive forms of direct rule including, in some instances, quartering British troops in American homes and shutting down colonial legislatures. But by then it was too late. The Americans had had several generations of experience in governing their own affairs, in their towns and their colonial assemblies. Never in human history had such a large fraction of a nation's population participated in its political life. Americans had acquired the habits of self-rule and the self-assertiveness that self-rule encourages. Without such habits they could never have endured the hardships involved in the five-year struggle to defeat the British. And, having so actively participated in political life, they could appreciate its difficulties and dangers, especially the need to reign in the passions of the moment. Thus, the majority were willing to support the restraints on simple majoritarian democracy that the Constitution imposed. They viewed such checks as promoting reasoned, deliberate decision making—not as plots designed to promote privilege and elite rule.

THE BRITISH HERITAGE

Americans benefited greatly from their British heritage. Britain was not a republic, and yet to a far greater extent than other monarchies it embodied a spirit of liberty. The Glorious Revolution of 1688–1689 had stripped the monarchy of any claim to absolutism. The monarch would rule in collaboration with an elected House of Commons and a hereditary House of Lords. The franchise for electing members of the Commons was very limited, but it did include a sizeable number of citizens who were not members of the titled nobility. Thus, long before the creation of the United States Congress, Britain had established a powerful legislature upon whose support the monarch depended for the resources needed to conduct the business of government.

The British legal system was rooted in the common law, the essential principle of which was respect for the habits and customs of the people. Judges were responsible for defending those habits and customs even if they conflicted with the will of the king or the letter of statutes. As James Stoner argues:

> Common law was, in the first place, the immemorial customary law of England.
> . . . Though a written code was lacking, the written evidence of common law

was to be found in the records of cases previously decided. To learn the law meant to learn these precedents and the rules of law they established, but also to understand the reasons behind them; it was a maxim of common law that a precedent that ran against reason was no law. It was the judge's duty to discover, not invent, what laws governed the case at hand.[27]

As the quote indicates, a critical means for invoking the common law was trial by jury. Judges declared the law in cases before them with the facts determined by a jury of "twelve good men and true."[28] Along with the judge's judicious application of custom, as embodied in their interpretation of precedent, trial by jury was the "distinctive mark of common law . . . for both customary law and jury verdict might be said to register the understanding of justice in the common mind."[29]

Jacobins and those they have influenced are apt to view "custom" as a barrier to freedom. But as applied by common-law judges, it is rather a check on abuse by the government, no matter how the government is constituted. Even in the absence of a full-fledged written bill of rights, the English people were understood to enjoy rights derived from "immemorial" custom.[30] Absorbed into custom were critical documents dating all the way back to the great thirteenth-century charter of rights, Magna Carta. Thus, despite the weight of aristocratic and royal dominance, the English were, among powerful countries, the freest in the world because of the complex combination of custom, reason, and rights exerted through the common law and the strength of Parliament. Because these principles were so fiercely adhered to, it is possible to speak of a British constitution even though there is no single document framing and enumerating these principles.

As the leaders of the movement for independence kept insisting, they only decided to separate from the mother country because they believed that their rights as *Englishmen* were no longer being honored. When it came time to create a constitution they were hardly likely to adopt a governing framework less devoted to liberty and restraint on government than the one they already knew so well. Indeed, the US Constitution explicitly incorporated such borrowings from England as trial by jury and elected legislatures. The common law, including English precedents, still serves as a legal underpinning in the states.[31]

It is difficult to overstate the importance of this legal heritage. It is why the authors of the Constitution could make some important assumptions about the political capacities of American citizens, and why Tocqueville believed

American democracy had been as successful as it had been up to the time of his visit. It is possible for people to learn a lot in five generations of self-government.[32] As Tocqueville argued, juries are the schoolrooms of democracy.[33] They require ordinary people to deliberate about weighty matters and thus to learn the skills and habits of mind that a decent political order requires. Trial by jury was guaranteed in all thirteen state constitutions and is protected in the original Constitution (Article II, Sec. 2), and in three of the first ten amendments (nos. 5, 6, and 7).

Because they were embarking on a new venture in self-government from which monarchs and aristocrats were absent, Americans saw the need to put their principles and their governing framework in writing. But as inheritors of British tradition they well understood that a constitution was not merely a written document. It was more than a set of rules. It was the fundamental assertion of guiding principles and practices on which all laws would be based, now and in the future. It could only succeed if it could inspire the same depth of veneration that its unwritten British predecessor inspired, which could only happen if it too became embedded in custom.

Poverty and ignorance are enemies of free government. Colonial Americans were fortunate to enjoy both widespread prosperity and literacy.[34] Their farms were sufficiently productive to allow them to produce surplus crops to bring to market. They developed an extensive commerce not only within and between the colonies but with Europe and the Caribbean as well. Americans also exploited abundant natural resources—timber, iron, furs, fish—for sale to Europe, where such commodities were in short supply. The abundant export trade encouraged the development of a large commercial shipping fleet that profited not only the ship builder and ship owners but also the merchants who financed the cargoes and profited from their eventual sale, as well as from the sale of the imported goods that Americans could afford to buy.

Most Americans could read and write and thus have access to politically relevant information. Literacy rates were especially high in New England but were also high in the Middle States. Even in the South, most free people could read and write. Books were in large supply. In 1776, its first year of publication, Tom Paine's *Common Sense* sold half a million copies, meaning that it was purchased by 20 percent of the free population. Since a single copy might well be read by more than one person, its total readership may well have risen to close to half the population.[35] This highly literate public was capable of digesting the subtle and sophisticated reasoning that produced the

Constitution as well as arguments made in support of its ratification, most notably in *The Federalist*.

As we have seen, the colonies had, in large measure, functioned as republics for many years. The one certainty about postrevolutionary life was that they would insist on sustaining republican government. And yet the 1780s experienced grave threats to continued republican rule. Dire conflicts had broken out between states, and within them. Shays' Rebellion had demonstrated the potential for domestic insurrection.[36] *Federalist* 9 argued that that these difficulties were not idiosyncratic but were endemic to small republics. All previous republics had been small. None of them had lasted very long. *Federalist* 9 admits that life in the republics of Greece and Italy could "dazzle" and have "momentary rays of glory," but these were, sadly, transitory. Publius marvels in No. 9 at

> the distractions with which they were continually agitated, and at the rapid succession of revolutions by which they were kept in a state of perpetual vibration between the extremes of tyranny and anarchy. If they exhibit occasional calms, these only serve as short-lived contrast to the furious storms that are to succeed. If now and then intervals of felicity open to view, we behold them with a mixture of regret, arising from the reflection that the pleasing scenes before us are soon to be overwhelmed by the tempestuous waves of sedition and party rage.[37]

These small republics all gave way to despotism. America could only avoid such a fate by creating a union of the states. We shall soon see that the "firm union"[38] the Constitution established preserved many of the virtues that attach to small republics, but it also created a central government strong enough to quell insurrection and preserve sufficient harmony among the states. To support the case for union, *The Federalist* quotes Montesquieu:

> This form of government [a union] is a convention by which several smaller STATES agree to become members of a larger ONE, which they intend to form. It is a kind of assemblage of societies that constitute a new one, capable of increasing, by means of new associations, till they arrive to such a degree of power as to be able to provide for the security of the united body. . . . As this government is composed of small republics, it enjoys the internal happiness of each; and with respect to its external situation, it is possessed, by means of the association, of all the advantages of large monarchies.[39]

THE CONSTITUTION AND THE CHALLENGE
OF MODERNITY

The Constitution could succeed in producing an enduring union because it was able to reconcile a profound understanding of human nature with an equally impressive understanding of the challenge modernity poses to republican rule. We enumerated the key politically relevant aspects of modernity in the introduction and at the beginning of this chapter. We return to them now to show how the constitutional order copes with them.

The first reality of the modern state is its enormous scale. A modern state operates at a scale previously attained only by great empires—whose citizens were not expected (even by themselves) to participate in their own governments. Modern states exist over vast territories encompassing huge populations. This is a nearly universal condition, because once a single state becomes large, its neighbors must emulate it or face conquest.[40] Small states exist only at the sufferance of the greater powers. Because the modern state numbers in the millions or even tens or hundreds of millions, direct participation is impossible—and this was true in America as soon as populations outgrew the "town meeting" ideal that was so important to the earliest colonial governments. Each citizen comes to compose an infinitesimal fraction of the whole citizenry. Not only does this place practical limits on participation, but it also makes it difficult to resist the conclusion that any one individual is simply too insignificant to matter politically and, therefore, one may readily succumb to political passivity.[41] As Henry David Thoreau is said to have complained in the 1820s, 1/20 millionth of a sovereign is not much sovereignty; each American now constitutes only 1/330 millionth of a sovereign. All modern states claim to rule in the name of the people, and so those who belong to it are called citizens rather than subjects, as they would be called in a monarchy. And yet, arithmetic reality threatens to turn them into subjects, in fact if not in name.

The American Constitution accepts that small republics are things of the past. It provides for a large republic, strong enough to protect its citizens while still preserving liberty. The key is *representation*. Indeed, Madison sees representation as the essential characteristic of a republic since those small enough to allow citizens to rule directly are doomed.[42] Note also that the ancient cities had highly restricted citizenship requirements, so that typically only about 10 percent of the city's residents could actually take part in its government, even under the most democratic constitutions. In Aristotle's time, the population of Athens was roughly 400,000, of whom approximately 21,000 were citizens. Estimates of how many actually attended meetings of the assembly are as low as 6,000.[43]

But modern democracies enfranchise all adult citizens, rather than the privileged few, which makes some form of representation inevitable. It makes a difference, however, how large the representative assembly is: the larger the number, the smaller the districts can be, magnifying the power of each citizen's vote. Yet there is an obvious trade-off—a larger legislature can have smaller districts (good for representation), but if it is too large it cannot function (which is worse for representation). Where should the line be drawn? A sharp debate took place during the Constitutional Convention over whether congressional districts would have populations of 30,000 or 40,000—the decision to stick with the smaller number was a concession to those who worried that larger districts would dilute the representative quality of the legislature. The House of Representatives is much larger now, of course, its size having been fixed at 435 in 1929, and the population of a House district has reached 710,677 (based on the 2020 census).[44] Are House districts now so large that citizens cannot make their own voices heard at critical moments? Is the legislature so large that not even a lone representative can make a difference?[45] This is an important question, since if the number of representatives is kept to a reasonable level, they can all get their chances to speak, during floor debate or in committee hearings—to *assert themselves*. And they have the opportunity to engage in the quintessential republican activity: they can deliberate.[46]

Deliberation gives vent to self-assertiveness because representatives can voice their concerns, their points of view, and their proposed courses of action. But it requires that self-assertiveness be "rightly understood." In order for me to have an impact on the other representatives, I must appreciate *their* self-assertiveness. To be heard, I must also be willing to listen. I must listen to others and even sometimes accede to their proposals, perhaps even at some cost to my own. Because in addition to being self-assertive and protective of one's interests, individuals have the capacity to reason. I might even learn something from my fellows, causing me to redefine my own interests (or the interests of my district) or to recognize that there is an overarching public interest at stake to which my narrow interests must conform in order for those interests to be protected over the long run.

As the contemporary Congress sadly demonstrates, representation is no guarantee that deliberation will actually occur. However, the odds of it occurring are better than in a strictly democratic assembly because popular views will be "refined" and "enlarged," Publius argues in *Federalist* 10,

> by passing them through the medium of a chosen body of citizens, whose wisdom may best discern the true interest of their country, and whose patriotism and love of justice will be least likely to sacrifice it to temporary or partial considerations. Under such a regulation, it may well happen that the public voice, pronounced by the representatives of the people, will be more consonant to the public good than if pronounced by the people themselves, convened for the purpose.[47]

It is true, of course, that representation implies that ordinary citizens will not have such an opportunity—but they need not remain entirely passive. They perform the vital political function of choosing their representatives. This is a lesser political role, but it is still an honorable one. *The Federalist* argues that the success of representation rests on the capacity of citizens to make "honorable determinations" of those who will represent them.

James Madison further explained the virtues of representation through his thoughtful distinction between *passions* and *interests*. Passions are what are mostly likely to provoke conflicts: passions inspired by religion, or loyalty to particular candidates for office, or issues of war and peace, are especially dangerous in a free country, because all citizens are entitled to speak their minds and engage in political activity.[48]

It would be far better, Madison argued, for citizens to concentrate on their *interests* instead of their *passions*. These days, when we hear the term "self-interest," we are likely to equate it with "selfishness," but this is a mistake in the context of the constitutional debate. When citizens are encouraged to think about their self-interest—to think seriously about what is *good for them*, especially in the long term—they are likely to think more clearly than when they are guided by their passions. In a similar way, it follows that legislators who share in making decisions will be inclined, more often than not, to think about what is in the long-term interest of the country itself, as well as each member's own district. Farmers need bankers; bankers need merchants; merchants need manufacturers; manufacturers need employees; employees need cheap food, which means they need successful farmers. And so on.

Because congressional districts are large, so much larger than state legislative districts, the particular interests, often conflicting, that they encompass means that a representative cannot always represent them all simultaneously.

Sometimes the representative will have to pick, from among the various interests in the district, which ones to speak for and which to ignore—and therefore disappoint. Obviously, those disappointed may well oppose his/her reelection—the two-party system makes this not only easy but inevitable—which gives the representative a motive for being as inclusive as circumstances will permit. Members will encourage their constituents to think about what it is they have in common. For however they may differ with respect to their immediate interests, they will differ far less with respect to their long-term interests. For example, creditors and debtors will differ regarding monetary policy, but they both have an interest in a healthy and growing economy and in a stable and solvent banking system. Similarly, various factions might differ with respect to tax policy, but they share a long-term interest in a government that has enough revenue to conduct its business without emptying the pockets of the citizens in the process—or piling up dangerous levels of debt.[49] Thus, the business of the Congress will be, collectively, the business of the nation, alive to parochial concerns but also attentive to the good of the whole.

But identifying the good of the whole is not the same thing as identifying what is good absolutely. That is the quest of philosophy and theology, not a task that can be safely entrusted to a legislative chamber or a political campaign. Thus, the Constitution neither establishes a religion nor empowers the Congress to interfere with either the "free exercise of religion" or the "freedom of speech." Nonetheless, concern for what is a good way of life is an essential element of any society that hopes to be, or to remain, a good society. There were many in the constitutional generation who worried about whether Americans as a whole were capable of maintaining a moral order robust enough to underpin a robust republican regime. John Adams said, "This Constitution was made for a moral and religious people; it is wholly inadequate to the government of any other."[50] Consequently, if the people ceased to be moral, the Constitution would fail. Yet how can a distant federal government supervise the moral education of millions of free citizens, under a constitution that forbids the establishment of religion?

Pondering this difficulty a few decades later, Alexis de Tocqueville was cautiously optimistic. Americans, he concluded, practiced "self-interest well understood," doing the right thing not because it is virtuous "but because it is useful," preferring "to do honor to their philosophy rather than to themselves."[51] That is, they believed that doing the right thing would help improve the community as a whole and therefore benefit themselves in the long run. To illustrate this idea with a contemporary example, some people whose children are grown and no longer use the local schools continue to support spending on the schools, not because it is the right thing to do (they say), but because a good school system will help keep up local property values, and therefore the value of what is, for most Americans, their most important investment.

But *The Federalist* pushes beyond "self-interest rightly understood" to insist that a virtuous citizenry is a necessary precondition for maintaining the constitutional order. This requirement is often ignored by constitutional critics, including Woodrow Wilson, who, as we will argue in chapter 2, viewed the Constitution as a "Newtonian" machine reliant on such interacting parts as checks and balances and separation of powers to keep the machine humming. A more recent scholar has referred to the Framers' belief that the Constitution would be "a machine that would go by itself."[52]

On the contrary: the Framers were no mechanics, Newtonian or otherwise. Citizen virtue remained a precondition for sustaining a republic. But it was not sufficient. The so-called mechanistic attributes, most notably separation of powers and checks and balances, were required to protect citizens *from the government*. *The Federalist* calls these provisions "auxiliary precautions." Despite the safeguards provided by the Electoral College, the indirect election of senators, and the large size of congressional districts, power-hungry and/or venal presidents and representatives might still come to power. "Enlightened statesmen will not always be at the helm," Publius warns.[53] Assigning separate and overlapping duties to the different branches was a vital additional means for ensuring the survival of republican government. In the famous words of *Federalist* 51, "men are not angels." Even a virtuous citizenry may cough up leaders with devilish tendencies.

> But what is government itself, but the greatest of all reflections on human nature? If men were angels, no government would be necessary. If angels were to govern men, neither external nor internal controls on government would be necessary. In framing a government which is to be administered by men over men, the great difficulty lies in this: you must first enable the government to control the governed; and in the next place oblige it to control itself.[54]

Far from presenting a "mechanistic" view of how a government might work, *Federalist* 51 presents a compelling argument about the *psychology of ambition*, and how that psychology might be used for salutary purposes—since there was no hope at all of abolishing ambition, which would be a self-defeating enterprise even if it were possible. A government without ambition is a government that can do nothing, even in the face of catastrophe. Or as General Washington put it after eight years of frustration under the Continental Congress, it would be "a half-starved, limping government that appears to be always moving upon crutches and tottering at every step."[55]

The greatest virtue of separating powers is not merely the carving up of governing responsibilities but the creation of strong independent political authorities whose leaders and members will jealously guard their powers. Since ambition is both vital to the republic and a danger—something we need in order for government to have energy—it cannot and ought not be stifled. Rather, "Ambition must be made to counteract ambition. The interest of the man must be connected with the constitutional rights of the place."[56] Thus, these vital auxiliary precautions provide an additional barrier to despotism while remaining faithful to human nature.

Nonetheless, civic virtue is the bedrock. The most fundamental question, whether republican government is even possible, is reserved to Americans to decide, *The Federalist* argued. That is, Americans have inherited the decisive moment—whether they like it or not. In the very first *Federalist* paper, Alexander Hamilton framed the question in the clearest possible terms:

> It has been frequently remarked that it seems to have been reserved to the people of this country, by their conduct and example, to decide the important question, whether societies of men are really capable or not of establishing good government from reflection and choice, or whether they are forever destined for their political constitutions on accident and force. . . . Happy will it be if our choice should be directed by a judicious estimate of our true interests, unperplexed and unbiased by considerations not connected with the public good.[57]

In his Farewell Address, George Washington acknowledged the overarching importance of civic virtue, whose underpinning is religion and which is inculcated through education. "'Tis substantially true," Washington noted toward the end of the address, "that virtue or morality is a necessary spring of popular government. The rule indeed extends with more or less force to every species of free Government. Who that is a sincere friend to it, can look with indifference upon attempts to shake the foundation of the fabric?"[58]

FEDERALISM

But if citizen virtue is the primary condition necessary to establishing and pre-serving republican rule, how is it to be nurtured and sustained? The Constitu-tion does not provide a direct answer to this question. The terms "education," "morality," and "civic virtue" do not appear in the Constitution itself, although they appear regularly in the debates about ratification and in numerous pub-lic addresses. At a minimum, the Framers faithfully observed the Hippocratic Oath: the Constitution would "do no harm" to the nurturance of civic virtue. They recognized the incapacity of the national government to inculcate vir-tue and the grave dangers of enabling it to try.[59] One has only to imagine the damage that would be done by a federal Department of Civic Virtue in order to appreciate the wisdom of this abstention.

Nurturing and sustaining civic virtue was a job best left to the states, the localities, and the private order.[60] The Constitution limits the powers of the federal government to those "herein granted" in Article I. As impressive as those powers are they do not include the "police power," which is left to the states, and which, in practice, the states largely devolved to the localities. The word "police" in this context means far more than law enforcement (this was, in fact, an era before professional police departments): it concerns the regulation of morals, public education, land use, business law, public works, family and marriage law, the protection of children, and of course enforcing the law.[61] Federalism's division of national and state responsibilities is an in-sightful response to the problem of scale, because it recognizes that certain matters *must* be decided by a national assembly but that many others *cannot* be satisfactorily dealt with on such a vast scale, as Anti-Federalists were always pointing out.

It is sometimes said that the Framers had no theoretical defense of feder-alism and that it was simply a bone that they tossed to those who feared a loss of state authority. As this quote from *Federalist* 9 makes clear, however, the Framers *did* have a clear-sighted understanding of the importance of leaving the police power with the states:

> So long as the separate organization of the members be not abolished; so long
> as it exists, by a constitutional necessity, for local purposes; though it should be
> in perfect subordination to the general authority of the union, it would still be,
> in fact and in theory, an association of states, or a confederacy. The proposed

Constitution, so far from implying an abolition of the State governments, makes them constituent parts of the national sovereignty, by allowing them a direct representation in the Senate, and leaves in their possession certain exclusive and very important portions of sovereign power.[62]

Such power is to be exercised locally because it pertains to the very fabric of local life. Those matters are not only important but are somewhat delicate: how children are raised and educated; how the law is enforced; how the land is used; how the quality of local life is protected. Localities are radically dissimilar from one another; each one has its own texture and needs and no one knows these needs as well as locals do. Thus, the citizenry in its local dimension is enabled to do a lot more than "honorably determine" the choice of its representatives. As Tocqueville would later describe, localities were often rife with political activity. This commitment to local authority was reinforced by the Tenth Amendment, which restates this division of powers even more emphatically. As a result, Americans would experience a level of self-government not found in any other large modern state, while making room for the creation of a powerful union of all the states.

The Framers were sanguine about leaving such critical responsibilities to the states. A great many of them had been involved in state and local government. They were well aware of the "nearly universal concern for the moral and intellectual qualities requisite in citizens and their representatives" that the preexisting thirteen state constitutions contained, including provisions for religious instruction and public education.[63] Stephen Lange provides these quotes from various state constitutions:[64]

"No free government, or the blessings of liberty, can be preserved to any people, but by a firm adherence to justice, moderation, temperance, frugality, and virtue." (Virginia Constitution 1776)

"A constant adherence to those [principles] of piety, justice, moderation, temperance, industry, and frugality, are absolutely necessary to preserve the advantages of liberty, and to maintain a free government." (Massachusetts Constitution 1780)

"A constant adherence to justice, moderation, temperance, industry, frugality, and all the social virtues, are indispensably necessary to preserve the blessings of liberty and good government." (New Hampshire Constitution 1784)

John Dinan shows that such provisions remained in state constitutions well into the nineteenth century.[65]

To accomplish these goals many states required that funding be provided to support public worship and religious education—a policy explicitly denied to the national government by the Bill of Rights. To sustain and expand the high rates of literacy enjoyed outside the Deep South, eight state constitutions explicitly provided for the creation and support of public or common schools, including New Hampshire, Massachusetts (in the constitution written by John Adams), Connecticut, Pennsylvania, New York, Delaware, North Carolina, and Georgia. Other states had similar provisions.[66]

In July 1787, Congress showed its concern for civic virtue by stating in Article 3 of the Northwest Ordinance that "religion, morality, and knowledge being necessary for good government and the happiness of mankind, schools and the means of education shall forever be encouraged." As we have seen, similar language did not find its way into the Constitution itself because the Constitution left such matters to the states. But the Northwest Ordinance created a territory rather than states. Until such time as the regions within the territory petitioned to become states, they were trustees of the national government, which therefore did exert a police power over them that it could not exert over the states themselves. In this role, like state governments, the Congress determined to promote civic virtue. The precursor to the Northwest Ordinance, the Land Ordinance of 1785, prescribed that land west of the Appalachians was to be divided into townships and reserved "lot No. 16 of every township, for the maintenance of public schools within the said township."[67] Notice also that the Northwest Ordinance banned slavery and promised to protect Indians within the territory.[68]

The Framers initially opposed a Bill of Rights, believing that the very concept of limited government that underlay the Constitution, bolstered by the strict enumeration of powers detailed in Article I, and further supported by separation of powers and checks and balances, offered sufficient rights guarantees.[69] They also worried that a list of things the national government would be forbidden to do might encourage future governments to insist that if an action was not on the "don't do" list, it would be legal. But they bent to the will of those who made the Bill of Rights their price for supporting the Constitution, and they were correct. More than a mere "don't do" list, the Bill of Rights provides a critical teaching about what it means to be a citizen of a republic.

Its advocates recognized that no other means was as critical for preserving a free people as the constant reminder of the rights they possessed. Having those rights in the forefront of their thoughts made it all the more likely that the people would resist any effort to impinge on them—and resist also the temptation to steal those rights from others.[70]

Premodern republics were homogeneous as well as small, and so were the relatively small kingdoms and principalities that made up Europe before the modern era. This did not imply that all the Athenians or New Englanders loved, or even liked, one another. But, because of common religious traditions and cultures, they did share similar values and could be expected to abide by similar codes of conduct. They spoke a common language, and most citizens were Christians of one sort or another—the Catholic/Protestant conflict that began in Europe was present also in America, yet it was never as violent. It is much easier to trust and cooperate with someone who is not profoundly different from you, and for this reason, different Christian denominations tended to group together and avoid "apostates." Puritans dominated in New England, Quakers were the dominant religion in Pennsylvania, Anglicans were the largest denomination in Virginia, and so on. Having common views on matters as important as religion made self-rule easier—less contentious.[71] That would change as the population grew and Americans began moving around, encountering social and religious customs very different from what they were used to. Under the circumstances, "tolerance" became at first a grudging necessity and then, gradually (and with important assistance from George Washington and Thomas Jefferson), a positive good.[72]

Because it was settled by such a diverse set of peoples (including the forced migration of Africans), America was the most diverse nation-state in the world. As Bosnia and many other places have shown, ethnic, religious, and racial diversity is too often a recipe for political breakdown. But federalism enabled the Framers to embrace diversity as well as size. Because they exercise the police power, states accommodate diversity by allowing for a very disparate set of policies with regard to such matters as education and family law, matters that differently composed populations would indeed choose to address differently. But the Constitution's version of federalism also provides for a powerful central government, supreme in its own realm as defined by Articles I and VI, and obliged to protect the integrity of the Union. When that integrity was breached, first in the Nullification Crisis of 1832–1833 and then by secession, the full power of the federal government was deployed to prevent a claim of diversity from destroying the Union. Sadly, a civil war had to be fought to forbid the ownership of persons as an allowable extension of the state police power.

The obverse of fractionalization is tyranny of the majority. The modern state dissolves many of the common bonds that rulers had always relied upon in order to keep the peace. Its profound cultural, racial, and religious diversity often breeds mistrust, misunderstanding, and prejudice, presenting political obstacles unknown before the modern age. (After all, if the people do not govern, it hardly matters if they get along with one another; all that matters is that they obey their sovereign.) And because the disparate groups do not exist in equal number, there is great temptation for the larger ones to seek to wield the power of the state to oppress the smaller ones. Such was the fate of Protestants in Bourbon France, Catholics in Britain, Jews in Nazi Germany and Soviet Russia, the Tutsis in Rwanda, and the Uighurs in contemporary China—to cite but a few examples of the fate of minorities in modern states. Even as it protects against the excessive conflict among diverse minorities, a large federal republic also provides insurance against tyranny of the majority. Feeling oppressed where one lives, one is free to move. And the states' police powers mean that different states will provide very different approaches to key aspects of life in common. Therefore, a person who feels devalued or oppressed by the police powers in one state or locale may well find relief by moving elsewhere.

As *Federalist* 10 explains, the large republic obviates tyranny of the majority because the very size and the diversity of its population produces so many different factions that they will be unable to combine to create a long-lived majority. *Federalist* 10 views property as the most "stable and enduring" source of faction (but not the only source). The welter of different property interests the United States encompassed—a variety of crops, fish, livestock, mining, manufacture, commerce—generated serious policy differences. The unstable coalitions that formed over the tariff are a good example of the difficulty of maintaining an oppressive majority coalition. Factions were not *only* property-based; they also formed over religion, ideology, and other aspects of social and cultural life. Here again the diversity produced by size came to the rescue. For example, the First Amendment protection of free expression of religion and its prohibition against the establishment of a religion not only reflect religious toleration, it is also the result of no single religious faction being able to dominate across the entire republic and therefore one's own religious faction could only be protected by allowing the others to be protected as well.[73]

ENERGY

Reliance on a multiplicity of factions sounds like a recipe for stalemate, a misapprehension easy to derive from reading *Federalist* 10 in isolation. To the contrary, appreciation of the many problems modernity poses impelled the Framers to recognize that a feckless republic could not stand. A government that is too weak is as dangerous as a government that is too powerful. Above all, there was the problem of national security. As the 1790s were to demonstrate, the United States was beset by dangers domestic and foreign. Britain had not relinquished its forts along the frontier, and it remained the world's dominant sea power. France was an ally, but would it always be? Citizen Genet's shenanigans and the "quasi war" would soon prove otherwise.[74] Spain had a powerful presence in North America and could threaten US commercial interests by denying access to the port of New Orleans to American ships. Shays' Rebellion revealed the dangers of domestic insurrection. The republic must have sufficient strength to cope with these exigencies. As Hamilton argued, it must have *energy*.

A legislative body, even if not beset by factional strife, is, due to its large size and diversity of membership, lethargic. Energy is a quality only possible in the executive. Hence, the Constitution establishes a *single* executive, rather than the plural executive urged by some of the delegates, who were worried about the emergence of a "republican monarch." The chief executive will be commander in chief of the armed forces, choose the executive team, preside over foreign relations, report to the Congress on the state of the union, and "take care that the laws be faithfully executed."[75]

But of the three branches, the powers of the executive are less precisely defined. Whereas Article I limits the powers of Congress to those "herein granted," Article II grants the "executive power" (undefined) to the president, with no additional stipulations, and therefore it does not set a clear limit on the extent of presidential authority. This is perhaps surprising, given that America had so recently rejected a king, and yet like the other aspects we have discussed, this provision reveals the Framers' acceptance of modern circumstances. The world has become too dangerous and unpredictable to hamstring the president's ability to respond. The president must retain the flexibility to address unforeseen circumstances that happen quickly and pose unpredictable perils. The Constitution provides sanctions for executive overreach, most importantly the ability of Congress to approve key appointments, to override presidential vetoes, and in the most extreme circumstance, to impeach the president and remove him from office. Indeed, over the years, vetoes have been overridden and appointments denied. But regarding those other vast areas that might inspire executive abuse, the only really impressive power of Congress is impeachment. But this process is, necessarily, too slow and cumbersome to effectively cope with executive abuses that threaten republican rule in real time.[76] The Framers expected that the real check on executive excess would be the Electoral College. The electors "honorably determined" by the citizens of each state would be sufficiently wise and well informed to select persons of sufficiently good character, republican commitment, and sobriety that they would resist whatever despotic temptations might arise.[77]

The Electoral College did not operate as planned because the Democratic-Republicans ran slates of electors pledged to Thomas Jefferson and Aaron Burr, who were bitter enemies. Instead, the very agents of the Electoral College's transformation—political parties—emerged to perform the filtering function, albeit in a much noisier way. The Constitution does not discuss political parties, because they are not part of the government, and, at least until Madison and Jefferson founded one, the Framers opposed them. And yet they were wiser than they knew. The Electoral College prescribed that the presidential election would be a conglomerate of state elections. It is this quality that enabled the parties to provide the wisdom that the college could not. Since the states would choose the president, and electing a president was the initial aim of creating a national party, parties had to be organized on a state-by-state basis. Although national party leaders would emerge, the key party figures were the state "barons," not the party "prince" at the head of the ticket. State party conventions performed the role originally assigned to the Electoral College. Controlled by seasoned politicians, they sifted through the would-be candidates, choosing not necessarily the best one but, at a minimum, those who would not threaten the political order in which the party leaders thrived. If some state conventions failed in this mission, the national convention added an additional filtering mechanism as the barons came together to negotiate the final choice. The barons no longer play a decisive role (or any role at all, in fact) in choosing their parties' presidential candidates. This crucial check on unsuitable candidates was eliminated by the party reforms of the 1970s (of which more below). The country therefore faces a much greater likelihood of choosing a president with despotic, or demagogic, tendencies.[78]

Ironically, the latitude the Constitution provides to the president is also a source of abuse prevention. In *Federalist* 72 Hamilton stresses the importance of a relatively long term and re-eligibility:

> With a positive duration of considerable extent, I connect the circumstance of re-eligibility. The first is necessary to give to the officer himself the inclination and the resolution to act his part well, and to the community time and leisure to observe the tendency of his measures, and thence to form an experimental estimate of their merits. The last is necessary to enable the people, when they see reason to approve of his conduct, to continue him in his station, in order to prolong the utility of his talents and virtues, and to secure to the government the advantage of permanency in a wise system of administration.[79]

Because presidents can enjoy a number of terms in office if they act well (capped at two only since the Twenty-Second Amendment was adopted in 1951), they have a strong motive not to act badly. Because they can run for reelection, the public is accorded an additional safeguard against despotism: a truly unsuitable president is unlikely to be reelected. The party leaders tried hard to avoid selecting badly, but they were not infallible—and neither, of course, are the voters who choose to take part in primaries. Neither the leaders nor the electorate can perfectly evaluate a candidate for the singular job of being president. But, having lived with a president for four years, both are much more able to "honorably determine" whether the president deserves to continue. Political scientists have long argued that the electorate is far better at making retrospective judgments than prospective ones—but then, who isn't?[80] The Twenty-Second Amendment denies the public the opportunity to cast a retrospective judgment in the wake of the president's second term, but the hope is that having survived one retrospective judgment the president has demonstrated sufficient dutifulness that a further retrospective judgment is not required to ensure that he will not abuse his power during his second term.

It is human nature to want to finish what one starts. This desire is especially strong among "the noblest minds," for whom the "love of fame" is the ruling passion. This passion "would prompt a man to plan and undertake extensive and arduous enterprises for the public benefit, requiring considerable time to mature and perfect them."[81] Re-eligibility is thus necessary in order to enable the completion of those enterprises. As much as one might hope that the "noblest minds" ascend to the presidency, one must also recognize the risks they pose. If stymied by term limits in their efforts to achieve lasting fame, such outsize characters would pose a greater risk of despotism than would more mediocre incumbents whose ambitions are not so great. Enabling presidents to pursue extensive and arduous enterprises has the added virtue of allowing the country to benefit from their success. This is a further example of the Framers' objective of both acceding to modernity and taming it. Among such enterprises, Hamilton had in mind the extensive and arduous fiscal and infrastructure projects required by a modern state, and that Washington's two terms in office enabled him to put in place. Adams's defeat in 1800 showed the importance of re-eligibility by permitting the people to peacefully and lawfully deny it to one they deemed to be inadequate.

As Hennessey and Wittes persuasively argue, another powerful inducement to presidential good behavior is the oath of office itself.[82] It is the only oath whose language the Constitution specifies: "I do solemnly swear (or affirm) that I will faithfully execute the Office of President of the United States, and will to the best of my Ability, preserve, protect and defend the Constitution of the United States." Such a profound pledge can have transformative power. Many of our presidents—Chester A. Arthur, Gerald Ford, and Harry Truman come to mind—had been relative mediocrities before becoming president. But, the awesome power they thus acquired did not corrupt them. Rather, their reverence for the office, as symbolized by the oath they took, brought out the "better angels of their nature" and impelled them to act in a manner far superior to what they had previously shown themselves capable of doing.

The example of Donald Trump shows just how far a president can stray from constitutional fidelity in a different way. As we will discuss in the next chapter, the Constitution conveys a spirit that guides republican rule, as well as the letter of specific powers and limitations. President Trump's transgressions were less about the letter of the Constitution or the law (for example, he did not, like other presidents, sick the IRS on his critics) than about the Constitution's *spirit*: here is where Trump's most egregious violations could be found. He rashly asserted that he had won the 2020 election "by a landslide," inspiring if not orchestrating an assault on the Capitol. He urged his vice president to refuse certification of the electoral votes in the states he claimed had been "stolen." He was careless in his relations with foreign leaders; he distorted or made up "facts"; he bullied his critics and defamed them in public, using as an excuse their frequent defamation of him (beginning with the false claim of collusion with the Russians to "steal" the 2016 election)—setting precisely the wrong example. He allowed his staff to ignore or even contradict his orders to them, and was disorganized and inconsistent in his presentation of public-policy directives.[83]

Thus, the executive remains the most dangerous branch of government— *as it must be.*[84] The Framers knew what they were doing when they chose not to circumscribe executive power as they did congressional power. There are simply too many trying circumstances that call for immediate unconstrained executive action. It is *more* dangerous to straitjacket presidents than it is to give them the very loose rein the Constitution grants them. So far, so good. Even Trump's outrageous exhortations to the January 6 rioters, the seditious behavior of the those who stormed the Capitol, and the incompetence of the Capitol Police did not prevent the constitutional order from functioning. Vice President Pence did his legal duty; the Electoral College voted; the new resident assumed the office in a timely fashion. We can do no better than to repeat the old wisdom that democracy requires eternal vigilance.

EXPERTISE AND AGENTS

The complex circumstances imposed by modernity place a great premium on expertise and administration. These two needs are related but not identical, and they both pose difficulties for republican rule. Because the esoteric knowledge that defines expertise (the expert's training enables him to understand problems that the rest of us don't) is critical for addressing many modern problems—health, environment, defense—to name just a few. It is, of course, very difficult for non-experts to evaluate such advice, especially since many questions are unsettled enough that experts will offer *conflicting* bits of advice. And experts often get it wrong. Consider the scientific consensus that formed around bleeding as the proper remedy for a myriad of different ailments, or the strong "scientific" support given to theories of racial inferiority in the 1920s. In the political realm consider the foreign-policy expert consensus that formed around no longer treating China as a dangerous adversary but, instead, enticing it into good behavior by overlooking its aggressive actions and seducing it by encouraging its penetration into the American market and providing access to American scientific data to Chinese scientists.[85]

The enemy is not science per se but the excessive political power exercised by what Michal Lind calls the "Mandarins."[86] This phenomenon is a type of "groupthink" that forms among the most politically influential members of the scientific community that causes them to underestimate contrary evidence.[87] We stress the importance of political influence because often the non-Mandarins have equally impressive scientific and academic credentials and they may have superior understanding. Consider climate change. William Nordaus is no "climate denier." He won a Nobel Prize for showing that the best scientific evidence suggests that climate change is a real problem, but not an apocalyptic one, and that it also offers some benefits to society (longer growing seasons in Canada, more arable land in Russia, to cite just two examples). Therefore, the net costs climate change imposes should be measured against the costs of combatting it. Only those measures should be adopted whose benefits outweigh their costs.[88] As sensible as this sounds, this perspective has failed to influence the thinking of the Obama and Biden administrations as well as such political and philanthropic heavyweights as Bill Gates. They have succumbed to the Mandarinate of scientists and engineers who persist in ignoring Nordhaus's more cogent and sober analysis.

It also follows that as the state grows, it will require not only the advice of experts but an increasing number of agents to carry out its policies. This complex mix of experts and bureaucrats has come to be called "the administrative state."[89] These bureaucrats are not mere automatons who do as they are told. They have minds and interests of their own, and are often themselves under the sway of various Mandarins.[90] Because no modern state can operate without a small army of such agents, as the welter of policies becomes ever more numerous and complicated it becomes ever more difficult for elected officials to exert meaningful control over what these agents actually do—especially when their numbers grow. According to the federal Office of Management and Budget, on the eve of World War II, the federal government workforce—not counting the Department of Defense—was 443,000. By 2014 that number had grown to 1,356,940. This number reflects the additional civilian responsibilities assumed by the federal government in the 1960s and 1970s (the number first topped one million in 1972.)[91] Every modern state must therefore find ways of controlling its own servants—or risk turning the government over to those who are supposed to merely administer the law rather than make it.

This is not to imply that bureaucrats are narrowly self-interested—although there is little reason to believe that they are reliably *less* self-interested than their private-sector counterparts, whose workplace incentives, and job security, are very different from those in the public sector. But their relative freedom from both political accountability and market pressures means that even when they are acting from altruistic motives, they have considerable room to impose their own vision of the public good, which might well be at odds with that of the broader citizenry or even the elected legislature. This is how the servants become the masters.[92] The growth of the American administrative state since the early twentieth century—both the sheer number of its servants and the range of their authority—is a phenomenon matched and sometimes exceeded in nearly every modern democracy. As we will see in subsequent chapters, this development has had a complex and often dangerous impact on the generation of the public policies that citizens must live with— even when they often have no clear idea of where those policies came from, or who decreed that they should now be the law of the land.

In a republic, ultimate policy control must rest with the people's representatives. The president and members of Congress possess critical forms of political wisdom that Mandarins and administrators, regardless of their claims to expertise, lack. Only the people's representatives have the capacity to evaluate "expert" recommendations in terms of their appreciation of the needs and wants of their constituencies. Hamilton anticipated the problem of excessive bureaucratic autonomy. In *Federalist* 68 he argues that, while good administration is very important, the idea that the best-administered regime is the best regime is a "political heresy."[93] In a real republic, experts and administrators must be subservient to politicians. Although the Constitution does not explicitly grant the president the power to remove administrators, neither does it deny him that power or make it subject to the advice and consent of the Senate. In the early days of its very first session, Congress gave President Washington the "removal power,"[94] and the president has retained it except for the period from 1867 to 1887, when the Tenure of Office Act denied it to the president with regard to certain key posts. Congress repealed the act in 1887, and in 1926 the Supreme Court affirmed the president's inherent right to remove executive officials, even those whose appointment required Senate confirmation.[95]

Neither does the Constitution explicitly grant Congress the power to oversee the bureaucracy, but it does so de facto by giving Congress the power of the purse. Article I, Section 9 states simply: "No money shall be drawn from the treasury, but in consequence of appropriations made by law."[96] This power enables Congress to call the various executive departments to account using such devices as hearings and investigation. If the Congress is displeased, it can withdraw appropriations from the offending bureau or agency. The failure of

Congress to make adequate use of this power is a matter to which we will return in chapter 4, but that fault does not rest with the Constitution.

THE PROMISE OF PROSPERITY

By the time of the Constitutional Convention, the United States was already engaged in an extensive commerce, and the prosperity commerce encouraged had become a popular expectation. But such an expectation was novel. In feudal times, only those at the very top of the wealth pyramid expected to live well. America was at the vanguard of this psychological transformation.[97] Merchants and other relatively prosperous individuals were prominent even among the early settlers. The lack of feudal constraints on land ownership, coupled with the widespread availability of good land, enabled the burgeoning of commercial farming. Here again, the Framers accepted modernity, recognizing that America would be not just a large republic but a *commercial* one whose citizens would demand that the state enable them to be prosperous. This was not the view of all of the framers—Jefferson and his allies were suspicious of "industry" and hoped to preserve the "yeoman farmer" as the model American citizen. But it was not to be—and would not have been, even without the strenuous efforts of Alexander Hamilton to promote both a stable banking system and a manufacturing sector. Americans were inventive and entrepreneurial from the beginning, and life on the farm did not have the same attraction to everyone. Furthermore, a vigorous manufacturing sector would be essential to the construction of an army and a navy strong enough to defeat whatever European powers might have continued designs on North America.

Accordingly, the Constitution protects private property and supports a competitive commercial economy. Article I grants Congress the power to regulate interstate and foreign commerce. This power was understood to foster commerce by preventing states or localities from impeding the free flow of goods across state lines or national borders. The Bill of Rights protects private property from usurpation by the government. The Fifth Amendment's "Takings Clause" states that "private property [shall not] be taken for public use, without just compensation." Article I, Section 10 prevents a state from impairing the obligation of contract. Since it was the states that regulated contracts, this clause had the effect of ensuring that if persons contracted with one another in good faith, no state government could intervene to void the contract or refuse to enforce it.

Although Madison, Adams, and Jefferson were worried about the excesses of commercialism, the Constitution did not address those concerns.[98] Because the states possessed the police power, they were the appropriate venue for reigning in such excess. And, until relatively recently, most states restricted commerce in various ways—with Sunday closing laws and prohibitions on gambling. Now the states tend to deny themselves such powers by doing away with most of those limitations, but that is a choice made by state legislators, and sometimes by the voters directly, through state referenda: it is not something imposed, or forbidden, by the Constitution.

This chapter focused on the Framers' ability to establish a constitutional framework that was well adapted to both modernity and human nature, and yet preserved liberty and republican rule. The next chapter explores the history of criticisms of the Constitution as those criticisms first arose during the ratification debates and have continued unto the present day.

CHAPTER 2

The Case against the Constitution

One of the oldest criticisms of the American Constitution is that it is fundamentally undemocratic. Although this argument took on new urgency after Donald Trump won a majority of the Electoral College vote while losing the popular vote to Hillary Clinton, it is actually a much older argument than most people realize, and it goes well beyond the alleged unfairness of the Electoral College. The claim that the Constitution fails the democracy test was first made at the Founding—although "democratic" was not the word that the Constitution's critics (or its defenders either) normally used. "Popular" government, or "republican" government—one that rested on the will of the people—were the preferred terms, since "democratic" often had the connotation of "mob rule" in the late eighteenth century. For example, the problems experienced under the Articles of Confederation were blamed on an "excess of democracy" by one delegate to the Constitutional Convention, and no one rose to object.[1] Still, despite the different nomenclature, and the passage of so much time, many of these early complaints about the Constitution, advanced by the faction that came to be known as the Anti-Federalists,[2] will sound remarkably familiar.

THE ANTI-FEDERALIST CASE AGAINST
THE CONSTITUTION

First, the Constitution did not allow for enough popular participation. All who took part in the constitutional debate agreed that the only good government was a popular government, but there were disagreements about what this could mean in practice, given the enormous size of the country, even in 1787. As we saw in chapter 1, one of the central facts about modern states, including the United States at the moment of its founding, is that they are very large, and great size imposes inevitable limits on the degree to which "the many" can directly participate in government. A common target of this criticism during the constitutional debate was the House of Representatives, which was said to be too small to be a genuinely popular assembly.[3] Given how large (for the time) the congressional districts were (30,000 persons), it would be unlikely, critics claimed, that a representative would have any real knowledge of the concerns and needs of most of his constituents. Furthermore, in order to secure election in such a large district, a candidate would have to be already well known, and this requirement would exclude many capable but humble citizens known only to their immediate neighbors.

The Senate was even worse. Appointed by state legislatures rather than directly elected, enjoying long terms, and "mixed" with the Executive in alarming ways (jointly appointing federal judges, ratifying treaties), the Senate might come to constitute an "aristocratic" tribunal. Everything about the distribution of responsibilities at the national level suggested to skeptics the likelihood of a "cabal" of "illustrious" men lording it over the barely representative House. In fact, the Senate and the House bore an obvious and unseemly resemblance to the House of Lords and the House of Commons in Great Britain. The federal courts came in for special criticism, since, once appointed, a federal judge could serve for life, with only the prospect of impeachment to restrain his aristocratic impulses. In any case, removal would require a judge to be convicted by the same institution that had confirmed him, and would for this reason be a very unlikely occurrence.[4]

The president, meanwhile, was obviously intended to be a monarch in all but name, with what would effectively be "life tenure," since there were no term limits in the original Constitution.[5] And the selection of the chief executive was far too removed from the voters, who would first choose the state legislature, which would in turn appoint the state's presidential electors, who would in their turn choose the president. But there was no direct way for the state's citizens, or the state legislatures either, to control how their state's electors actually voted. The electors would have the final say. (Obviously, this arrangement has changed, in a more democratic direction, for reasons to be taken up below.)

Meanwhile, critics argued, the states, although they appeared to have been left intact and self-governing, would now have only a secondary role to play in American government, with the most important questions—foreign policy, war, public finance, the interpretation of the Constitution itself—left in the hands of the Union, which would mean, in practice, the president, the Senate, and the courts. The Constitution was also too *complicated*—an elaborate arrangement of offices and powers meant to put limits on those in authority, according to its defenders. But how could ordinary people work such an intricate piece of machinery? There was considerable sentiment in favor of a proposition advanced by Thomas Paine in his famous 1776 pamphlet, *Common Sense*: "I draw my idea of the form of government from a principle in nature, which no art can overturn, viz., that the more simple any thing is, the less liable it is to be disordered, and the easier repaired when disordered."[6]

To make a long story short, things did not work out in quite the way that either the Federalists or the Anti-Federalists anticipated.[7] The nation rather quickly developed a set of arrangements for choosing the president that made the office much more popular than it was originally intended to be. Once the two-party system developed—and a rudimentary party system was visible as early as 1796, when Thomas Jefferson lost to John Adams in the race to succeed President Washington—the selection of presidential electors became a partisan selection, and once the party system was fully developed, the selection of the president became a partisan *campaign*, with most of the features we have long been used to. And rather than becoming subordinate to the Union, as so many Anti-Federalists feared, the states became in many ways the center of American political life, because the states were both older than the Union and the part of the political order most amenable to popular participation.

Many states embraced practices more democratic than those at the national level: elected judges, larger legislatures, broader suffrage rules, weaker executives. Some states, such as Rhode Island and New Hampshire, were small enough to have something approaching direct democracy. For the first century of American government, nearly everything that passed as "governing" took place in the states, and this is what "popular government" came to mean to most Americans. In consequence, the word "democracy" soon lost most of its negative connotations. This pattern lasted well into the twentieth century, and has not, even now, entirely disappeared. On both sides of the current political divide, for example, partisans push their state governments to enact policies that depart from the national consensus, whether it be abortion laws in Georgia or gun laws in California—even while being critical of the other side's choices, and sometimes, as we'll see, critical of the very possibility that states could be allowed to adopt different policies of any kind.[8]

As a result, the old concerns of the Anti-Federalists faded into the background, although they never disappeared entirely. Sometimes the president seemed too powerful (Andrew Jackson threatened to hang the governor of South Carolina for obstructing the tariff); sometimes the federal courts seemed imperious (*McCulloch v. Maryland* permitted the government to establish a National Bank immune to state control); and the Senate frequently behaved as if it were a "cut above" the "people's House." (Many contemporary members of the House would probably say that it still does.) But as property and wealth restrictions on the franchise were loosened in state after state, the American republic became, by the time Alexis de Tocqueville studied it in 1831, the world's most genuinely popular regime. In fact, even as early as 1790, "the qualified electorate" in the various states ranged "from about 60 to 90 percent of adult white males, with most states toward the upper end."[9] By contrast, only one out of five adult males exercised the franchise in the United Kingdom even *after* the electorate was expanded by the Reform Act of 1832.[10]

In the early nineteenth century, the constitutional authority of the federal government only occasionally came into conflict with the powers left to the states. Some states felt aggrieved by the nation's tariff policies, others by the power of the federal courts to void state laws that conflicted with the Constitution. This did not mean that the states were uninterested in gaining help from the federal government, however, in the form of subsidies for things like roads and canals. What the states were *not* interested in was being told what to do by the federal government—and the federal government had not yet gotten into the habit of using money to influence behavior in those areas of policy (local schools, for example) where the Constitution gave the federal government no direct authority.

As time passed, states themselves were pushed in the direction of devolving more and more authority downward, to cities, towns, and counties. All over the country—following the lead of the Massachusetts Constitutional Convention of 1820—states enacted provisions allowing for local referenda to determine both public policies and new forms of local government.[11] This movement left a profound impact on state and local government that has lasted well into modern times. Much of what state governments were formally responsible for—law enforcement, land use, education, economic regulation—has been handled on a regular basis by municipal governments, the level of government closest to the voters, following the pattern originally set in the New England townships of the seventeenth century.

Were it not for the conflict over slavery, the relations between the national government and the states would have continued to be mildly contentious but well within the usual give and take of everyday politics. But when the slavery conflict became unmanageable—as it did fairly quickly—the result was an appeal, not to the Constitution, but to arms. Yet while the Civil War ended slavery, it did not end federalism, nor was federalism the war's target. Even with the extra authority that wartime presidents normally command, President Lincoln could not, on his own, abolish slavery, but could only use his powers of persuasion to get the Thirteenth Amendment through the Congress and into the hands of the state legislatures.[12] And even Lincoln could not get what he needed from the Congress or the states without an assiduous use of his influence over federal patronage. When the war ended, however, the ambitious plans to "reconstruct" the South failed in the face of public indifference, exhaustion, and partisan maneuvering. In fact, one of the war's most important legacies was an acute sense that the complex machinery of American government had only just managed to survive the crisis intact, and from then on, political and constitutional reforms of varying sorts were never off the agenda.[13]

At the same time, however, the victory of the North was very clearly a victory for the Constitution, and for the Declaration of Independence as well—in Lincoln's words, the "apple of gold" for which the Constitution provided the "frame of silver."[14] Central to this view was the complicated doctrine of natural rights that stands at the heart of Jefferson's famous words: "that all men are created equal, [and are] endowed by their Creator with certain unalienable rights," and that among these are the rights to "life, liberty, and the pursuit of happiness." Among the forces that might threaten those rights, government itself stands at the top of the list: the same government that might threaten natural rights is at the same time the only force capable of protecting those rights—so long as the citizenry is wise enough to hold it within certain limits. But the nineteenth century saw the birth of many movements whose followers were deeply suspicious of "limits" on the will of the people, and these movements left their mark on the United States as well as Europe.

THE ANTI-SLAVERY CRITIQUE OF THE CONSTITUTION

However, the first post-ratification attacks on the Constitution came from abolitionists, who insisted that the document's toleration of slavery made it anathema. That the Constitution made various compromises with slavery in order to keep the country together is widely known, and it continues to be a source of criticism even today.[15] Although the Constitutional Convention managed to keep the words "slave" and "slavery" out of the document, the delegates were forced to accept various compromises with the institution: a twenty-year delay in the authority of Congress to ban the slave trade (Article I, Sec. 9), agreement to a "fugitive slave" clause (Article IV, Sec. 2), and conceding to southern delegates the right to count three-fifths of their slave populations for the purposes of determining how many congressional districts a state would receive (Article I, Sec. 2).

These compromises were made by a convention the majority of whose members were not slave owners (of the fifty-five delegates, twenty-five owned slaves).[16] Yet even for some of the slave-owning delegates, such as James Madison and George Washington, the ultimate end of slavery was an outcome they desired and anticipated. This was true also of the absent Thomas Jefferson. But neither the slave-owning delegates nor Jefferson chose to hasten slavery's end by freeing their own slaves in their own lifetimes, closing down their plantations, and finding other ways of making a living.[17]

By contrast, slavery had been abolished in five of the seven northern states by the time of the convention: Pennsylvania (1780), Massachusetts and New Hampshire (1783), and Connecticut and Rhode Island (1784). New York and New Jersey would not abolish slavery until 1817 and 1804, respectively, but anti-slavery sentiment was strong in both states.[18] Midway through the convention—in July of 1787—the Congress passed the Northwest Ordinance, providing a path to statehood for the vast Northwest Territory—while prohibiting slavery in what would become the states of Ohio, Michigan, Indiana, Illinois, and Wisconsin. It was clear that the North and South were profoundly different, and that northern views about slavery would soon become dominant—and that this difference would make a successful Union even more of a challenge than it would otherwise have been.

As we discussed in the introduction, a number of writers have argued that the Constitution's central purpose was to preserve slavery, or that slavery was the "central" institution in American life at the time of the Founding. Yet this claim is hard to square with the *abolition* of slavery in many northern states, or with the fact that the Constitutional Convention came very close to breaking up over the slavery question, agreeing to the slavery compromises only reluctantly, and only to keep the southern delegates from bolting. The idea is also contradicted by a fact that should be obvious: it was not necessary to organize a constitutional convention in order to preserve slavery; slavery could easily have been preserved by doing nothing. If the country had remained under the Articles of Confederation—and assuming the country did not simply break apart—the "United States of America in Congress Assembled" would have had no authority to abolish slavery in the *existing* states—even though they had done so when organizing the new Northwest Territory.[19]

As Sean Wilentz argues, the Constitution did not *authorize* slavery, it merely tolerated it—which is why the words *slave* and *slavery* never appear in the document. This absence was hardly accidental. Even the fugitive slave provision does not require the return of "slaves" but rather of "person(s) held to Service or Labour."[20] Wilentz demonstrates that this was not "merely" a hypocritical effort designed to present a less obnoxious truth to the world but rather was part of a carefully planned out project to avoid supporting the proposition that slaves were a legitimate form of property. "This exclusion, insisted on by the majority of delegates, was of profound and fateful importance. It rendered slavery solely a creation of state laws. It thereby opened the prospect of a United States free of slavery—a prospect some delegates deeply desired and many more believed was coming to pass. Above all, it left room for the new federal government to hinder slavery's expansion."[21] Opposition to the expansion of slavery was the central cause of the war that finally ended slavery.[22]

The only defense of these compromises is that, without them, there would not have been a United States of America. There would have been *something*, however: either two separate countries, north and south, one with and one without slavery; or thirteen (or more) disunited states, with slavery continuing wherever it currently existed, or wherever it might be subsequently planted. In either of these cases, there would not have been a Civil War; but in either of these cases it is also not clear how slavery would ever have been abolished. That slavery would have ended *somehow* is almost certainly true; *how* it would have ended in this alternate timeline must always remain a mystery.

But the compromises with slavery were a serious charge against the Constitution, and powerful arguments were made that the compromises made the Union unworthy of support, or even of continuation. William Lloyd Garrison, a cofounder of the New England Anti-Slavery Society (1833) and founder of the antislavery journal *The Liberator*, declared the Constitution to be a "covenant with the Devil," and then ceremoniously burned a copy.[23] His hatred of slavery led him, ultimately, to reject the idea of living in a nation with slaves and slaveholders, and he advocated that the *North* secede from the Union.[24]

This would, of course, have done nothing to help the slaves, in what would now be an independent nation based in the South.

Opponents of slavery were quite often devoted to other reform causes, as well—most commonly temperance and women's suffrage—and usually argued from a Christian perspective on equality. There was a considerable overlap, then, between political and social reform, on the one hand, and various schools of "reformed religion," on the other. Thus, from multiple perspectives, the political order established by the Constitution was found to be severely wanting. It was not only a "covenant with the Devil," it was also said to be hostile to the rights of women and working men, and increasingly solicitous of the interests of the wealthy: an oligarchy, in other words, rather than a republic—arguments that would be revived, as we will see, once the conflict over slavery had come to its end.

Opposition to slavery was widespread in the North, but it was especially acute in New England, where there was sometimes violent opposition to any effort to enforce the Fugitive Slave Act.[25] When John Brown came north to raise money for what he hoped would be a successful armed slave insurrection (led by him), he found a warm welcome in Concord, the home of Henry David Thoreau.[26]

HENRY DAVID THOREAU

Thoreau is most famous—at least in the context of the conflict over slavery—for his essay "Disobedience to Civil Government," published in 1849.[27] Thoreau began the essay with a familiar liberal idea: government is a regrettable necessity—the less of it the better. In fact, if human beings were better—or, as Madison said, "if men were angels"—no government would be necessary at all. But Thoreau did not follow this thought down the same path that Madison followed, that is, to a consideration of what kind of government most suits human nature as we find it (that is, non-angelic), or the particular circumstances that Americans find themselves in, or what kind of government is most conducive to human happiness. Madison and others among the Framers would have agreed immediately that only a republican, or popular, government could promote human happiness, because only in such a government would men be free. Instead, Thoreau appeared to question whether the American government, or any government, could have *any* legitimate claim on his obedience, especially if it has involved itself in the commission of acts of great injustice, and the two he had in mind in were slavery and the Mexican War.[28] No one should cooperate with governments involved in such evils; no one could claim to be free, or virtuous, who paid taxes to such a government, to be *spent* on such evils. Indeed, no one could "without disgrace be associated with" the United States government. "I cannot for an instant recognize that political organization as *my* government which is the *slave's* government also. This people must cease to hold slaves, and to make war on Mexico, though it cost them their existence as a people."[29] Nor did Thoreau have any apparent interest in promoting reform. "It is not a man's duty," he insisted, "as a matter of course, to devote himself to the eradication of any, even the most enormous wrong; he may still properly have other concerns to engage him; but it is his duty, at least, to wash his hands of it, and, if he gives it no thought longer, not to give it practically his support."[30]

The occasion for another reflection on slavery—"Slavery in Massachusetts"[31]—was a meeting in Concord called to oppose the admission of Nebraska as a slave state. The question this event prompted Thoreau to ask is: Why should Concord care about Nebraska? Why should the town meeting discuss slavery in Nebraska and not slavery in Massachusetts?

Thoreau's reference to "slavery in Massachusetts" was of course didactic rather than literal. Slavery had been illegal in Massachusetts since 1783, and the only slaves in the commonwealth were escaped slaves trying to evade the federal marshals. When Thoreau wrote that there were a "million" slaves in Massachusetts, he was referring to all of the state's citizens; they are all slaves. What does he mean by this?

The immediate occasion for these comments were events at the Boston Court House, where a federal judge was trying to determine whether an escaped slave was really a slave or not. These proceedings were necessary in order to enforce the Fugitive Slave Act, and some abolitionists were trying to use the evidentiary requirements of the law against the law—after all, if you are asked to return an escaped slave, shouldn't someone have to prove that the person really was a slave?

Thoreau was impatient with this; no one can have been a slave, ever, since slavery is unnatural and obviously wrong. The clear impression given by this essay is that Thoreau was simply tired of trying to figure out how to live an honorable life in a country that practiced slavery. The governor is useless; the courts are useless; the parties are useless; politics is useless. But so is the "liberty" of Concord, and of Americans. These things are merely a joke. "Every humane and intelligent" citizen of Concord, when hearing the ceremonial bells on April 19—to celebrate the beginning of the American Revolution—thought instead of April 12, 1851, when a fugitive slave was returned, by the militia, to his so-called owner.

In fact, the nation is corrupt to its core; it worships money, not liberty—if it cared about liberty it would not send so-called slaves back to their so-called masters. Massachusetts "can find no respectable law or precedent which sanctions the continuance of such a union for an instant." A union in which slavery is legal cannot be the object of anyone's loyalty or even obedience.

So central was opposition to slavery in the judgments made about the Constitution that when southern secession came, many (though not all) abolitionists welcomed it. William Lloyd Garrison and Wendell Phillips, the most well-known of the white abolitionists, both welcomed secession, as did Horace Greeley, the most prominent anti-slavery journalist of the time.[32] Whatever America had been before secession, it would be no longer; it would be something utterly different—and, presumably, something worthy (at last) of a decent man's loyalty. But *what* America would be—other than a much smaller nation that no longer practiced slavery—was not clear.

FREDERICK DOUGLASS

The most prominent African American abolitionist was unquestionably Frederick Douglass, born on a slave plantation in 1818, and sent to Baltimore in 1826 as a servant to the family of Hugh Auld. Auld's wife, Sophia, began to teach Douglass to read but was stopped by her husband—yet Douglass had by then learned enough to continue learning on his own, although secretly. In some way he learned of John Quincy Adams's anti-slavery petitions to Congress, and determined to find some way of escaping to the North. He managed his escape in 1838, traveling to New York under a false name, dressed in a sailor's outfit. There he married Anna Murray, who had helped him escape from Baltimore, and together they moved to New Bedford, a city filled with abolitionist sentiment. It was after moving north that he took the name Frederick Douglass.[33]

Douglass met William Lloyd Garrison at one of Garrison's speeches in New Bedford and by 1841 had become an agent of Garrison's Anti-Slavery Society.

At the time, he shared Garrison's, and Thoreau's, disdain for America and its institutions, saying, "I have no love for America, as such; I have no patriotism. I have no country. What country have I? The institutions of this Country do not know me—do not recognize me as a man."[34]

He published his first book, *Narrative of the Life of Frederick Douglass, An American Slave*, in 1845. Unfortunately, the book revealed enough details about his life to attract the attention of slave catchers, so Douglass decided to leave the country for a while, embarking on a speaking tour in England and Ireland, where he started a friendship with the Irish Republican Daniel O'Connell. O'Connell campaigned for Irish independence but opposed violence as incompatible with the establishment of a successful free Irish republic. Douglass, too, was opposed to violence, believing that it would prevent the creation of an American nation in which whites and Blacks could live as fellow-citizens of a free nation. Accordingly, he turned down an invitation from John Brown to help lead an armed slave insurrection in the South, but only after the two engaged in a day-long argument over the relative merits of peaceful agitation and armed rebellion.

But despite his association with Garrison, Douglass came to see the Constitution not as a document founded in slavery, but as a document that did all it could to hide slavery—not to deny its existence, but to deny it constitutional sanction. This, of course, was also Abraham Lincoln's view. Lincoln said, in his Peoria address of 1854, that the Framers of the Constitution hid slavery, "just as an afflicted man hides away a wen or a cancer, which he dares not cut out at once, lest he bleed to death."[35] Douglass's most famous anti-slavery speech, "What to the Slave Is the Fourth of July?," delivered before an anti-slavery convention in 1852, excoriates *America* in no uncertain terms, but, like Lincoln, exonerates the Constitution itself. That is, *Americans* need to accept the shame of slavery as their *own* shame, chosen by themselves—including the current and disgraceful Fugitive Slave Act—and not forced upon them by the Constitution or by the Framers.

> "In *that* instrument," he concludes, "I hold there is neither warrant, license, nor sanction of the hateful thing, but interpreted as it *ought* to be interpreted, the Constitution is a glorious liberty document. Read its preamble, consider its purposes. Is slavery among them? Is it at the gateway? Or is it in the temple? It is neither. . . . Now, take the Constitution according to its plain reading, and I defy the presentation of a single pro-slavery clause in it. On the other hand it will

be found to contain principles and purposes, entirely hostile to the existence of slavery."[36]

Douglass returned to this theme in an address given before the Scottish Anti-Slavery Society in Glasgow, in March 1860. Much had transpired since the Fourth of July address, including the fateful Dred Scott decision in 1857, and the Lincoln/Douglas debates in Illinois in 1858, in which Abraham Lincoln established himself as the Republican Party's most eloquent anti-slavery advocate. The question on the table in the Glasgow debate was whether the American Constitution did or did not give explicit sanction to the institution of slavery. If the Fourth of July speech was an opportunity for Douglass to challenge his fellow citizens to live up to the high promise of American independence, the Glasgow speech was a direct rebuttal to his former ally William Lloyd Garrison. To the question chosen for debate—"Is the Constitution of the United States pro-slavery or anti-slavery?"—Douglass gave an unequivocal answer: It is clearly an anti-slavery document. But there was now another question on the table, and this is where Douglass made his cleanest break from the faction he refers to as "the Garrisonians." Should the Union be dissolved by the opponents of slavery? Should anti-slavery Americans refuse to vote, pay taxes, or hold office under the United States government?

> To these questions the Garrisonians say Yes. They hold the Constitution to be a slaveholding instrument, and will not cast a vote or hold office, and denounce all who vote or hold office, no matter how faithfully such persons labor to promote the abolition of slavery. I, on the other hand, deny that the Constitution guarantees the right to hold property in man, and believe that the way to abolish slavery in America is to vote such men into power as will use their powers for the abolition of slavery.[37]

The Constitution, in other words, is not the problem; the problem is the American people, who have not yet faced up to the enormity of the task before them, which is simply that slavery must end. It would not be enough for Americans to "wash their hands" of the problem by separating from the slave states—a tactic that would do nothing for the slaves, however it might salve the tender conscience of the Garrisonites. Even the so-called fugitive slave clause, Douglass pointed out, does not use the word "slave." Though those who introduced it certainly intended it to apply to slaves, it was rewritten "because the convention would not consent that the idea of property in men should be admitted into the Constitution."[38]

THE UTOPIAN CASE AGAINST THE CONSTITUTION

The utopian speculations originating in Europe in the wake of the French Revolution—vaguely or explicitly communist or socialist, and often tinged with the mob-rule Jacobinism that the revolution provoked—were finding followers in America. During Washington's first term, the emergence of "Republican" and "Federalist" parties owed a great deal to contrasting reactions to the violence in France. In 1793 first the king, and then the queen, went to the guillotine, as did thousands of other "enemies of the people." Federalists were appalled, but many Republicans—most prominently, Thomas Jefferson and Thomas Paine—were prepared to look the other way, believing that the French Revolution would ultimately be as salutary an event as the American Revolution had proved to be.[39] Even in the United States, in other words, utopian abstractions about "the rights of man" could veer off into support for, or toleration of, violent struggles against property and even life.

But America is not France, and one reason is the far greater strength of militant Protestantism in the United States, which provided an alternative outlet for dreams of a better world. Tocqueville made special note of the many experimental religious communities in America in the early nineteenth century, and even worried about the "fierce spiritualism" he found in some quarters: "Religious follies are very common there."[40] Whether secular or religious, however, all of these movements shared a common desire for the "collective" or "communal," especially the collective ownership of property—and offered "communism" in some form as a path to happiness far superior to the constitutional regime of individualism, rights, liberty, free markets, and private property.[41]

As all modern states, including the United States, grew ever more populous, a natural reaction against the impersonality of the modern state became an increasingly common theme in political commentary. As America became larger, the individual citizen seemed to shrink to an arithmetically tinier piece of the whole. This might explain the heightened interest in "community"—a modern preoccupation with a very long history.

But in their more extreme versions, reform movements aimed at a reconstruction not just of the political community but of human nature itself, in order to eliminate the "self" (and thus the "selfish"). This was perhaps the most obvious influence of the French Revolution, which aimed to begin the world over again—including human nature itself—from "Year Zero." Such movements yearned for the establishment of a national, or even universal, community of feeling, in which all souls would join together to pursue communal goals. "Public" property rather than "private" property; "collective" decision making about economic questions, as opposed to market-based decisions; simple majority rule, or even "consensus" decision making as a substitute for the "complex" modes of "politicking" that were, the critics claimed, inevitably corrupt and corrupting. Such were the themes of the numerous utopian speculations that contributed to the birth of modern "progressivism" in the nineteenth century—and these dreams have survived into modern times, forming the basis for contemporary spiritual and political movements.[42]

But perhaps the most notable example of this trend is an astonishing piece of writing that became the third-best-selling American novel of the nineteenth century (after *Uncle Tom's Cabin* and *Ben-Hur*)—*Looking Backward: 2000–1887*, by Edward Bellamy, published in 1888 and rarely out of print since. *Looking Backward* is best understood as a utopian romance. Bertrand de Jouvenel has noted that utopian speculation begins by painting a lovely picture of how the world might be, if only certain steps could be taken—but the steps are always subordinate to the vision (and sometimes the steps are left out altogether), because the reader must learn to love the vision before facing the hard work of realizing it.[43]

In Bellamy's novel, our hero, Julian West, hypnotized in 1887 Boston, wakes up in 2000 to a world that has become a communal utopia. In the world of 2000 there is no private property, and no market for goods and services. "Work" as conventionally understood has disappeared, as has money: everyone gets a credit card from the government, which shifts credits from one employer to another should a worker change jobs. The cards can be used to purchase food and other necessary items. The credit cards, however, are not an invitation to shop: the citizens of 2000 are so removed from acquisitiveness or competition that they rarely use up all the credit on their cards. One character, Dr. Leete, says: "According to our ideas, buying and selling is essentially anti-social in all its tendencies."[44]

The heart of the economy is the Industrial Army, divided into ten "sectors," each run by a director, who has, in military fashion, moved up from the ranks to a position of leadership. "The machine which they direct is indeed a vast one," Dr. Leete observes, "but so logical in its principles and direct and simple in its workings, that it all but runs itself."[45]

Vocations can be chosen, but only after several years of service in the Industrial Army have given the individual a taste of various jobs, which reveal to his superiors the range of his or her talents. There are private residences, provided by the government (which has become simply a committee of experts), but people usually take their meals in communal dining halls. Labor conflict has disappeared, of course, since there are no longer separate classes of "owners" and "workers": everyone starts out as a private in the Industrial Army. All workers are content with their jobs (because the tests reveal what they will excel at)—although they are free to try out something different if they so desire. War has disappeared, since there are no longer nations in the conventional sense—just bits of territory supervised by different committees, which are in turn governed by an International Council. Crime has also disappeared—as have juries and lawyers—since there is no longer any reason to steal. There is therefore no more law enforcement than is necessary to handle those few citizens whose "medical problems" cause them to be violent.

What is most remarkable about this novel is the complete absence of politics. There is still a "Congress," but it has only the power to make recommendations. There are no more states or municipalities, Dr. Leete informs Julian, because "state governments would have interfered with the control and discipline of the industrial army, which of course, is required to be central and uniform."[46] Even the emergence of this new utopia was not the result of politics, but of a gradually dawning realization that once all property had fallen into the hands of a single private syndicate—the inevitable result of the natural process of monopolization—it was but a simple step to nationalize the syndicate. It was natural as well to give the management of the new "public" syndicate to experts. In fact, decisions in 2000 are all made by experts, because every problem has a single correct solution, which only the expert will know. This view of expertise was extreme even at the time the book was published, and it remains extreme—but it is not without a family resemblance to the growing reliance on administrative and professional expertise by governments at all levels from the late nineteenth century to the present, and not, of course, only in the United States. It was especially important in the policies of the New Deal (see below), and it continues to be the most obvious way in which contemporary American government departs from the original constitutional framework, which is why the bureaucracy is so often referred to as the "fourth branch" of government.

Twentieth-century reformers adopted Bellamy's faith in expertise, and also (to a lesser extent) his disdain for politics. But politics remained, unfortunately, because in our real, non-Utopian world, elections are not optional. Yet elections could be conducted in a different way, by curbing (if not eliminating) the influence of political parties, which nearly all turn-of-the-century reformers believed had hopelessly corrupted American politics, and which were (along with monopolies) a major obstacle to good government. The parties could be circumvented by referenda and initiative petitions in the states, and during the early decades of the twentieth century, many states adopted laws allowing citizen initiatives to place laws on the ballot.[47] Some progressives imagined *national* referendum campaigns either to adopt legislation by circumventing the Congress, to reject legislation adopted by the Congress, or even to reject decisions of the Supreme Court.[48] In this way, majoritarian democracy could be used as a weapon against the parties—but majoritarian democracy was never an end in itself. The people, after all, are not experts. As we will see below, this conflict between politics and expertise is a problem that has not gone away, because it is always possible that the majority will not choose the correct solution—or the correct candidate—and it has not yet been possible to avoid having elections.[49]

The birth of modern industry is unquestionably the "Big Bang" from which all modern reform movements have emerged: but it is important to remember that the communal aspirations of American reformers long pre-dated the rise of modern industry. Yet by the time of Bellamy's novel the American economy had undergone a profound and rapid transformation, and these changes almost certainly explain some of the novel's appeal. The economy had grown enormously; measured by output, the American economy was 11 times larger in 1899 than it was in 1839—although the population was only 4.5 times larger. During the same period, the outputs of agriculture and manufacturing switched places: agriculture was 72 percent of output in 1839 but only 33 percent in 1899; manufacturing grew from 17 percent to 53 percent of output during the same period.[50] Although the workforce was still heavily engaged in agriculture, more and more labor was industrial, and more and more employers were large corporations rather than "shops."[51]

Second, industrial corporations were now larger than anything the nation had experienced in the past, and they often grew so large by absorbing their competitors. As "consolidation" increased, and as their products became a more significant chunk of the national economy, large corporations acquired a presence that business concerns had never possessed in the past. Whole sectors of the economy fell under the control of the largest corporations, who were able to buy up competitors and form monopolies. While many reformers complained about monopolies, and sought to break them, others (Bellamy was one) saw in consolidation a natural process that should not be resisted but T. R . regulated. After all, weren't the larger businesses more efficient, more productive, than the small shops of the past? And how could modern manufacturing be conducted in any way *other* than by large industrial corporations? As Dr. Leete, Julian West's impossibly smug host, explains: "The movement toward the conduct of business by larger and larger aggregations of capital, the tendency toward monopolies, which had been so desperately and vainly resisted, was recognized at last, in its true significance, as a process which only needed to complete its logical evolution to open a golden future to humanity."[52]

Third, as industrial operations became national rather than local, states lost the ability to regulate them through the exercise of the police power, even at a time when regulations were far less onerous than they have since become. "Bigness" was now normal, rather than unusual, and "interstate commerce" had become the rule rather than the exception. These facts presented a challenge to a regime that, even a generation after the Civil War, was still largely "federal" in its orientation, rather than "national." Bellamy, in fact, chose to call the phenomenon portrayed in his novel "nationalism"—because the "nation" is in charge, rather than private actors, states, or municipalities. Bellamy's use of the word "nationalism" may also have been an attempt to avoid association with "socialism," which was now coming to be linked not with communal farms and utopian religious communities but with violent revolutionary agitation in Europe. But the term "nationalism" suggested what seemed to Bellamy, and many others, obvious: in a modern industrial economy, "federalism" is obsolete, and the sprawling, disorganized circus of American politics would have to be replaced by something more orderly, rational, scientific—and national.

But this vision does not condemn only federalism. It also condemns the very idea of a constitutional regime that at one and the same time places complicated limits on popular rule and on the government itself, while protecting liberty, including the liberty to own and manage property—the very root of the evil afflicting us, according to Bellamy and other reformers. To deal effectively with the modern world, American government would need to catch up, and this aim became the heart of the program of modern economic and political reconstruction, in all of its varied forms, none of them as radical as Bellamy's romantic Utopia, but all of them similar in one or more ways.

THE BIRTH OF MODERN PROGRESSIVISM

Playing catch-up meant, first of all, increasing the authority of the national government over the states *and* the economy, and liberating state and national politics from any reliance on "party machines" and other forms of political baggage left over from the past. Modern government would be streamlined, efficient, and scientific—but it would also be (paradoxically, as we will see) "democratic," by channeling the "voice of the people" through the institutions of a newly enlightened national government, and especially through an enlightened executive. It would also mean transcending the legal restraints placed by the Constitution on the actions of public authority, as well as the political restraints imposed by the party system. Here's where reform notions of "community" bumped up against the reality of partisan politics, a conflict that would divide American reformers into two camps: those who accepted the two-party system (so-called regulars), and those who rejected it because it implied an artificial division of the "national community" over trivial or corrupt concerns ("reformers").[53]

Among reformers, the champion of the party system was Woodrow Wilson. The champion of "the national community" was Theodore Roosevelt. Roosevelt served seven years as president, having succeeded to the office after the assassination of President McKinley in 1901, just six months into his second term. During TR's time in office, he popularized the notion of the president as the "tribune" of the people, and he used the visibility of the presidency to push a variety of ideas about national control of the economy. Among his other accomplishments, he campaigned for new laws to regulate railroad rates (the Hepburn Act), to protect the nation's forests (the National Forest Service), to regulate the quality of food and medicine (the Pure Food and Drug Act), and to create the Department of Commerce and Labor. He used the "bully pulpit" of the White House to negotiate an end to a coal strike in Pennsylvania, and his Justice Department prosecuted J. P. Morgan's Northern Securities

Company—the beginning of a long process of regulating the sale of stocks and other securities.

In 1912 Roosevelt came out of retirement to seek another nomination by the Republican Party. But the Roosevelt of 1912—though he still had many admirers in the Republican leadership and in the electorate—was far more radical than the man who had succeeded President McKinley. He was now a more forthright opponent of the old constitutional regime, which he had come to see not just as a relic but as a menace. No regime of limited government could possibly deal with the pressing problems of 1912, he believed, and Roosevelt was eager to endorse the most radical proposals for getting around the strictures of constitutional limits. Where others had endorsed state referenda, for example, TR now embraced the idea of *national* referenda, including for the purpose of overturning inconvenient Supreme Court decisions.[54] This idea in particular struck the leaders of the Republican Party as a dangerous tinkering with the constitutional design, and they quickly moved to reject his candidacy. Having been rebuffed by his old party, TR then helped to found a new party, the Progressive Party, and entered the 1912 presidential campaign, along with Democrat Woodrow Wilson, Republican William Howard Taft (running for a second term), and Socialist Eugene V. Debs. The 1912 presidential campaign, in fact, was a showcase of what was now being called "progressivism," from all three of the factions that reform had generated: political and industrial reform, the favored theme of "Teddy"; full-out (but "democratic") socialism, the ultimate aim of the Debs campaign; and "modernizing" the political order, the favored approach (most of the time) of Woodrow Wilson.

No one stressed the "modernizing" theme more consistently than Wilson, who, long before he entered the White House, was castigating American government for its outdated reliance on the constitutional restraints that stifled both the popular voice and the ability of "enlightened" statesmen to act effectively. America, progressives in both parties agreed (and both major parties had progressive factions), could not prosper in the twentieth century with an eighteenth-century constitution, because the Constitution as written imposed too many obstacles on decisive action by the national government in pursuit of the national public good. And because there is only one national good, something would have to be done to overcome the ability of the nation's states (and their party organizations) to ignore this single national good, or to articulate competing visions of what the national good might be.

How did these early twentieth-century progressives define the national good?

The changes in the American economy in the generation following the Civil War had, progressives believed, decisively changed the environment of American government: large corporations, unprecedented inequalities in wealth, hard times in both rural and urban America, an increasingly global market, political corruption, an unpredictable economy—what these developments suggested was that either the government would take control of the market or the market would take control of the government. In fact, critics often claimed that corporations had *already* taken control of the Senate, by bribing legislatures to choose the friends of business for available Senate seats—an argument that led to the adoption of the Sixteenth and Seventeenth Amendments, both ratified by the states in 1913, the first authorizing the imposition of a federal income tax, and the second providing for the direct election of members of the Senate.

A related measure was the Nineteenth Amendment, forbidding the exclusion of women from voting rolls, which was passed in 1919 and ratified by three-fourths of the states in the following year. Supporters of female suffrage frequently claimed that the addition of women to the voting rolls would improve the moral tone of American elections—substituting for crass self-interest a "feminine" concern for the public good.[55] In the same year as the Suffrage Amendment came the Eighteenth Amendment, banning the sale of alcohol. Prohibition, too, was largely a popular reform enthusiasm, although not as consistently popular as the other three—perhaps for obvious reasons. More than a public health measure, Prohibition was an effort to purify public morals, defeat the stratagems of corrupt political machines, and elevate the quality of public life. Coupled with the Suffrage Amendment, the nation would see more women and fewer drunks on election day—all by itself a sign of progress.

In the generation following these major constitutional amendments, American politics reflected the progressive influence in a number of ways, some more prominent than others at different times. Initially, the emphasis of progressives was on the problem of "corruption," which meant many different things simultaneously. There was the more-or-less open and obvious corruption of the political machines that ran the big cities (both Democratic and Republican), typified by the attitudes portrayed in another popular book (also rarely out of print), *Plunkitt of Tammany Hall*, by a former newspaper reporter, William Riordan.[56] In Riordan's telling, Assemblyman George Washington

Plunkitt (an actual New York State assemblyman) ran his district by carefully attending to its many and varied needs, and by the collection and distribution of "honest graft"—jobs, contracts, favors available to those in the know. This was a time when, in most big cities, all public jobs, from school teachers to police officers, were heavily influenced by party organizations. All over the country, state and city governments were said to be under the control of "grifters" like Plunkitt, with the result that America was (reformers claimed) one of the worst-governed countries in the civilized world. But the most important complaint about such "machines" was that they were incapable of attending to *real* problems, so intent was their focus on the *petty* needs of local constituents. They could not see the Big Picture; worse, they did not even know there *was* a Big Picture.

The most important consequence of the campaign against corruption was the effort to reduce the role that political parties played in American politics—to zero, if possible. This had been one of the aims of the movement to require popular election of Senators, since "corrupt" interests could more easily buy the votes of a few state legislators than influence the choice of millions of voters. What we now take as given—that candidates will be chosen in primary elections, rather than by party conventions—was first proposed before the First World War. But it was not until the 1970s that this hope became a reality, and primary elections have by now spread throughout the electoral system, most notably, of course, with respect to presidential nominations. Parties as such take a back seat in these contests, and as we learned in 1972 (George McGovern) and again in 2016 (Donald Trump), a party's nominal leaders may end up with a presidential candidate not entirely to their liking.[57]

The campaign against parties also involved a campaign against the very idea of partisanship. Here is where the vision of Bellamy met the vision of more established reformers, such as Theodore Roosevelt. The first party named "Progressive" was the party that made Roosevelt its candidate in the presidential election of 1912. This was perhaps the first campaign (but as we will see, not the last) to make the "party system" an object of scorn, and to make "partisanship" itself—the idea that some Americans support one set of ideas and other Americans, equally virtuous, support a very different set of ideas—a problem, rather than a condition; something to be regretted and overcome, rather than an inevitable consequence of the human condition. Especially in a large nation, where people will differ quite sharply about the wisdom of various public measures (in part because they will be affected very differently by such measures), and where they are free to promote their own opinions, it is essential that some means be found by which one set of ideas will (temporarily) triumph, legitimately, over another. But political reformers in the early twentieth century became increasingly entranced by the notion that this arrangement was wrong, and that if there is a single "national community" it must embrace a single idea of the national good.

Meanwhile, industrialism, critics claimed, was turning employees into "workers"—even into a working "class" with interests and experiences different not only from those of their immediate employers but from much of society as a whole. Coupled with the arrival of millions of mostly poor immigrants from Europe and elsewhere, either fleeing oppression or simply seeking higher wages, American society seemed to be changing its shape in fundamental ways. In colonial and republican America, there were wealthy citizens, to be sure: bankers, merchants, plantation owners, shipbuilders. But those who were not rich were rarely destitute, and opportunities could nearly always be found in a different town or, in a pinch, in a different state. And there was room for innovation, growth, and economic expansion. By the turn of the twentieth century, that pattern appeared to have stalled, and for the first time the nature of the American economy became a central issue in political debate.

This experience suggested an idea that progressives especially took to heart. As long as the wealthy are free to manage the economy, they will naturally take the lion's share for themselves, leaving less and less for the many. The problem, in other words, is private property.[58] Taking away some of the "surplus income" of the rich through taxation—the openly stated purpose of the income tax amendment, since the federal government had been collecting more than enough revenue from the tariff—did not seem to make much of a difference.[59] Even after taxes, the rich were still rich, and the poor were still poor. What was needed, clearly, was a rearrangement of the economic system; but to achieve such a goal, it would first be necessary to change the common American understanding of constitutional government. Standing in the way of such a reimagining was, of course, the Constitution.

Not the original Constitution, however. The period since the Civil War had seen a revolution in constitutional government through the process of amendment: ending slavery; forbidding "unequal" treatment under the law for the former slaves (and by implication others as well); extending the franchise to women; ending the "undemocratic" method of choosing Senators in favor of direct popular elections; substituting taxes on the wealthy for the tariff as the main means of generating revenue for the government; and even the most radical effort at constitutional *moral* reform, the (temporary, as it turned out) prohibition of alcohol. None of it seemed to have changed things very much, and some progressives believed it was because Americans continued to think along the obsolete patterns inspired by the Constitution, which was, as critics continually pointed out, written for an America vastly different from the America of the early twentieth century. Fixing this problem would require more than a few amendments, but the fixing could not begin until Americans were weaned from their slavish devotion to constitutional forms.

This was a theme stressed by two men who could not have been more different, but whose ideas about American politics were to have a major impact on the coming century: Woodrow Wilson and Herbert Croly. Neither of these figures would be claimed by modern progressives—Wilson because of his apparent racism, and Croly because very few even politically active Americans have ever heard of him (despite his having cofounded the *New Republic*). But there is little in the modern progressive argument that does not owe a recognizable debt to these figures from the beginning of the twentieth century. Progressivism, too, has its Founding Fathers.

HERBERT CROLY

Herbert Croly was a New York journalist and reformer whose 1909 book, *The Promise of American Life,*[60] was one of the most influential progressive tracts of the early twentieth century, influencing, in different ways, the presidencies of both Theodore and Franklin Roosevelt. *The Promise* is a long and complex book, but for the purpose of understanding its relation to modern political debates, two of its qualities stand out.

First, Croly attempted to link the past and future into one harmonious explanation, for this purpose praising and then recruiting the most famous of the Founders—Thomas Jefferson and Alexander Hamilton—into a seamless new philosophy of government.

Second, and at the same time, Croly insisted that the constitutional founding, praiseworthy as it might have been at the time, was now obsolete, and incapable of dealing with or even noticing the changed circumstances of twentieth-century America. Thus the Framers could be recognized as noble statesmen, while their work could be safely scrapped and replaced with something entirely new—and yet something in tune, somehow, with the larger purposes of the Framers themselves. In a famous passage, Croly notes that "the better future which Americans propose to build is nothing if not an idea which must in certain essential respects emancipate them from their past."[61] To emancipate Americans from their past, it would be necessary for them to give up their devotion to certain principles and institutions that had been rendered obsolete, according to progressives, by the passage of time.

Croly was certain that the most important changed circumstance was the economy. What made *The Promise of American Life* such an important contribution to *modern* liberalism was its focus on economics and its dismissal of constitutionalism. Like Wilson before him, and others who would come later, Croly believed that an eighteenth-century Constitution could not adequately govern a twentieth-century nation because that nation now had a twentieth-century economy. The Constitution, after all, was meant to put durable limits on the powers of the national government, in part to protect the states (more than some of the Framers would have wished, as we noted earlier). But the limits were also meant to protect the citizens themselves from *any* government action infringing their rights: to speak, argue, worship, own property, move about the country at will, even to own firearms.

Croly believed that no progress could be made until Americans gave up these eighteenth-century habits and the affection for limited government. "Emancipating" Americans from their past meant abandoning old ideas as well as old institutions. Conventional liberalism—and by this Croly meant both the Hamiltonian and Jeffersonian versions—was too preoccupied with the defense of private property and the liberty of the individual. It would have to give way now to a "social" liberalism more attuned to the good of the nation as a whole. "Worship" of the Constitution would have to be replaced by more flexible institutional arrangements that would unmistakably be more national than federal. Whereas the Constitution was designed to place effective constraints on the rulers (including the voters who had chosen them), letting the society run itself, the future America would have to be "planned and constructed," or as a modern progressive might say, "transformed": a process that would involve important new questions and important new arrangements, both political and economic. The most important question, obviously, would be: Who will be doing all of this planning, constructing, and transforming? Croly had a simple answer: a reformed national government.

America would also need a new way of life to match its new mode of governing. One of the ingredients that we could no longer afford to keep, Croly insisted, is the traditional American belief in individualism, because the confidence in individual freedom has led to a "morally and socially undesirable distribution of wealth."[62] The country was founded on the idea that prosperity and democracy would both follow from liberating the people to pursue their own self-interest according to their own lights. That would no longer do. We would no longer be able to rely simply on "enlightened self-interest" to automatically produce the general good. Instead, we must rely on other virtues: planning, discipline, self-denial. Of these three, planning was the easiest to understand and to institute through legal and administrative actions taken by the federal government. But Croly's understanding of planning was expansive, to put it mildly, and it introduced a conflict of perspectives that would divide reformers throughout the twentieth century and into the present. These conflicting perspectives would become clearer as the nation moved into the troubled twentieth century, with its unique political, economic, and even military challenges.

WOODROW WILSON

Woodrow Wilson was one of the nation's first political scientists, among the founding members of the American Political Science Association in 1903. By training a historian, Wilson took a historical view of the Constitution, seeing it as an event that happened at a particular time, and that could only be understood in terms of the time in which it was written—with the clear implication that different times might require a different constitution. Because that time is no longer our time, Wilson insisted; political and economic circumstances have changed so radically that "veneration" of the Constitution blinds us to its increasingly dangerous limitations.

In his first work on politics, *Congressional Government*, published in 1885, Wilson's focus was not only the Congress per se but the entire constitutional environment in which the Congress tried, but failed, to govern. Wilson compared the United States Congress to the British House of Commons—unfavorably, because the Commons was a place where the great questions of the day could be debated extensively and publicly. Unlike the Commons, however, the Congress spent most of its time *legislating* rather than *debating* legislative measures, and hardly any time at all on "understanding, discussing, and directing administration."[63] This may seem an odd complaint to throw at a legislature, but it is revealing, since it is a preface to a larger argument about the new centrality of *administration*. Instead of worrying about the details of legislative measures, the Congress ought to spend its time bringing before the public, in vigorous back-and-forth debate, the essential *principles* of legislation. The details should be left to those who administer the laws, that is, to the bureaucracy.

The ultimate cause of this disability—the focus on details rather than principles—is the "separation of powers," which the Framers adopted because they were concerned about one branch swallowing another. Thus, the legislative branch passes laws and the executive branch enforces them. But the problem is that the Constitution has fixed the shape of the government for all time, preventing it from "evolving" (as the British government has allegedly done for centuries), and this is why the Congress—the entire national government—is outdated. "The government of a country so vast and various [as America] must be strong, prompt, wieldy, and efficient."[64] Instead, the government is slow, cumbersome, divided, and inefficient. In fact, it is doubtful, Wilson argued, that the country can be governed at all under the existing Constitution, and it is clear that what Wilson meant is that the country cannot, under the present circumstances, be efficiently *administered*.

This is perhaps the central complaint of modern reformers: the government cannot adequately respond to the problems of the modern age because the Constitution is a relic of a bygone era, and it only gets in the way of doing the things that must be done. That was then; this is now. "The Constitution is not honored by blind worship. The more open-eyed we become . . . to its defects . . . the nearer will we approach to the sound sense and practical genius of the great and honorable statesmen of 1787. And the first step . . . is a fearless criticism of that system."[65]

In a 1912 campaign speech, extended into an essay and published as part of *The New Freedom* (1913), Wilson offered what readers would probably have described as a "scholarly" critique of the Constitution, one that attempted to find the Constitution's fundamental and fatal flaw. Wilson believed he knew what it was.

> It came to me . . . that the Constitution of the United States had been made under the dominion of the Newtonian Theory. You have only to read the papers of *The Federalist* to see that fact written on every page. They speak of the "checks and balances" of the Constitution, and use to express their idea the simile of

the organization of the universe, and particularly of the solar system—how by the attraction of gravitation the various parts are held in their orbits; and then they proceed to represent Congress, the Judiciary, and the President as a sort of imitation of the solar system. . . . Politics in their thought was a variety of mechanics. The Constitution was founded on the law of gravitation.[66]

Wilson believed that "government is not a machine, but a living thing. It falls, not under the theory of the universe, but under the theory of organic life. It is accountable to Darwin, not to Newton." The Constitution cannot work because it cannot *evolve*.

Wilson combined the scholar and the politician, but in 1912 it was the politician's task to offer a picture of a better future, and Wilson warmed to the task. He asked his audience to imagine a family remodeling a house by adding, haphazardly, this room and that room, "an office here and a workroom there, and a new set of sleeping rooms . . . until we have a structure that has no character whatever. Now, the problem is to continue to live in the house and yet change it." Change it how? Here Wilson, returning to the architecture analogy, imagines taking away the haphazard scaffolding in a generation or two, to reveal at last a "great building whose noble architecture will at last be disclosed, where men can live as a single community, co-operative as in a perfected, co-ordinated beehive, not afraid of any storm of nature, not afraid of any artificial storm . . . knowing that whenever they please they can change that plan again and accommodate it as they please to the altering necessities of their lives."[67] Here is, among other things, clear evidence that Wilson has been seduced by the idea of America as a "single community" with one idea—if not a legacy of Bellamy, at least a meeting of the minds.

But is there a model for this "noble architecture"—other than the not very appealing (but very revealing) image of the beehive? Where should we look? President Wilson does not hesitate to direct America's gaze eastward, back to the Old World that is now becoming a newer, more up-to-date world than America: to France, surprisingly, "where men can now hold up against us the reproach that we have not adjusted our lives to modern conditions to the same extent that they have adjusted theirs." Or northward, to Canada, where "they [have] adjusted their regulations of economic development to conditions we [have] not yet found a way to meet in the United States."[68] Beyond America, the rest of the world was catching up to reality, while Americans were stuck in the era of buckle shoes and powdered wigs.

THE NEW DEAL

Reformers were ultimately disappointed in Wilson, and Theodore Roosevelt died in 1919. American participation in the Great War in Europe disillusioned some reformers while it inspired others, but when the war ended and "normalcy" returned, the economy expanded, unemployment declined, and the stock market boomed—and then crashed, for reasons that are still unclear,[69] and the economic collapse that followed, the worst in American history, became a second "Big Bang" that breathed new life into the old reform debates of the pre-war period. And, of course, the crisis ushered onto the stage another Roosevelt, who had eagerly followed the debates of the 1910s and 1920s, and was certain that the moment had come when the dreams of reformers could at last be revealed as the logical, practical way to a better future.

In one of his earliest "Fireside Chats" on national radio, President Roosevelt laid down a clear marker: "The old reliance upon the free action of individual wills appears quite inadequate. And in many directions, the intervention of that organized control which we call government seems necessary to produce the same result of justice and right conduct which obtained through the attrition of individuals before the new conditions arose."[70] From his inauguration in 1933 to the advent of the Second World War, FDR moved the theory and practice of American government farther down the reform road—more specifically, down the progressive road—than ever before, with results that even those who pay no close attention to American political history can recite. Retirees were supported by a Social Security program administered by the government in cooperation with employers. The unemployed poor were helped by federal grants to overwhelmed state and municipal welfare departments. Unemployment was attacked with public programs that put able-bodied workers into public service jobs, doing everything from road-building to planting trees on Cape Cod and writing histories of local communities. The chronic problem of unpredictable crop prices was addressed by a price support program and more aggressive regulation of farm outputs by the Department of Agriculture.[71] The chaotic struggle between industrial workers and their employers was brought under the regulation of the Department of Labor. Government power plants brought electricity to the Tennessee Valley, establishing a public power company to compete with private power companies, a model that the president hoped would spread.

One New Deal program stands out as illustrative of the New Deal's roots in the progressivism of Croly and Wilson. The National Industrial Recovery Act (passed in 1933) was the most ambitious New Deal reform effort, and the one that brought the full panoply of progressive-era ideas to bear on the central challenge of the Great Depression: how to get the economy moving again; how to keep it moving, smoothly, into the future; and how, finally, to overcome the nation's obsolete devotion to free enterprise. The National Recovery Administration—the agency created to enforce NIRA—was to organize every piece of the American economy, from steel to macaroni,[72] into a network of administrative committees representing government, employers, and employees (and in some cases also consumers), for the purpose of "rationalizing" industrial and commercial competition, which New Dealers always described as "destructive" and "chaotic." These committees would be responsible for reaching agreements about market shares, wages, product specifications, prices—and entry into the market by new companies. Every decision touching on the sector's business would be made by administrators, with what would now be referred to as "buy-in" from every interest involved. All of this would be administered through an exhaustive set of "codes" written by NRA subcommittees—an enormous undertaking that ultimately produced 150 volumes of codes covering 557 separate industries.[73]

The NRA and other reform initiatives of FDR's first term were the practical outcomes of ideas broached most clearly in a famous campaign address Roosevelt delivered to the Commonwealth Club in San Francisco in 1932.[74] This was, in a sense, a pre-election inaugural address, in that it laid out the political justification for the policies FDR promised to follow should he be elected. This speech was probably the most purely *progressive* statement made by a presidential candidate since the 1912 campaign, when pieces of the argument were made by both the *official* Progressive candidate, Teddy Roosevelt, and the Democratic candidate, Woodrow Wilson. But the true progenitor of the Commonwealth Club address was Herbert Croly, who was the first to make the case that in order to be faithful to the Constitution's purpose it would be necessary to overturn the Constitution's limitations on the power of the national government.

The first evidence of Croly's influence in FDR's address is the pairing of Alexander Hamilton and Thomas Jefferson as the yin and yang of America's founding, which was one of Croly's central conceits.[75] But FDR brought something new to this theme, stating frankly that Hamilton was among those who "surrendered to the belief that popular government was essentially dangerous and essentially unworkable." In fact, Hamilton was "the most brilliant, honest, and able exponent of this point of view," and he concluded that "the safety of the republic lay in the autocratic strength of its government, that the destiny of individuals was to serve that government, and that fundamentally a great and strong group of central institutions, guided by a small group of able and public-spirited citizens could best direct all government."[76] Jefferson, on the other hand, "turned his mind to the same problem and took a different view." The people have two sets of rights, Jefferson believed: "personal competency," meaning the right of "free thinking, freedom of forming and expressing opinions, and . . . living each man according to his own lights." But the people also possessed the rights of "acquiring and possessing property." Yet "even Jefferson realized that the exercise of the property rights might so interfere with the rights of the individual that the government, without whose assistance the property rights could not exist, must intervene, not to destroy individualism but to protect it."[77]

Jefferson won, in FDR's view of history, and thus the government of the United States, rather than becoming a Hamiltonian autocracy, grew into a Jeffersonian democracy, and a "new day" began, "the day of the individual against the system, the day in which individualism was made the great watchword of American life." But then something changed, toward the middle of the nineteenth century, and a "new force was released and a new dream created." The new force was the industrial revolution; the dream was the possibility of an "economic machine" capable of raising living standards, putting an end to drudgery, "bringing luxury within the reach of the humblest."[78]

But with the new dream came also a new reality: the new economic system gradually became highly centralized, and the powerful industrial corporation became the "new despot" of the modern age. Both Teddy Roosevelt and Woodrow Wilson sought to tame this power, the first by putting the trusts under the authority of federal administration, the latter by breaking them up, and both were castigated as "radicals." And now, FDR concluded, we have seen how much worse our own situation is than the one that they had to face.

> In retrospect we can now see that the turn of the tide came with the turn of the century. We were reaching our last frontier; there was no more free land and our industrial combinations had become great uncontrolled and irresponsible units of power within the State. As long as we had free land; as long as population was growing by leaps and bounds; as long as our industrial plants were insufficient

to supply our own needs, society chose to give the ambitious man free play and unlimited reward provided only that he produced the economic plant so much desired.[79]

Equality of opportunity "no longer exists." America's industrial plant is already built, and may actually be "overbuilt." The frontier is no more; we cannot even make room for immigrants from Europe, given how straightened our current circumstances are. There is no more free land. All of this requires, FDR concluded, that we reassess the relationship between the government and the economy, and admit that circumstances are not what they once were. Above all, we need a "reappraisal of values." In one of the most famous passages of this speech, FDR redefined the task, not just of the government but of the nation itself: not "discovery or exploitation of natural resources, or necessarily producing more goods. It is the soberer, less dramatic business of administering resources and plants already in hand, of seeking to reestablish foreign markets for our surplus production, of meeting the problem of under consumption, of adjusting production to consumption." These tasks point in one unmistakable direction: "The day of enlightened administration has come."[80]

We will take another look at the policies of the New Deal, along with those of its successors in the 1960s, in chapter 4. But it is worth pausing, for a moment, to consider the implications of FDR's address. Among its assumptions is that there will be no more growth because there is no more "frontier"—that is, no more land for the taking. We know, of course, that this is a primitive understanding of "growth": farms can become more productive even if they do not acquire more acres; businesses can become more profitable even if the population has stopped growing, by making things that people wish to buy. FDR was right that there was no more frontier; the West was settled in fact.

But where did the idea come from that because there is no more "free land" the population will stop growing, companies will no longer be able to find markets for new products, and the market will therefore no longer be able to function without government supervision? We will come back to this speech in subsequent chapters, but the notion that both the country and the economy had stopped growing is perhaps the most peculiar of the ideas that shaped New Deal thinking, and not only by President Roosevelt. It is obviously false: using Real GDP as a measure, the economy in 2019 was more than twenty times larger than the economy of 1933.[81] And, of course, less than two decades after the president gave this speech, the postwar "baby boom" began, and the American population soared.

FDR's speech reflected a profound pessimism, but the same pessimism was often found hidden inside the most "forward-looking" progressive arguments, including those of Herbert Croly—the man even readers of the *New Republic* have forgotten, but whose ideas have had nearly as much influence on contemporary American government as the ideas of Publius.

As with Woodrow Wilson, so with Franklin Roosevelt: the effort to enact a modern reform agenda was interrupted by a war, but not before the New Deal had delivered to the federal government considerably more authority over economic life than had ever been the case in peacetime. Only a "reactionary" Supreme Court kept that control from being even greater. When the Second World War ended, America once again returned to something like "normalcy." President Harry Truman displayed some of the enthusiasm for reform that characterized the mid-1930s, and was especially eager to achieve what the British Labor Party had just managed overseas: the nationalization of health care. Yet with the Depression and the war both over, millions of Americans were eager for some peace and quiet. The eight years of President Eisenhower's administration were, relatively speaking, "wilderness" years for aging reformers, who were in any case about to be shoved aside by their children and grandchildren of the 1960s and 1970s—the next great wave of reform enthusiasm.

But the constitutional government of the pre–New Deal era had been transformed. The visible sign of this fact was the transformation of the District of Columbia itself from a hot, swampy quasi-Southern town into the capital city of the world's most powerful nation. Already crowded by the building boom required by the growth of a huge national bureaucracy (which began even before the New Deal), the capital spilled over its borders into neighboring Virginia and Maryland. The government that Presidents Eisenhower and Kennedy presided over was not only bigger and busier, but institutionally more complex than it had ever been before, in order to handle the manifold tasks that the government had acquired over the previous decades, including its new international responsibilities as the most powerful victor in history's most terrible war. The federal government now regulated labor relations; constructed housing for the poor; and supervised the construction of a new interstate highway system, making it easier for workers and products to get into and out of America's cities, and to link each part of the country with the rest. The "feds" sent checks to the elderly, policed the stock market and the nation's banks, and would soon acquire significant authority to protect the environment. The federal government grew enormously—as did the population and the size of the economy, contra the expectations of FDR's Commonwealth Club address.[82]

THE NEW LEFT

And then, all of a sudden, a new generation of reformers began to worry about the enormous size and power of the national government, and the daunting scale of American society as well as the private and public institutions that governed it: schools, corporations, the military, the bureaucracy. The founding document of the so-called New Left (new because its members—of the SDS, Students for a Democratic Society—were young, and also because it differed sharply on many questions from the "Old Left" of the New Deal era) stated in its first sentence: "We are people of this generation, bred in at least modest comfort, housed now in universities, looking uncomfortably to the world we inherit."[83] Clearly, something was amiss.

Some of what the New Left would go on to demand was not actually very new: for example, that the nation keep the promises it had already made—to care for the poor and the elderly, to achieve world peace, to keep the economy from trampling the little guys and enriching the well-connected. Above all, the New Left demanded the completion of the revolution begun by the abolition of slavery and the passage of the Fourteenth and Fifteenth Amendments—but that had been short-circuited almost before it began, with disastrous results for the nation's African-American citizens, and for all who cared about equality.

But along with the old came something that appeared to be both new and somewhat contrary to previous reform campaigns. Twentieth-century liberals had consistently pushed the center of gravity of American government upward. The New Left insisted instead (in a somewhat contradictory way, as we will see) on the importance of "the community" as the proper locus of politics. The phrase "participatory democracy" made the distinction (if not the basic idea) clear, implying that the changes to American government made since the beginning of the twentieth century had left out an important requirement of democracy, namely, that decisions be made in a way that allowed citizens to debate and decide on their own, rather than live as the mere "recipients" of largess from above, whether from federal officials or powerful private corporations. Liberal students, in reply, began to denounce "corporate liberals" for their willing participation in the "military-industrial complex," whose finger-prints were easily found all over the modern university, where faculty members were eager recipients of research money from the Department of Defense and major corporations—for example, the Dow Chemical Corporation, which was chastised for creating chemical weapons for use in the war in Vietnam.

The New Left, which began quietly with the SDS's 1962 manifesto, grew rapidly and then burned itself out. Quiet demonstrations against racism and war became larger, noisier, and finally turned violent, with street fighting and disruptions of the kind that contemporary Americans had not seen, except in news footage about revolutions abroad. As early as 1969 the SDS had broken in two, with the violent Weather Underground faction turning to domestic terrorism as a way to end "American imperialism." The election of Richard Nixon in 1968 and his reelection in 1972—when the "progressive" Democrat George McGovern carried only one state—was a hard blow, not softened even by President Nixon's resignation in the wake of the Watergate scandal in 1973.

But while the New Left got the headlines, the older version of "New Deal liberalism" had a spectacular revival in the 1960s, in the Great Society pro-grams of the Lyndon Johnson administration. Although Johnson's prosecu-tion of the war in Vietnam ultimately caused reformers to desert him—and they had never really warmed to Johnson, given his checkered background in Texas politics and the wheeling-dealing Senate—the years of his presidency saw a remarkable expansion of federal programs whose debt to reformers of the past was obvious.

First in importance was the "War on Poverty," meant to raise up those at the very bottom of the income ladder to a standard of living that could make them full members of society. But rather than simply giving financial aid to the poor, the War on Poverty stressed "participation." There was a clear "dem-ocratic" theme running through the War on Poverty, whose administrators were to encourage the formation of "community action programs" involving local residents. (This emphasis owed a great deal to the influence of politicians with links to, or sympathies with, the pre-Weatherman SDS.)[84]

Meanwhile, the Model Cities Program aimed to rebuild not just buildings but also neighborhoods. One of the most lasting elements of the Johnson ad-ministration's activism was the Elementary and Secondary Education Act of 1965, which began what became a steadily increasing amount of federal aid to public schools—with the expectation that federal money would be accom-panied by federal ideas about how schools could be improved. Public welfare also came under the supervision of the federal government, even more so than during the Depression, a time when federal "relief," although appreciated, was still so novel as to be suspect, even by some of its recipients.

The Social Security Act of 1938 had been one of the most successful of the New Deal programs for the assistance it was able to deliver to the elderly—a major form of assistance as well to the children of the elderly who were so often responsible for taking care of them, even though many of them were unemployed. The Social Security Act of 1965 added medical care to cash payments, creating the Medicare program, and in 1966 a health program to aid the poor (Medicaid) was added. It is ironic, of course, that a president who progressives and liberals never liked, and who they came to dislike intensely, can be credited with extending the political philosophy of the New Deal farther than any Democratic president since FDR himself.

And then, as on the previous two occasions of reform excitement, "normalcy" returned in the form of Presidents Reagan, Ford, and George H. W. Bush. The economy, which had not stopped growing since the end of the Second World War, grew even faster. The computer revolution, unleashed by old-fashioned antitrust actions against both IBM and what everyone in those days called "the phone company" (aka AT&T), gave birth to an entirely new sector of the economy, in the meantime creating enormous fortunes—as well as millions of new jobs and entirely new careers.[85]

But the new century began with a wholly new and unexpected challenge. Nothing about the 9/11 attack fit the reform paradigm, either the old one or the newer one from the 1960s. Twentieth-century liberals had paid scant attention to religion, except in its "Social Gospel" forms, which disappeared from reform discourse sometime in the 1950s. It was wholly unprepared for a challenge from inside the Islamic world. The instinct of modern reformers, no longer committed to a religious perspective on the world, has been to translate this challenge into purely secular terms: America had become an "empire," and now the victims on the empire's periphery were fighting back. Peace would only come through interfaith understanding, not through reliance on the same old "military-industrial complex" that had brought us wars in Asia and "police actions" in South America. Domestically, liberals urged America to continue even farther down the roads first pointed out by Croly, Wilson, and FDR, with contemporary proposals for compulsory national health insurance, higher taxes on the wealthy, greater control over the economy to protect the environment and combat climate change, and (although this is not something earlier progressives had ever contemplated) reparations for slavery. There is even some talk about breaking up monopolies again, this time aimed at the new "malefactors of great wealth" who sit on top of the tech industry.

Yet it is unmistakably the case that modern liberalism has taken a sharp turn in recent years—although the roots of this new direction can be traced to the 1960s. A favorite New Left saying—"the personal is the political"—was a way of pointing out that what individuals actually experienced was connected to, even caused by, the political arrangements that surrounded them. This is obviously true, although it is the hope of constitutional liberalism that most of life will be *immune* to political intrusions. That is, although we live in an environment defined by laws and institutions, these do not entirely define us, nor do they tell us how to live every moment of every day. But there was an element of the New Left that was uncomfortable with the idea of respecting some separation between private and public life. Also, if it is true that the personal is the political, then we must *necessarily* focus on what is private, and what is most private of all is one's "identity."

The most politically important identity in the 1960s was race. The struggle of African Americans for the protection of their civil rights defined the decade. Even before the war in Vietnam became the most urgent political problem on the New Left's agenda, support for the civil rights movement was the very definition of what it meant to be in "the movement." Yet despite the remarkable successes of the civil rights movement—most importantly, the protection of voting rights in the South—some members of the movement wondered whether Black Americans should even want to be Americans. Some of the most well-known leaders of the time, such as Stokely Carmichael and H. Rap Brown, insisted that Black identity could not include identity as an American citizen.

This rupture in the civil rights movement began to spread to other identifiable groups, whose members began to wonder whether they too could really consider "American" to be part of their identity. Groups then began to split and subdivide, as "identity" came to be defined in ever more precise and exclusive ways. "Women" were no longer a group; instead, there were "Black women" and "white women." Then there were "straight" and "gay" women in each subgroup, making for even smaller slices—and then, inevitably, "Black men" and "white men" and "gay men" and "straight men"—and white and Black versions of each. It's clear that this development was fueled by at least two different motives. The first motive was to avoid guilt, as if to say, "Just

because I'm white doesn't mean I'm one of the oppressors. I'm a victim too."
The second motive was to find comfort in an identity that separated you from
the great herd and made you special. Who can doubt that in a modern society,
finding one's "identity" can sometimes be a daunting task—especially so, perhaps, for the young.[86]

The fracturing of the civil rights, women's, and anti-war movements into
"caucuses" based on "identity" was not a phenomenon confined to the 1960s
but has gradually emerged as the most important difference between modern reformers and their not-so-long-ago ancestors. The result is a surprising
rupture in the movement to "transform America." On the one hand, the traditional complaints about the limitations of the Constitution continue. Why
can't America be like Canada, or France, or Great Britain, free countries where
the national government can, nevertheless, do more or less whatever it wishes,
without all of the fuss and bother about federalism or the Bill of Rights, from
nationalizing health care to banning guns?

On the other hand, modern reform movements have developed an intense focus on the "personal as political," with a heightened interest in matters of gender, race, sexual orientation, and many other "identities" that are
said to define Americans as "different." Where the older reformers were eager
to tame the modern economy by submitting it to "rational decision-making"
by government experts, many modern reformers tend to look inward rather
than outward, and are more interested in pushing particularistic claims for
the groups with which they identify. Where the older liberals argued for "fulfilling" the American dream in more modern ways—almost always by giving
the national government more authority over both the states and the private
economy—the newer critics have essentially rejected "America" as a nation because, they say, its history is exclusively a history of oppression and crime.[87]
Yet those who proclaim their "progressivism" are eager as well to remove the
constitutional restraints on majority rule that stand in the way of progress,
as they understand it. Like their forebears who struggled to "get around" the
Constitution, modern reformers have increasingly set their sights on breaking
the chains that the Constitution puts on the power of a presumptive majority
to have its way and work its will unimpeded—but only, of course, to do good.

POLITICAL SCIENCE CRITIQUES THE CONSTITUTION

Yet the emergence of identity politics has not stemmed the flow of constitutional critiques squarely in the progressive tradition. Indeed, the most influential political scientist of the second half of the twentieth century, Robert Dahl of Yale University, wrote a book whose very title—*How Democratic Is the American Constitution* (first published in 2001)—places the author squarely in that tradition. Notice: he did not title the book "How *Republican* Is the Constitution?" because he saw no real tension between republicanism properly understood and majoritarian democracy. "For my part, I believe that the legitimacy of the constitution ought to derive solely from its utility as an instrument of democratic government—nothing more, nothing less."[88] In this vein, he establishes four standards by which to judge whether a constitutional *system* (his word) is promoting democracy. Does it: (1) Maintain a democratic system; (2) Protect democratic rights; (3) Ensure democratic fairness; (4) Encourage democratic consensus; and (5) Promote effective problem solving?[89]

Dahl excuses the Framers for the myriad "errors" the Constitution makes. Their ignorance was understandable because they had no model to build on. But subsequent experience should encourage us to remedy those mistakes. "My question, then, is this: Why should we feel bound today by a document produced more than two centuries ago by a group of fifty-five mortal men, actually signed by only thirty-nine, a fair number of whom were slaveholders, and adopted in only thirteen states by the votes of fewer than two thousand men, all of whom are long since dead and mainly forgotten?"[90]

Dahl's most original addition to the tradition of progressive critique is to place his question in a comparative context. He asks: How does the US Constitution stack up as compared to twenty-two other mature democracies? His answer is: not well. He notes that none of these peers has adopted the US model.[91] They either lack an upper house or have one with very limited powers. Most are parliamentary in nature, with the prime minister being both a legislator and chief executive (they are not granted that title because there is a nominal head of state, a powerless monarch or a so-called president who enjoys very little power). France is the only one with direct election of the chief executive, and it does so on the basis of popular, not electoral college, election. With the exception of Canada and the UK, none of these countries adopts the "first past the post," winner-take-all form of election to parliament. Instead they rely on proportional representation. None provides life tenure for judges.

And yet, by Dahl's standards, those countries are *more* democratic and egalitarian than the United States. Since this is not the result of copying the United States, Dahl attributes the difference to political culture. Somehow the citizens and leaders of these other countries have acquired the beliefs and "habits of the heart" required to establish and sustain egalitarian, democratic government.

> The links between political equality and democracy, on the one hand, and fundamental rights, liberties, and opportunities, on the other, run even deeper. If a country is to maintain its democratic institutions through its inevitable crises, it will need a body of norms, beliefs, and habits that provide support for the institutions in good times and bad—a democratic culture transmitted from one generation to the next. People who share a democratic culture will, I think inevitably, also endorse and support an even greater sphere of rights, liberties, and opportunities. Surely the history of recent centuries demonstrates that it is precisely in democratic countries that liberties thrive.[92]

He views these findings as a refutation of Tocqueville's prediction that, unless checked deliberately, democratization will lead to despotism.

> When we examine the course of democratic development over the past two centuries, and particularly over the century just ended, what we find is a pattern of democratic development that stands in total contradiction to such a prediction. We find instead that as democratic institutions become more deeply rooted in a country, so do fundamental political rights, liberties, and opportunities. As a democratic government matures in a country, the likelihood that it will give way to an authoritarian regime approaches zero.[93]

Dahl mentions that some scholars and intellectuals support the other aspect of Tocqueville's prediction: that rather than falling victim to the "hard despotism" entailed in autocratic rule, democratic nations may well succumb to "soft despotism," a herd-like mentality. Dahl does not refute, nor even address, this alternative prediction.

As an astute political scientist, Dahl recognizes that insuperable constitutional and/or political barriers exist to prevent meaningful constitutional change. Yet he makes clear that if he could, he would abolish the Electoral College, turn the president into a prime minister (thereby ending the separation of the legislative and executive branches), allocate Senate seats on the basis of population, place curbs on the Supreme Court, and vastly restrict the powers of the states. With virtually unlimited democracy as his objective, he would turn the US political system into that of the Scandinavian countries, Israel, or Great Britain, but without the "first past the post" voting system.[94]

LAWYERS AGAINST THE CONSTITUTION

In more recent times the locus of constitutional criticism has shifted to the legal profession. The 2022 quote from two Ivy League law professors at the beginning of our introduction is only the most strident of the legal professoriate's efforts, inspired by a book by the prominent University of Texas law professor Sanford Levinson, entitled *Our Undemocratic Constitution*. As the title announces, Levinson believes the central problem of the Constitution is that it is profoundly undemocratic, so much so that he would no longer be willing to sign it.[95] In a subsequent volume entitled *Framed: America's Fifty-One Constitutions and the Crisis of Governance*, Levinson discusses the relationship of a republic to a democracy and emphatically comes down on the side of democracy.[96] Thus his specific objections to the document focus on what he takes to be the insurmountable obstacles that the Constitution puts in the way of true democracy. The Senate is undemocratic because the small states get as much representation as the large ones.[97] The Electoral College is undemocratic because it makes it possible to thwart the will of the national majority (witness 2000, and 2016).[98] The need for a supermajority of both houses of Congress to overturn a presidential veto is emphatically undemocratic.[99]

The Judiciary and the Executive, Levinson argues, can only be rendered compatible with democracy if they can be held accountable for their actions. Thus, he opposes lifetime tenure for federal justices. Although the reelectability of presidents and the impeachment process provide some presidential accountability safeguards, they are inadequate. The two-term limit provides no accountability protection during the president's second term. The impeachment process is too cumbersome and accords too much power to the undemocratic Senate. The "high crimes and misdemeanors" standard for impeachment is a bar set too high, and does not enable removing a president simply on the basis of the public's loss of confidence in the president's performance. Instead of impeachment, Levinson proposes adopting the no-confidence approach deployed in various ways by parliamentary regimes as diverse as the United Kingdom, Germany, and Israel. Although the specifics differ, each of those countries enables its parliament to declare "no confidence" in the current chief executive by a simple majority vote, requiring the chief executive to step down. Levinson would substitute a slightly less democratic version that would require a two-thirds vote of the combined Congress, thus weighting the process in favor of the more democratic House of Representatives.[100]

Since he finds that the amendment processes contained in Article 5 erect insurmountable barriers to democratization, Levinson's most important reform proposal is to make constitutional change easier and more responsive to the popular will. He would institute a "national referendum calling Congress to consider . . . a new constitutional convention whose new constitution would be put to the people for ratification by national majority vote."[101] Thus the piecemeal process of amending the Constitution by requiring a two-thirds vote of both houses of Congress and ratification by three-fourths of the states would be abolished. Article 5 also provides an alternative to piecemeal amendment by enabling two-thirds of the states to petition Congress to call for a constitutional convention, whose product would also require ratification by three-fourths of the states. Levinson's version requires only a simple national majority vote to call for a convention and a simple national majority to ratify it.[102] To further insure the democratic nature of the process, delegates to the constitutional convention would be chosen by lot.[103]

Levinson recognizes that the greatest difficulty his convention plan faces is the veneration with which the present document is held.[104] Public attachment to the Constitution is not entirely rational; rather, it is based on a deep emotional and spiritual devotion that treats the Constitution almost as if it were scripture. The subtitle of the section in which he discusses this matter is entitled "Overcoming Veneration."[105] In the next chapter we will return to the issue of veneration as it emerged in a great debate between Jefferson and Madison. Levinson emphatically agrees with Jefferson about the necessity of holding periodic constitutional conventions in opposition to Madison's conviction that for the democratic republic to survive, the Constitution must become an object of devotion, and not something to be fought over on a regular basis. Levinson quotes a famous passage from Madison's *Federalist* 49: "Frequent appeal to the people would carry an implication of some defect in the government [and] deprive the government of that veneration which time bestows on everything and without which perhaps the wisest and freest government would not possess stability."[106] A few pages later Levinson attacks "thoughtless veneration" rather than veneration per se, but does not explain how that seemingly more moderate formulation provides an adequate response to Madison.[107]

Lest one think that this chapter has overrated the links between earlier constitutional critics and contemporary ones, Levinson makes our case for us by ending the book with a coda consisting of one long quote from Woodrow Wilson. It reads, in part:

> The Constitution is not honored by blind worship. The more open-eyed we become, as a nation, to its defects, and the prompter we grow in applying with the unhesitating courage of conviction all thoroughly tested or well considered expedients necessary to make self -government among us a straightforward thing . . . the nearer will we approach to the sound sense and practical genius of the honorable statesmen of 1787. And the first step towards emancipation from the timidity and false pride which have led us to seek to thrive despite the defects of our national system rather than to deny its perfection is a fearless criticism of that system.

In an earlier section of this chapter, we discussed the tension in progressive thinking between faith in democracy and faith in nonpartisanship and expertise. This tension continues to surface among the law professors who criticize the Constitution. Although Stephen Griffin dedicated his book *Broken Trust* to Sanford Levinson, and had Levinson write the foreword, Griffin nevertheless takes a different tack, stressing the need for greater disinterested expertise in government. Indeed, expertise seems to be more important to Griffin than the need for increased majoritarianism.[108] As the title indicates, Griffin's critique centers on the damage done by radically declining public trust in government, rather than its alleged democratic deficit.[109] "Constitutions are not just about preserving individual rights—they concern and fundamentally so, the establishment and maintenance of effective governance by creating a constitutional order that is trustworthy."[110]

Griffin attributes a significant portion of that decline to "broken" elements of the Constitution. He provides a case study of the response to Hurricane Katrina to demonstrate that the horrific failures of that response were not just the result of poor decision making and partisan politics but were failures of the constitutional design relating to federalism, separation of powers, and in-sufficient executive agency autonomy.[111]

To remedy the egregious policy failures that are largely responsible for pub-lic distrust in government, Griffin proposes establishing a new fourth branch of government. Contrary to Levinsonian majoritarianism, however, Griffin focusses on the need for a branch of government characterized by nonparti-sanship and expertise. He would establish a set of nonpartisan, expert "super regulators who would be able to gradually build confidence in the political system. There is so much ongoing misconduct, outright corruption, undue in-fluence and dysfunction in politics and government that a set of independent permanent regulators is required to police them."[112]

The first form of "super regulation" he proposes would be a "National Elec-toral Commission." The current joint national and state supervision of federal elections would be replaced by a strictly national entity that would "super-vise national elections including matters of voting rights and registration." It would substitute for state legislatures in redrawing congressional districts, dis-placing a partisan process with a nonpartisan one.[113] The commission would also possess greatly expanded power to regulate campaign finance.[114] The other form of super regulation he proposes would create a set of expert, pro-fessional, nonpartisan commissions to perform the oversight functions that Congress no longer adequately performs, and to oversee the internal work-ings of Congress itself, thus holding Congress accountable in a way that the electoral process fails to do. These commissions would enjoy broad subpoena power. To perform their mission to restore public trust, these commissions would not include public officials. Instead they would be composed of former federal judges. He takes as self-evident that legal training and judicial service provide an adequate basis for the disinterested expertise such diverse tasks as drawing congressional district lines and probing the inner workings of Con-gress require.[115]

In their 2022 book, entitled *The Anti-Oligarchy Constitution*, Joseph Fishkin of UCLA Law School and William Forbath of the University of Texas declare that the current state of constitutional understanding is the product of an "an-tiquated inherited constitutional world that has created an America in which democracy has been displaced by oligarchy."[116] However, they emphasize nei-ther direct democracy nor nonpartisan, expert super-regulation and oversight. Unlike Levinson and Griffin, they would rely on representative institutions, but only if congressional and presidential elections are further democratized.

They focus most of their anger, in fact, on the federal judiciary. The key to victory in the war for a more democratic regime is letting Congress and the president work their will. Unfortunately, as things now stand, the authors claim, the judiciary has so expanded its range of authority that it thwarts attempts by the elected branches to sufficiently advance vital progressive reforms.[117]

To ensure that progressive majorities control Congress and the presidency, they demand that Congress make major changes to campaign finance and election law. Skeptical of the possibility of repealing *Citizens United*, and thus remaining unable to limit private campaign contributions, they advocate that the federal government provide "large unconditional sums of campaign money" to "any serious candidate for office" and/or match all small donor contributions. They do not define who would qualify as a serious candidate. To provide further aid to underfunded candidates, Congress should require internet platforms and media outlets to supply inexpensive or even free advertising to candidates. To maximize voter turnout, Congress should require universal voter registration.[118]

Thus liberated, Congress should and could enact laws to democratize the oligarchic political economy, expand welfare benefits, and combat gender and race discrimination. Congress could increase the power of organized labor to combat "oligarchy" by freeing unions to conduct secondary boycotts, thus enabling unions with strong economic power (teamsters, longshoremen, stagehands, etc.) to strike their employers on behalf of striking workers in other jobs and industries, especially those in which workers have less economic power (grocery workers, farm workers, packinghouse workers, etc.).[119] This would vastly enhance the latter's chances for success. Furthermore, Congress would greatly limit the ability of companies to claim that their workers are independent contractors and therefore not subject to federal employment law.[120]

Congress would extend the reach of antitrust laws to rein in the current "winner take all" monopolistic economy by treating oligarchy per se as an antitrust violation. It would be less tolerant of mergers, provide a more stringent definition of monopolies, and restrict corporate political activity. It would provide a basic universal income and universalize health insurance.[121] Congress would greatly constrain the Religious Freedom Recovery Act to keep it from acting as a "super statute" preventing a claim of religious freedom from being used as a weapon for enabling race and gender bias.

Democratizing Congress is insufficient to enact Fishkin's and Forbach's progressive agenda, because as currently constituted, a conservative Supreme

Court would declare many of these initiatives unconstitutional.[122] The great hero of their book is FDR, who both championed the passage of a tidal wave of reform initiatives and then proposed a means for ensuring that they would not be overturned by the Supreme Court[123] They endorse FDR's effort to pack the court by adding additional liberal members, and they offer their own proposal for working around the obstacle that life tenure poses, by having Congress pass legislation "causing individual Justices to rotate into a secondary role after a set term of years so that new Justices may be appointed. Congress could also strip the Court of the right to consider certain forms of challenges to its legislation.[124]

Now that we have traced the development of anti-constitutional criticism from the Anti-Federalists until the present, we proceed in the following chapter to defend the constitutional order against both specific criticisms raised and of the ethos that pervades them.

CHAPTER 3

The Case against the Constitution, Reconsidered

In chapter 2 we identified the most important critiques of the Constitution, from the Anti-Federalists through the birth of modern progressivism and its progeny, the New Deal and the Great Society. It is time now to answer those criticisms—some of which concern specific aspects of the Constitution (e.g., federalism, or the unrepresentative character of the Senate), while others mount a broader critique of America as a regime: as a particular way of living politically. In one way or another, nearly all of these attacks on the Constitution involve a defense of what the critics insist is a superior understanding of popular government—defined as "democracy"—than the one advanced by the Framers of the Constitution, which creates a regime in which the people choose who will govern, without governing directly.

Some of what appear to be critiques of the Constitution are at bottom critiques of an American "way of life." Because the Constitution undergirds that way of life, the Constitution must be overcome or at least radically transformed. As written, so goes the claim, the Constitution is undemocratic; it fosters excessive individualism, greed, inequality, and corruption; it is insufficiently protective of rights; it was founded in slavery and exploitation; it is excessively fixed and rigid; and it forces the present to be governed by the past.[1]

MITIGATED POPULAR GOVERNMENT

As we noted above, the Constitution *is* undemocratic, if "democratic" is assumed to mean majority rule simply. This criticism implies that if all the obstacles to majority rule that the Constitution establishes were removed, the American people would be freer and better governed. But the Constitution is undemocratic, not because it wishes to oppose popular rule, but because it seeks to *discipline* popular rule, by enforcing restraints on public action. It enables the majority to have its way, but only if that majority is durable enough to produce majorities in the Senate as well as the House, *and* elect a favorable president: only then will it be able to enact the policies it supports—provided that they do not violate the Constitution, which permits the people to *choose* while at the same time limiting what the government so chosen may do. Furthermore, the more consequential a proposal is, the larger the majority required to adopt it: thus, constitutional amendments require supermajorities. (Traditionally, the Senate requires a supermajority for shutting down debate, although this is not a constitutional rule.) Therefore, the case against the Constitution involves not a defense of democracy but a defense of *impulsive* democracy, the idea that majorities should obtain their goals in real time, no matter what those goals are, and no matter how narrow the majority.

Properly understood, however, the Constitution's checks on democracy are not intended to *obstruct* it but to *restrain* it. Herbert Storing referred to the result of these efforts as "mitigated popular government."

> Mitigated popular government is itself altogether consistent with democracy: it is not something foisted on the people from outside. Just as any one of us is likely to arrange one's own affairs so that circumstances will help resist one's own vices, so a people might anticipate its own probable future flightiness or foolishness and try to build into its constitutional institutions [means] to counteract those tendencies. The anti-democratic or non-democratic devices in our Constitution are democracy's own inventions of prudence to deal with its own harmful tendencies.[2]

Unfortunately, mitigated democracy—including the complex and time-consuming procedures involved in amending the Constitution—provides no absolute guarantee against foolish judgments. The decision to prohibit the sale of alcohol survived both houses of Congress and ratification by three-quarters of the states. But one can only imagine what decisions abhorred by progressives might have survived the amendment process if amending the Constitution required a mere legislative majority, or even a majority (rather than a supermajority) of the states. Until recently, a majority of Americans opposed same-sex marriage. What if we had had an up or down national vote on this question as late as 2010?[3] Or, what if at the height of twentieth-century racism, perhaps the 1920s, there had been a constitutional amendment passed to enable employers, landlords, and restaurants to discriminate on the basis of race—in effect repealing the Fourteenth Amendment the way the Twenty-First Amendment repealed the Eighteenth (Prohibition). Such a proposal could not have been approved by three-fourths of the states; but it might have been approved by a simple majority of the states or, had we passed a national referendum amendment, as Teddy Roosevelt proposed, a simple majority of the nation's voters.

Supermajorities are accused of being "anti-democratic," but they are often necessary in order to enable enforcement of controversial laws, which if supported only by a bare majority would be wildly flouted (as was, in fact, the Prohibition amendment, even *with* the approval of three-fourths of the states). Many, perhaps even most, bills that survive the legislative process and end up on the statute books are different in important ways from the versions first introduced, because of the need to broaden their support beyond their authors and original supporters. At a time when many Americans profess an abhorrence of "polarization," it is useful to note what that word actually means: to divide into "two sharply contrasting groups or sets of opinions." The solution to polarization, obviously, is compromise—a meeting of opposites somewhere closer to the middle, a practice that is more likely to take place if action requires *more* than a simple majority.

The aspect of the Constitution that Americans most cherish is the Bill of Rights.[4] As the Declaration of Independence boldly states, rights are "unalienable," meaning that we cannot be deprived of them without suffering an act of theft. This applies to all those rights that even the Constitution's critics cherish—free speech, freedom of the press—as well as at least one they do not cherish—the right to "keep and bear arms." Protecting these rights requires severe limits on majority rule. It is precisely because diverse minorities depend on one or more of these rights that their "unalienability" is so valuable. Of course, most citizens will appreciate some rights more than others. But placing these rights beyond the reach of simple majorities means they are nearly untouchable, and therefore, despite the great controversy over gun rights, there is no serious possibility of repealing the Second Amendment. "Gun control" therefore means various measures taken by Congress and the states to regulate gun ownership and the manufacture and sale of firearms without being so restrictive that the right to "keep and bear arms" is effectively abolished.[5]

We have discussed how the diversity of the modern state poses challenges to free government. The inability of the majority to deprive minorities of their rights—at least, not without violating the Constitution—is one of the crucial ways in which those challenges are met. The original Constitution did not include a bill of rights. The Framers believed that the constitutional blueprint alone would protect the most important rights. Hamilton, for example, insisted (correctly) that "the constitution is itself in every rational sense . . . A BILL OF RIGHTS."[6] But the Framers bent to the will of those who made the Bill of Rights their price for supporting the document, and those advocates were correct.

Perhaps the greatest importance of the Bill of Rights rests in its educational value.[7] Its advocates recognized that no other means was as critical for preserving a free people as the constant reminder of the rights they possessed, so that they would be alert to efforts to undermine them. Having those rights in the forefront of its thoughts made it all the more likely that the people would resist any effort to impinge on them—and resist also the temptation to steal those rights from others. This is one reason the Bill of Rights appears as a separate list of guarantees, rather than being folded back into the original document (e.g., in Article I, which outlines the powers of the Congress as well as the original limitations on those powers). To play its educational role, the restrictions on the government contained in the Bill of Rights ought to be listed together, supporters believed, separate from the original text of the Constitution, so that they would stand out.[8]

But why this list, and not others, or at least a couple more? Right to vote?

CONSTITUTIONALISM AND INEQUALITY

The Constitution, it is true, does nothing to protect against greed, materialism, and inequalities of wealth, the prevalence of which so deeply disturbs many Americans, including these authors. The Constitution protects private property and supports a competitive market economy—both of which are essential to the preservation of liberty as well as prosperity.[9] Article I grants Congress the power to regulate interstate and foreign commerce. This power was understood to foster commerce by preventing states or localities from impeding the free flow of goods across state lines or national borders. The Bill of Rights protects private property from usurpation by the government—and this is the foundation of the liberty to keep the income and property you have earned, even if some people think it "unseemly" to have more than others. The Fifth Amendment's Takings Clause states that "private property [shall not] be taken for public use, without just compensation."[10] Article I, Section 10 prevents a state from impairing the obligation of contract, meaning that if you make a legal promise you are expected to keep it, and can be held liable if you do not. Since it was the states that regulated contracts, this clause had the effect of ensuring that if persons contracted with one another in good faith, no government could intervene to void that contract or refuse to enforce it. Constitutional critics have not attacked these specific clauses. Rather, as we demonstrated in chapter 2, they lament the *spirit* that the Constitution's defense of free enterprise underpins.[11] And, for the first time since the Depression, large segments of the American public sympathize with the anticapitalist critique and evince deep skepticism about free markets, a free economy, and private property.[12]

To assess the validity of this critique it is necessary to disentangle its various strands. One claim is that capitalism is responsible for keeping the poor in their poverty.[13] This idea echoes FDR's observation in his Commonwealth Club address that the economy had matured. It would no longer grow—indeed, it *could* no longer grow—and therefore the interplay of market forces could no longer be counted on to make people better off, including those currently at the bottom. If the pie cannot get bigger, then any increase in the size of my slice means your slice gets smaller. This was the dominant understanding among progressives, and it was based on what in retrospect appears to be a gloomy and even naïve assumption: that neither the economy nor the population would continue to grow in the future. The severe contraction of the economy in the early 1930s, therefore, was said to be not a mysterious aberration but the result of a new reality. This new reality would require a fundamental reconstruction of the relationship between the federal government and the economic order. As FDR put it in his famous Commonwealth Club address: "The age of enlightened administration has arrived."[14]

This view might be excused by the enormous economic shock of the Depression, but as a prescription for fixing the nation's economic problems it was shortsighted and counterproductive. The evidence for this is the remarkable growth of the American economy in subsequent decades, during times of war and times of peace alike, compared to the sluggish economic growth and double-digit unemployment rates of the 1930s.[15] Of course, market forces no longer operate in as unfettered a manner as they did before the New Deal. The national government regularly intervenes in the economy, establishing a federal minimum wage, providing health care and pensions for the elderly and the poor, regulating banks and securities firms, and controlling pollution of the air, land, and water. Most importantly, given the origins of the stock market crash that preceded the Great Depression, the government now regulates the stock exchanges more effectively than it did in 1929. And ever since the New Deal Court shifted its definition of "interstate commerce," the Constitution no longer serves as an absolute barrier to the federal regulation of the full range of industrial, commercial, and agricultural activities. Although there have been some serious economic downturns since the Great Depression, including the stagflation of the 1970s, the aftermath of the stock market crash in 2008, and the rocky period beginning in 2022 influenced by the onset of the war in Ukraine and the continued impact of COVID-19, economic growth has been the norm, and the bulk of the American population has continued to enjoy low rates of unemployment and high living standards.[16]

Even poor Americans live far better than poor Americans in the past, partly because of government benefits, but in larger part because of the decline in the prices of what once were considered luxuries. Many Americans officially categorized by the government as "poor," for example, own what the poor even in Western Europe do not own: air conditioners, computers, and cars.[17] America appears to have more poor people than other rich countries because it has a higher percentage of the population below 60 percent of the median US income. However, US median income is quite high compared to other nations. If one compares the percentage of the population below 60 percent of the European Union's considerably lower median income, the United States enjoys a lower percentage of citizens in poverty than Sweden, Great Britain, and France.[18] Most of the time the free enterprise economy creates ample numbers of jobs. Thus, the persistence of poverty amid plenty does not indicate a failure of the market but rather a social failure, involving a variety of factors including bad schools, broken families, substance abuse, and high rates of crime that blight the chances of children succeeding before they are even out of school.[19] Despite hundreds of billions spent on improving the education of the poor and trying to ameliorate the debilitating conditions of life in very poor neighborhoods, these problems persist, and in chapter 4 we offer an explanation for this failure. Thus, the problem of poverty remains unsolved, a stain on the society but not one to be blamed on capitalism or the Constitution, but rather on the failure of public policies supported, for the most part, by both political parties, for most of the past century.

Those who seek greater government control of the economy often (and mistakenly) point to Sweden and other Scandinavian countries as an example of the success of "democratic socialism."[20] But these are not socialist countries.

The private sector thrives there. Sweden and Norway have more billionaires per capita than the United States and charge no inheritance tax. The United States charges a 40 percent inheritance tax rate; Denmark's rate is only 15 percent. In response to its economic stagnation of the 1990s, Sweden initiated a whole series of deregulatory efforts and initiated a 33 percent cut in the size of its government.[21]

In Sweden, education vouchers can be used at private schools.[22] Patients can receive medical services from private suppliers. Sweden does have higher taxes and greater welfare spending, but in other ways it is more capitalistic than the United States. It has no minimum wage, and it imposes fewer but more efficient regulations on industry, trade, and banking. Property rights are well protected. According to the Heritage Foundation, a staunch defender of free enterprise, "[Sweden's] efficient regulatory framework strongly facilitates entrepreneurial activity, allowing business formation and operation to be dynamic and innovative."[23] Heritage's Economic Freedom Index assigns Sweden slightly lower scores than the United States because of its higher government spending and taxation, but it assigns higher scores for all other components of economic freedom.[24]

The taxation gap between Sweden and the United States is not great. Swedes pay on average 12.3 percent of their income in taxes while the average American pays 10 percent.[25] Indeed, very wealthy Americans, the top 10 percent, pay 45 percent of the total tax burden, while their Swedish counterparts pay only 27 percent. Overall, the Swedish tax system is far less progressive than that in the United States.[26] Nor is Sweden an outlier. According to the Organization for Economic Cooperation and Development (OECD), the top 10 percent of earners in France in 2015 paid only 28 percent of the total tax burden, and in Germany they paid 31 percent. Conversely, the bottom 90 percent of earners in the United States paid only 55 percent of the tax burden, while the bottom 90 percent of earners in France paid 72 percent; in Germany they paid 69 percent; and in Sweden they paid 73 percent.

Thus, in Sweden and other modern democracies, the cost of a generous welfare state falls squarely on the middle class, as it would in the United States if favorite progressive schemes such as free higher education and a government monopoly on health-care insurance were adopted. Instead, the tax burden in the United States falls largely on the wealthy and on corporations. As a result, the OECD rated the American tax system the most "progressive" among the developed nations.[27]

Critics of capitalism also abhor the impact of the free enterprise economy in fostering inequality, and they point to the Constitution's numerous protections of private property as inequality's source and foundation.[28] Economic inequality is a reality, not only in America, but in modern nations generally. Income inequality in the United States has gotten more pronounced in recent years, in large part because of the rapid rise in incomes at the very top of the income pyramid. That is, the rich have become much richer than they were a generation ago, without causing the poor or the middle class to become poorer. According to the Congressional Research Service, "Rising income inequality [since the 1970s] is driven largely by relatively rapid income growth at the top of the income distribution." Whereas in 1975 the top fifth of income earners had average incomes 10.3 times greater than the average income of the bottom fifth, by 2019 the top fifth had incomes that were 16.6 times the incomes at the bottom.[29] It follows, as well, that as the income of the wealthy has increased, their share of federal income taxes has also gone up: the top 1 percent of income earners paid 33.2 percent of all federal income taxes in 2001 and 40.1 percent in 2018.[30]

But the incomes of the middle class have also risen, and living standards have increased for everyone, including the poor.[31] To determine how deep a problem inequality actually is, one must distinguish among the various charges against it, some of which are pragmatic in nature, while others are ethical. Inequality is accused of interfering with economic growth, but it is criticized as well because it is indecent. It is also criticized for its alleged impact on the political system: that is, the wealthy are said to have an unfair influence on the outcome of elections—a topic to be taken up more fully below.

The pragmatic case is much weaker than the ethical one.[32] The practical argument for enabling a class of very rich people to flourish is that precisely because they have so much wealth they are more prone to invest, and especially to invest in risky ventures—risks that do not simply grease the wheels of the economy but provide for technological and conceptual breakthroughs.[33] If this form of surplus were taxed away, substitutes would need to be found—or else the economy would simply stop innovating. The two most available substitutes are employee and union pension funds, and the government itself. Pension funds are already huge investors in stocks and bonds, and government can use its taxing power to generate capital. But pension funds are not venturesome. Because their primary responsibility is to protect the present and future retirement income of their members they must, for the most part, act cautiously. They cannot afford to take a flier on an unknown computer geek operating out of a garage. Government does indeed provide valuable seed money for technologically and conceptually advanced ventures—but these tend to be confined to those investments that have a plausible connection to national defense. For example, the Defense Department's Advanced Research Projects Agency (DARPA) provided funding that was crucial for the creation of the internet. But here the intention was to find a way to maintain a nationwide communications network in anticipation of a war that might disable the nation's capital. Military planners were not dreaming of cat videos and Twitter.[34] This example is the exception to the general rule that government investment tends to be risk averse for the same reason that pension funds are risk averse: after all, the government is not spending its own money, but the money of taxpayers, and the use of each tax dollar competes with other potential uses. Spending on national defense might very well justify risks that could not be tolerated by investment firms handling retirement accounts or ordinary government agencies. But it is unlikely that those risks would have included startup funds for Apple or Microsoft.

The willingness of wealthy investors to risk even heavy losses enables a multitude of cutting-edge efforts to launch. Many will fail, and it is only the ability of the rich to suffer financial loss that sustains such economic dynamism. This is the entire explanation for why the internet is an American invention: once the basic framework was established by the Defense Department, everything that followed—Xerox, IBM, Microsoft, and Apple, followed by hundreds of companies taking the risks that created the "technology sector"—was a product of private capital. According to a recent Brookings Institution study, the United States leads the world in technological innovation.[35] Inevitably, some of those investments paid huge dividends and some were a net loss. The same thing can be said about the extraordinary investments in medical technology financed by private capital, which is why the American pharmaceutical industry plays such an outsize role in the global market for new medicines.[36] Because this pharmaceutical industry was already in place, it was available to perform an unprecedented achievement, albeit with substantial government financial help: the rapid development of not one, but (as we write) three COVID-19 vaccines in less than a year.

In addition to investing and consuming—both sensibly and frivolously— the very rich are crucial supporters of the great private institutions that serve the public, such as museums, hospitals, social services, churches, "think tanks," and universities. Private philanthropy operates on such a vast scale in the United States that when it is added to government spending it enables the United States to achieve virtually the same level of welfare, cultural, and education spending as that of its European counterparts, where private philanthropy is less extensive.[37] If the wealth of the wealthy is reduced, they will contribute less, and either the recipients of private philanthropy will face greatly decreased income, or government funds will (some people hope) make up the loss. In this way, with regard to both investment and philanthropy, reducing the wealth of the rich creates a much more intrusive role for government.

It would be pleasant to believe that such a substitution of political for private control increases the political power of ordinary people, but that is naïve. Neither Congress nor the president has the time or the expertise to provide meaningful control and oversight over the bureaucracies that would have to make the complex and subtle choices involved in choosing which cultural, educational, and social service activities to support. Federal government bureaucracies are already deeply involved in such efforts. The question is whether increasing their dominance at the expense of private philanthropy advances a public good. Individual Americans give far more money to charity than their wealthy European counterparts.[38] The United States also engages in far more social welfare tax expenditure, meaning tax deductions for various policy objectives including aiding the working poor. For example, the Earned Income Tax Credit provided more than twenty-five million taxpayers with almost $63 billion in federal Earned Income Tax Credits during the 2019 tax year.[39] When the accounting is done properly, by combining tax expenditures with charitable and philanthropic spending on social welfare, the United States actually spends more on social welfare policy than its "welfare state" counterparts in Europe.[40] Does society benefit more by increasing bureaucratic authority and discretion (which, as we will argue in chapter 4, is already greater than it should be), or by maintaining considerable discretion in diverse private hands? The contrasting experience of American technological innovation and that of even advanced European economies supplies the answer. There is no European counterpart to either Apple or Microsoft, or, for that matter, the Ford Foundation or any of the other philanthropic institutions that have contributed so much to American cultural and educational life.

One cannot ignore that some percentage of the wealthiest Americans may have achieved their wealth through inheritance, dumb luck, or unscrupulous dealings. But the vast majority of America's wealthiest citizens are as wealthy as they are because they did something useful, not because they had wealthy parents or because they are unscrupulous. *Forbes Magazine* publishes annually a list of the four hundred wealthiest Americans, and in 2018, 67 percent of those on the list were self-made.[41] Unfortunately, apart from punishing criminal behavior, no objective standards exist to discriminate between the deserving and underserving rich. Should Lady Gaga or Tom Brady be richer than a school teacher? If not, why not? And who could be trusted to make such judgments? The Congress? The Department of Health and Human Services? Furthermore, the attempt to use government to make such discriminations would violate a constitutional stricture that nearly all Americans cherish: the equal protection of the laws, which forbids the government from deciding who should be wealthy and who should not. And how could any government be trusted to decide, on its own, who should have how much money—especially when the people in control of that government are likely to be replaced two or four years hence? Would the people disinherited by the Smith administration get their wealth back under the Jones administration? For that matter, what is to stop the members of the Jones administration from deciding that it is the members of the Jones administration who should be wealthy?

A related criticism of the super-rich is that of indecency. Not only do they not deserve their money, it is argued, but they flaunt it through indecent or silly behavior and consumption, as graphically depicted in popular magazines from *People* to the *New Yorker*.[42] Is there any moral justification for yachts the size of ocean liners or mansions that could house dozens of families? Or $20,000 bed sheets and $500,000 cars? No. And yet, how is one to distinguish between the decent moral outrage such consumption inspires and just plain envy? Would you like to own a yacht? If so, how big should it be? Since it is not possible to distinguish between the "good" and the "bad" super-rich, the only means for eliminating the undeserving and the indecently consuming super-rich is to have no very wealthy citizens at all—not even in Hollywood, the source of many of the worst offenders among the wealthy—eliminating them as a class through confiscatory taxation and accepting the expansion of state power, economic stultification, and cultural conformity that such a change would entail.[43]

The materialism and greed that progressives deplore are indeed defects in American life. But changes in the Constitution and the free enterprise spirit it embodies will not remedy those defects. Materialism is not an American phenomenon but a modern one, and greed is one of the oldest of sins, preceded only by envy.[44] In any case, although modern socialist regimes preach a higher regard for economic justice than capitalist ones, they do not provide them. The revolutions that broke out in Eastern Europe in the 1980s and 1990s were motivated by a desire for political liberty, but also by an understandable desire for a better standard of living, one that none in the Soviet bloc enjoyed except those in power. Those who revolted against the Soviet regimes understood the connection: in a socialist regime, only the rulers will be rich—or even have enough to eat.[45] This is true of all of the socialist regimes that have emerged since the beginning of the twentieth century, from the original Russian version to its contemporary Asian and Latin American imitators.[46]

There was a time when society was far less materialist and individualist, a time prior to the birth of the modern world.[47] That world was based on hierarchy, custom, religion—and very short life spans. There is no going back to such a world even if one wanted to sacrifice the gains in liberty, equality, prosperity, and technology (and longer life spans) that modernity has made possible. In the contemporary context, brotherly love and rejection of materialism thrive best in those communities that most decisively *reject* modernity, such as the Amish and monastic orders. The freewheeling American constitutional order allows such communities to thrive and even to invite imitation. The limits the Constitution places on government intrusiveness leave room for private life to move in any number of different directions, both salutary and pernicious. For example, if parents want to organize to discourage children from abusing Facebook, they are free to do so. If they don't like the public schools they can choose a private school—or lobby their local state and city government to improve the local educational offerings. Government does not stop professors from encouraging their students to seek satisfaction from reflection and contemplation rather than from shopping. Precisely because such efforts go against the prevailing culture they will not, at least initially, garner majority support. But private initiative, not democratic majoritarianism, offers the most promising avenue for curbing the vices of modernity that many progressives, and many conservatives, abhor.

THE CONSTITUTION AND RIGHTS

Progressives accuse the Constitution of being insufficiently protective of rights because they have a very broad understanding of what constitutes a "right."[48]

In the Commonwealth Club address and the Four Freedoms speech, Franklin Roosevelt introduced an important alteration of the idea of rights found in the Constitution and the Bill of Rights, shifting the focus from what the government is *forbidden* to do to what it *must* do in order to help citizens cope with the modern economy. The new idea is *economic* rights: a right to security in one's old age and, more broadly, "freedom from want." In the 1960s Medicare, taking up FDR's challenge, expanded the concept of old-age security to include the right to government-provided medical care. The key difference between the older and the newer rights is that while the older ones guaranteed freedom *from* government intervention—that is, any attempt to limit speech, assembly, or the practice of religion—the newer idea of rights required the government to *provide* something—pensions, medical insurance, prescription drugs, and so on. The popularity of these programs has encouraged progressives to couch other demands for government intervention in terms of rights—a right to health care for all (not just the elderly), a right to a safe and healthy environment, a right to a guaranteed income—and in 2021, free community college, day care, and kindergarten.[49] As the Declaration of Independence states, the essence of a right is that it is "unalienable," meaning that it cannot legitimately be taken away. This does not mean that it is entirely unmodifiable. As the Supreme Court has ruled, though the Congress may not deny freedom of speech, people are not free to falsely "cry fire in a crowded theater," among other restrictions. But the First Amendment *does* mean that there is a very strong presumption against limiting speech. One is free to shout curse words and even racist epithets during a protest demonstration, to make unfounded criticisms of a public figure, or to worship the devil. Thus, one cannot apply a utilitarian calculus regarding free speech. One cannot simply add up its costs and compare those to its benefits.[50]

In principle, however, if one has a right to health care *one should be given as much of it as one wants*, regardless of the costs. Nor is one free to ask whether granting such a right creates a moral hazard, that is, whether it leads to perverse behavior. Thus, if there is a right to a guaranteed income, the public is not free to ask whether providing that income creates a serious disincentive to work. As programmatic rights become more numerous—rights that depend on government *programs*, which exist only because the Congress has appropriated money for them—the less possible it becomes to make rational spending decisions. Government only has so much revenue. The more it spends on one program, the less it has to spend on other ones: unless it decides to borrow the money from future generations in the form of deficits, as the federal government has been doing, in fact, since the 1960s—with the result that the national debt (defined as the ratio of debt to gross domestic product) is now larger than it has been since the end of the Second World War.[51]

The freedoms protected by the Constitution are not like this: your right to free speech does not interfere with my right to free speech, and no one has to decide how much of it you deserve, or who will give it to you, or for how much. You can exercise this right at no cost to the taxpayers—or you can decline to exercise the right at all. Health care is, generally speaking, a good thing. But is an additional dollar spent on health care really more socially beneficial than one spent on education or public transportation? Are there more and less efficient ways of providing good health care? Conceptualizing health care as a right makes it impossible to ask such questions—and as entitlement spending consumes an ever-larger share of the total national budget, those responsible for running the government have an ever smaller say in what it is that the government is actually doing.

THE CONSTITUTION FORCES US TO BE
GOVERNED BY THE DEAD

Contemporary critics frequently make the claim that a written constitution, especially one that is difficult to amend, forces the present to be governed by the past.[52] This claim is not new. In fact, it was the subject of a famous exchange of letters between James Madison, who had just returned to Virginia from the Constitutional Convention, and Thomas Jefferson, who was serving as the American ambassador in Paris. Madison had sent Jefferson a copy of the proposed Constitution for his comments, along with a lengthy defense of the convention's work and some observations on the problems the delegates had to overcome.

Jefferson was generally sympathetic to what the convention had done, but he was uneasy about the difficulty of amending the Constitution, which required two-thirds majorities in both houses of Congress, as well as the approval of three-fourths of the state legislatures. In fact, Jefferson was uncomfortable with the very idea of a Constitution meant to be permanent, believing (as many do today) that the past should not have such a tight grip on the present and the future. But Madison understood that for the new nation to be successful, future generations would need to see the Constitution as a document worthy of their devotion, even though they could have had no role in approving it. That is why public officials swear an oath to defend the Constitution, rather than the nation: a certain amount of "veneration" must be encouraged, as if the Constitution were an honored ancestor. But in Jefferson's view, being governed by a document made by the hands of others did not deserve to be called "self-government" at all.[53]

Accordingly, Jefferson worked out a scheme for holding a constitutional convention every nineteen years—a number derived from a complex formula involving birth rates and average life spans—and asked Madison to submit the idea to the Congress for its consideration. "The earth belongs always to the living generation. . . . Every Constitution, then, and every law naturally expires at the end of 19 years. If it be enforced longer, it is an act of force and not of right."[54] Jefferson took this idea so seriously that he was still promoting it years later. "We may consider each generation as a distinct nation," he wrote in 1813, "with a right, by the will of its majority, to bind themselves, but none to bind the succeeding generation, more than the inhabitants of another country."[55]

Madison's reply aims, however gently, to demolish his friend's idea—for its impracticality but more importantly for its fundamental premise that each discrete generation owes nothing either to those who came before or those who will follow. Each generation, after all, has received a permanent and unearned gift from previous generations, and therefore owes some measure of respect to the decisions made in the past. Likewise, each generation is morally bound to act in ways that will work to the advantage of generations yet unborn.[56] We hear such arguments all of the time, but we often fail to notice the logic behind them. What is the argument for combatting climate change if not an argument for acting now for the benefit of those who will follow us? In turn, our descendants will look back in gratitude (we hope) for what we do now, just as we look back in gratitude to those whose past contributions have been so important to our own freedom and prosperity. In Madison's time, those would have been the settlers who originally framed the colonial assemblies and wrote the constitutions that had taught generations of Americans how to make a free government work properly. Madison's generation was now profiting from their labors, paying them back by paying the debt forward in time. In our own time, we might think of those who fought the war against Hitler—or who pushed the civil rights movement, often at the risk of their lives, to its great successes in the 1960s. How can we ignore the debt we owe them?

But Madison also stressed some practical arguments against a regular over-throw of the Constitution and its continual replacement.

First, in anticipation of the entirely predictable moment when all the rules would suddenly change, political actors would focus on that moment to the exclusion of everything else—just as opposing parties in Congress have recently ceased the effort at bipartisan compromise in anticipation of the next congressional election, less than two years away. All useful deliberations would cease as all parties hedged their bets. Making a new constitution would be a moment of opportunity for self-interested groups to pursue their own aims amid the general confusion and uncertainty. If the rules can change every nineteen years, there will be plenty of time to plan ahead, and faithful deliberations on the problems of the day would go out the window as the most ambitious partisans prepared for their next big chance.

Second, having a new constitution once in every two decades would deprive each document, Madison wrote, of the "prejudice in its favor which is a salutary aid to the most rational government."[57] That is, no constitution will be perfect; it will therefore be helpful if the public has a bias in its favor, drawn partly from the fact of its age, allowing them to give it their effective support despite its faults.

The argument about the Constitution being "fixed" and "rigid" is also overdone. The Constitution has been amended twenty-seven times (including the original Bill of Rights), and at least twenty of these amendments represent highly consequential reforms of basic institutions or practices. These amendments created the modern presidential election system; extended voting rights to Black Americans, women, and eighteen-year-olds; guaranteed the "equal protection of the laws" to all Americans, banned "demon Rum" (for a while), provided for the direct election of senators, created the modern income tax, fixed a two-term limit for the president, and abolished the poll tax, which had become nothing more than a means of keeping Black Americans from voting in the South.[58]

Does not recognize Madison's doubts about veneration

PARTIES

As important as these amendments have been, an extra-constitutional development—the advent of political parties, and more particularly the two-party system—has also been crucial for adapting the constitutional order to the

exigencies of popular government.[59] The Constitution does not mention political parties; indeed, the Framers were initially opposed to them.[60] The root
of the word "party" is *part*, which in some circumstances is a synonym for "faction." The Framers recognized the potential of parties to breed divisiveness,
thus obstructing the establishment of a "more perfect union." Their models
for good politics were the Electoral College and the Senate. State legislatures
would choose prudent electors who would meet collegially in each state to
deliberate over who they considered to be most suited to the presidency—on
the plausible assumption (at the time) that only the most attentive citizens
would be aware of suitable candidates outside their own state. The same state
legislatures would also choose members of the Senate—and once again, the
assumption is that the Senate is less of a popular body than an instrument of
federalism, since its members were not directly elected (until the Seventeenth
Amendment) but appointed by the state legislatures.

This expectation is an example of how even the most clear-thinking real-
ists can misread human nature. In their longing to keep factions at bay, the
framers of the Constitution did not fully account for the *political* character
of human beings—even though they were, themselves, superlatively political.
In a popular government the people will insist on playing a major role in the
choice of *all* their national leaders—not only the members of the House of
Representative, but also the national chief executive. But it would be essential
to prevent such a choice from becoming the occasion for "tumult and disorder."[61] Thus the choice of an Electoral College to make the final choice, by
citizens chosen by a popularly elected state legislature, appointed for the sole
purpose of making a single decision, and then retiring back to the obscurity
of private life.

The Framers might be forgiven for their naivete since theirs was the first
truly popular government in human history and therefore they had no precedent to rely on. It was therefore inevitable that by 1800, in most states, the
voters would choose among competing slates of electors pledged to support
specific candidates. Indeed, the Electoral College never really performed its
deliberative function. George Washington was the undisputed choice of the
people, and the electors were eager to ratify that choice. The 1796 election was
held even as the Democratic-Republican Party was in its infancy but not yet
sufficiently developed to mount slates of pledged electors to challenge the candidacy of John Adams. However, by 1800 it had developed the organizational
capacity to do so successfully.[62]

Despite the antipartisan outlook of the Framers, the Constitution does not actually obstruct party formation, especially after the Twelfth Amendment required that electors cast separate ballots for president and vice president, thus encouraging the creation of a president–vice president ticket. Indeed, the Framers unwittingly provided a vital stimulus for the development of the distinctly American party system: federalism. Because states have elected governors with significant powers, parties needed to organize at the state level to win the valuable prize of the governor's political support for a presidential candidate, as well as the support of important state legislators. And because the president is chosen by state-designated electors and not by a national plurality, the winner must form a coalition among states with a majority of electoral votes. In fact, the first party-dominated election was the 1800 state coalition that formed behind Thomas Jefferson.[63]

Because of this state focus, national parties, at least until 1968, were really congeries of state parties. In a sense, they resembled feudal monarchies. Like medieval monarchs, presidents wielded power, but were beholden to state party "barons" for support. The barons were the powerful city and county leaders, governors, or state party chairs, who sometimes wielded more concentrated power than their nominal chieftains in public office, albeit over a much narrower sphere. This arrangement was almost as old as the Constitution itself: Jefferson invented the so-called spoils system, and the team of Martin Van Buren and Andrew Jackson greatly expanded it.[64] This system enhanced presidential power by giving the president a reservoir of support, at least in a plurality of states, *and* was at the same time a vital check on the president, because to win reelection, the "king" had to maintain the loyalties of a sufficient number of "barons" by acceding to their demands to channel jobs and other forms of government largesse to their supporters, and to support national policies that would be popular in the crucial states. "Spoils" is a misnomer for a system that rewards party loyalty while checking presidential power, but the term "patronage" is even worse, since it implies a top-down relationship rather than the system of reciprocity that came to characterize the relationship between "barons" and "monarch." Milton Rakove captures the essence of this reciprocal relationship in the title of his book on Chicago politics in the heyday of the Daley machine: "*We Don't Want Nobody Nobody Sent.*"[65] In this way federalism enabled the creation of a decentralized party system, while the vitality of that system reinforced federalism.

Parties sustained popular government in other ways as well. Despite the excellence of both the Declaration of Independence and the Constitution, the former is highly abstract in its declaration of rights and the latter is schematic, perhaps not fully anticipating the often tumultuous nature of popular choice. As they developed from the start of the nineteenth century, the parties were able to cultivate subjective forms of loyalty to supplement the more rational forms of attachment fostered by those two formal documents. The word *party*, significantly, also means "convivial socializing," and for most of American history, parades, rallies, Jefferson-Jackson Day and Lincoln dinners, and other ceremonial occasions suffused party life. As the aforementioned dinner name demonstrates, parties also create heroes. Jefferson, Jackson, Teddy Roosevelt, Lincoln, FDR, and Ronald Reagan instilled pride and admiration in party identifiers, thus nourishing their emotive attachment to the political order.[66]

Although the Framers worried about the size of the country, they did not anticipate how the sheer size of the Union would make it difficult for voters to make reasoned electoral choices. As the population expanded, the size of congressional districts grew, making it ever more difficult for voters to know how to evaluate congressional candidates, since the likelihood that most of them would have any personal knowledge of the candidates had evaporated. The failure of the Electoral College to perform a deliberative function meant that voters would have to choose among presidential candidates who might come from hundreds if not thousands of miles away, whom they would never meet and about whom they had only scant and often unreliable information. Here again parties came to the rescue. Because they differed on important political principles and provided strong sources of attachment, they reduced the complexity of voter choice to a manageable level. Voters might not always *like* the candidates of their party, but most of the time they would support them, because even though they were voting for strangers, those strangers had been vouched for by a trusted local source.[67]

The Constitution requires that congressional seats be apportioned among the several states based on the decennial census, but it does not specify that the states elect their congressional delegation on the basis of districts. Nonetheless, dividing a state into districts quickly became the norm except in those states not populous enough to have more than one representative, in which case the single House member is elected statewide. States probably adopted the district system because the only model they knew for a national representative assembly was the British Parliament, whose members were elected from "constituencies," and because they had long ago adopted that model for electing the lower houses of colonial legislatures. This method also was consistent with the view of representation that prevailed in the nation and that is defined by Madison in *Federalist* 10. The Congress will be, Madison argued, a "chosen body of citizens," through which the views of the voters will be "filtered." The Senate represents the states; the House represents the people, and for this reason the districts needed to be as small as was practical.

Though unintended, this decision also greatly encouraged the emergence of a two-party system. Had the states opted for statewide at-large elections, this would have encouraged the advent of a multi-party system, as is to be found in many modern democracies. The two-party system is a bulwark of American democracy because it enables elected officials to be held accountable. Multi-party systems encourage the formation of coalitions of unlikes, which deprive voters of any ability to know what the coalitions actually stand for. A glaring example of the antidemocratic nature of multi-party systems is Israel, where the governing coalition in 2021–2022 contained some parties that advocate the annexation of the entire West Bank, as well as parties that advocate the creation of a Palestinian state there.[68] Whatever the faults of the two-party system, there is not much doubt about what differentiates a Republican from a Democratic administration, and voters can therefore have a reasonable expectation of what each will offer.

Of course, the Framers' fears were not unfounded. If the divisiveness that parties encourage exceeds a bipartisan commitment to fundamental constitutional principles, then the constitutional order is genuinely threatened. Party politics did not save us from a civil war. Indeed, Tocqueville thought that while America had once had "great" parties, based on fundamental principles, it was in the 1830s threatened by parties that were concerned with "material interests" only (e.g., conflicts over the tariff).[69] Contrary to Tocqueville's fears, however, for most of our history the parties have found a middle distance between these two extremes, remaining faithful to the broad principles of the republic, providing material benefits for party supporters, while still embodying important differences regarding serious matters.

Over the past decade, however, party conflict has moved in a dangerous direction. In the 2020 presidential election, 147 Republican senators and House members voted against certifying the election results.[70] Similar though less serious conflicts followed the elections of 2000, 2004, and 2016, when many Democrats insisted that various "irregularities" had illegally denied the victory to Al Gore, John Kerry, and Hillary Clinton, respectively. The 2000 election was decided in Florida, when the Supreme Court ruled that, based on the relevant federal election law, the Florida legislature—not the state courts—had the statutory authority to certify the victor. The 2004 election was also close, and Democrats challenged (unsuccessfully) Ohio's Electoral College votes.[71] The election of Donald Trump in 2016 was also challenged by Democrats, who charged that Russian influence had somehow shifted the vote to Trump over Hillary Clinton—an accusation that led to a two-year investigation by a special prosecutor, who found that the claim had no basis in fact.[72] And, of course, the 2020 election was said by many Republicans—most vociferously, former President Trump—to have been stolen in states controlled by Democrats. As the title of this book suggests, the problem of "keeping the republic" persists.

FEDERALISM

Beyond its specific provisions for how American government will work, the Constitution envisions a particular kind of "regime"—meaning, a particular way of understanding how government should be conducted, but also how citizens should live, and how they should conduct their political lives. Central to this understanding are the ideas of *limited* government and *federal* government. Both of these ideas have become suspect in progressive circles: that the government should be "hampered" in its efforts to deal with "crises" by fussy concerns about federalism, or the limitations imposed by the Constitution, is a source of irritation in progressive circles.[73]

Federalism, critics argue, enables the states and localities to deviate from national majority sentiment. Equal representation in the Senate for small and large states alike deprives citizens from large states of the superior voice in the passage of legislation that their numbers should give them. The Electoral College enables the election of a president who is not the choice of the majority.[74] Life tenure for Supreme Court justices means that the Court may not reflect the "popular will" at any given moment in time.

As we have argued previously, greater democracy will not make Americans more virtuous or less greedy. It might bring about the enshrinement of more rights, but that is not necessarily wise. However, even if the mitigating institutions the progressives attack are not perpetrators of evil, what good are they? To fully appreciate the implications of this question, we must remind ourselves of the fundamental problem the Constitution was designed to address:

the problem of establishing popular government in a large modern state. Our discussion of the problem in the introduction and chapter 1 stressed three specific difficulties the modern state poses: size, diversity, and power. The Constitution's "undemocratic" institutions each provide indispensable means for keeping those problems in check (they can't simply be made to go away) and therefore making popular government possible.

First, consider the phenomenon of American federalism.[75] Some of the Framers were no great fans of the states. At the Constitutional Convention, Alexander Hamilton gave a long speech in which he confessed two worries: the "great extent of the country," which alarmed him, and the power of the states.[76] To the first problem there was no obvious solution: the country was already very large, and was bound to become larger. To the second problem there was a solution in theory: states might become, in effect, administrative districts of the national government; their borders could even be changed to make them similar in size, which would obviate the difficulties of each state having the same representation in the Senate. Neither, he acknowledged, was a realistic possibility: but he reminded the assembly that "some men present may have changed their mind on these questions" and would secretly agree with him.[77]

But the convention conceded so much power to the states because that was the price of winning the Constitution's passage. The states had already written and ratified their own constitutions well before the convention. Americans were simply too attached to their former colonial polities to deprive them of the central political role in their lives now that they had achieved independence. They would only vote to establish a strong national government if it left the state constitutions and state polities more or less intact. Borne of a political bargain, the complex sharing of power between states and the national government that we call federalism has nonetheless proven itself indispensable for addressing the difficulties posed by the modern state. It enables diversity, preserves liberty, encourages self-reliance, sustains national cohesion, and enhances citizenship.[78]

When composing *The Federalist*, however, its authors took a more positive view of the federalism "bargain." Conceding that small republics were the sphere for "internal happiness," *Federalist* 9, for example, envisages the states and the localities as providing for the good life, while the large republic guarantees protection against foreign powers and domestic insurrection, and guarding the free flow of commerce. "The proposed Constitution," Publius argues, "so far from implying an abolition of the State governments, makes them constituent parts of the national sovereignty, by allowing them a direct representation in the Senate, and leaves in their possession certain exclusive and very important portions of sovereign power."[79] American federalism thus embodies both the virtues of a confederacy and the virtues of a centralized government. Dividing power between the states and the national government has proven to be a critical means of enabling free government to cope with the extraordinary diversity that the United States encompasses—a diversity that the growth of online communication has made more apparent than ever before.[80]

Although the populations of the individual states are not homogeneous, only the largest approach the level of diversity that exists nationally. In general, therefore, the states are better able than the nation as a whole to find common ground regarding contentious issues.[81] Thus, Colorado can choose to legalize marijuana while the neighboring state of Nebraska continues to ban it. Massachusetts can impose stringent laws regulating firearms, whereas neighboring New Hampshire does not even require a permit to own or carry a handgun or rifle.[82] Thus, federalism's approach to the problem of diversity is not to try to solve it but to develop ways of living with it. Live and let live! Accept that the social fabric is made up of many different threads and that it can be kept from tearing only if the threads are loosely woven together.

As dreadful as the COVID-19 pandemic has been, and as many stumbles governments at all levels have made, this catastrophe has revealed the virtues of federalism. In one crucial respect the COVID crisis resembled the Great Depression—no one in authority saw it coming, and no one really knew how to deal with it. Only the federal government has the financial resources to address the fiscal aspect of such a cataclysm—but the pandemic was much more than a fiscal challenge. As during the Depression, the federal government poured out huge sums to prop up the economy—in the COVID case several trillion dollars.[83] But COVID required a much more complex set of responses than the Depression did, ones that had to be made in the absence of sufficient data and understanding. Should schools, factories, churches, and stores be closed? If facilities were to remain open, what restrictions should be placed on them? How should scarce medical supplies be allocated? In the face of these difficult choices, the United States was lucky to have fifty-one chief executives instead of only one.[84] As we have repeatedly noted, states, not the national government, possess the police power, that is, the power to "regulate the health, welfare, and morals" of the people. Regardless of various statements made by Presidents

Trump and Biden, most of the crucial decisions regarding how businesses and individuals were to function rested with the governors and not with the White House. It was governors who had the authority to determine how and under what conditions people could go out in public. It was governors who determined the rules about the wearing of masks, the extent of quarantine, how hospitals were to operate, which businesses could stay open, what restrictions would be imposed on (or merely recommended to) houses of worship, and how vaccines would be distributed.[85]

In the face of the pandemic, federalism promoted both learning and liberty. The decentralization of authority that federalism establishes allowed the different states to approach these problems in ways that responded to local circumstances—including differences in risk preferences—more or less successfully in different states. In the face of ignorance and uncertainty, experimentation is the only way to learn, and the existence of fifty state governments allowed for, indeed encouraged, a wide variety of experiments. States could and did learn from what other states did right and what they did wrong. And, because failed experiments were confined to the states in which they took place, other states did not suffer from them. Nationwide uniformity could well have led to nationwide disaster.[86] *Or, the opposite*

It is well to remember how large this country is and therefore how diverse. In general, the most densely populated areas faced the greatest threat from the virus, whereas some lightly populated areas saw few cases initially. North Dakota did not require the kind of draconian shutdown that crowded cities like New York, Boston, Los Angeles, and Washington, DC, needed to adopt. States varied widely regarding both incidence of and death from the disease, and also in the means by which the disease was spread. In New York City, the subways were a problem; in South Dakota, it was meat-packing plants. In principle one could expect even a highly centralized government to allow for variation in how different places are treated depending on local conditions, but such an expectation flies in the face of how "enlightened administration" actually operates. Federal officials always claim that they take local conditions into account when formulating regulations, but such claims are just as often disputed by those who must obey them. As we have pointed out before, local knowledge is the hardest thing for decision makers to come by. Those who are the farthest removed from a place are most likely to misunderstand what it needs, and what it is capable of. State and local officials are hardly immune from misunderstanding such conditions, but because they are closer to the

this isn't anything like how things actually work most of the time

situation they stand a better chance of making more accurate assessments—and of noticing quickly if those assessments are incorrect. Those affected are their constituents, and therefore they are more highly motivated to listen to what locals are saying—if only because the locals have the power to end a public official's career. And if the authorities make a mistake, the consequences are localized—and other states are able to learn from the mistakes.

Central planners are biased in favor of uniformity.[87] If one is responsible for making rules for an entire country, the only way to make that task manageable is to simplify it. One size may *not* fit all, but settling on a single size is a far easier challenge for a federal agency to manage than writing rules that account for the extraordinary degree of diversity the United States encompasses. Federal bureaucrats are neither more virtuous nor more venal than the rest of us. But like the rest of us, they have a strong incentive to get the job done and avoid censure. Not only are uniform rules easier to devise and enforce; they also make their formulators less susceptible to charges of bias and favoritism.[88] Whatever happens, at least the experts can claim that they were enforcing the same rules for everyone, or "following the science"—even when enforcing the same rules for everyone is exactly the wrong thing to do, or when the actual scientists disagree on the nature of the problem and what solutions make the most sense.[89]

Ironically, progressives loudly proclaim the virtues of diversity, but they limit themselves for the most part (especially these days) to diversity of *identity*—race, gender, sexual preference—and seek to make intrusive use of the national government to impose uniform regulations on how those forms of diversity are to be protected—or even understood or discussed.[90] Yet they show far less interest in diversity of opinion about how to live or how to govern. They do not show the same appreciation for enabling whole subsets of the population, as defined by state borders, to go their own way regarding matters of deep religious, ethical, and cultural importance. The survival of such a robust role for the states does not imply a return to confederation. The Articles of Confederation gave states a free hand and minimized the role of the national government—which, in any case, barely existed. Constitutional federalism blends the two and, most importantly, the Supremacy Clause of the Constitution leaves no doubt about where ultimate power lies: with the Constitution itself, and not with any particular level of government. Over time, the Supreme Court has determined that virtually all of the rights contained in the Bill of Rights impose obligations on state legislatures as well as the Congress, and therefore the national government is empowered to enforce them *against* the states if necessary.[91] The Fourteenth Amendment forbids any state to deprive "any person of life, liberty or property without due process of law nor deny to any person within its jurisdiction equal protection of the laws." The states must therefore treat each person fairly and equally. Admittedly there will be hard cases in which one side claims that a state is violating rights while the other side claims that it is exercising its proper, constitutionally granted, decision-making power. So be it; such disputes are inevitable.

Such hard cases are the reason that passage of the Fourteenth Amendment was such a critical improvement on the original document, and why the Supreme Court, after too much hesitation, became its vigorous champion. We rely on the Court to sort out the hard cases. These are the exceptions. For the most part the division of labor between state and national government has enabled each level to concentrate on what it does best. The states don't raise armies, they may not create barriers to trade with other states, and they may not conduct their own foreign policies. Meanwhile, the national government did not tell states how to educate their children, or how fast to drive their cars, or how to handle ordinary criminal and civil matters.

Yet this is no longer the case. The national government has now become involved in many activities that were once exclusively the province of the states and their local governments: public education, law enforcement, environmental regulation, and much else besides—often using the carrot (federal grants) when the stick (the Fourteenth Amendment) is unavailable.[92] To use a fairly recent example, if a state refuses to allow "right turn on red" (promoted by the EPA as a means of reducing exhaust fumes from idling cars), then the federal government will withhold federal assistance for developing mandated conservation programs.[93] But often the means of achieving control is an expanded understanding of what it is *appropriate* for a government to control—a larger subject to which we will return below.

Because states differ, people who are unhappy with the policies of one state can move to another.[94] In order to combat climate change, protect wildlife, reduce sprawl, and reduce pollution, California state government has made a number of very expensive public investments and imposed very stringent environmental regulations. To support these endeavors, Californians pay very high taxes. Indeed, their income tax rate is the highest in the nation. Texas has a much less intrusive government and no state income tax.[95] Between 2007 and 2016 almost 300,000 more Californians moved to Texas than the other way around. In 2018 the exodus amounted to just over one-tenth of California's population.[96] One cannot say for sure that most of those migrants did so to embrace less regulation and lower taxes—but we know they did not move to Texas to enjoy better weather.

In fact, the contrasts between how the two states govern themselves are stark, and the out-migration number is large and getting larger; it is therefore quite likely that the two phenomena are related. Americans are therefore free to choose between very different ways of life simply by crossing state lines, a liberty not enjoyed by those who live in countries where the central government imposes a uniform set of laws everywhere.[97] A French citizen moving from Paris to Marseilles will experience exactly the same government in his new home as in his old. An American citizen moving from New Jersey to Florida will not, quite: the federal government will be the same, of course, but the state government in Florida will be quite different from the state government in New Jersey—and so will many of its laws and regulations.

Federalism copes with the problem of size in several different ways. The responsibilities of national government agencies extend to more than 330 million people spread over a continent. Sophisticated information gathering makes these agencies awash in data. But because they are so far removed from conditions on the ground, they struggle to determine which data is pertinent for dealing with the specific problem at hand. Knowing so much, they know so little, because they cannot be more than superficially familiar with any specific set of local circumstances. They lack what the economist Friedrich Hayek called "local knowledge"—the sort that is only obtainable by familiarity with local conditions and deep immersion in the particularities of individual cases.[98] All but the smallest states are too big to enable their officials to enjoy sufficient local knowledge. Consider, for example, how many building sites a particular state has at any given time and how rapidly such sites appear and disappear as some are completed and others begin. And yet, miraculously, every day, nickel-plated trucks or vans will appear at these sites so that hungry construction workers can enjoy a mid-morning snack.

How do these snack vans know where to go? They know because the amount of information any one vendor needs is limited. The vendor only needs to know where the sites are that are close enough to him to make serving them profitable. Because the learning task is limited and they have a powerful incentive to master it, they do. As long as there is money to be made, vendors will keep seeking and finding sites until, in all likelihood, all sites get served.

They do not rely on public data. They ask around. They talk to their friends and neighbors. They cultivate contractors. They drive the territory in search of construction sites.

The value of such local knowledge is so great that it calls for devolving decision making to the lowest possible level.[99] Imagine if the central government or even a state or local government tried to establish and regulate fixed routes for snack vendors? Their lack of knowledge would leave hordes of hard-hats hungry. Therefore, the presumption should be that discretion is best left to private actors because they have the most local knowledge, and a reliable incentive—the profit motive—to use it. If that is not possible then authority should pass to the next lowest level of government because it has the next most amount of local knowledge. If that is insufficient then discretion should pass up the governmental chain, only reaching the national level if it cannot be settled lower down, or if it concerns the relatively few but profoundly important tasks for which the central government was intended. Since so many states are too big to enable their officials to exert much in the way of local knowledge themselves, the preference for state rather than central government decision making hinges on the lesser distance that separates them from the localities and therefore on the likelihood that they will prove more accommodating of and deferential toward localities than the central government would be.

Federalism is also vital for the promotion of citizenship.[100] Critics of the Constitution argue that since the document does not discuss either the need for civic education or how it is to be fostered, the Framers must not have recognized how important it is for the maintenance of the republic.[101] These critics describe a caricature of the Constitution, in which the capacity of the different branches to check each other is said to be entirely sufficient to make mitigated democracy tick. On the contrary, the Framers knew that such clever institutional arrangements could not sustain free government by themselves. They needed to rest on the secure foundation of an active, involved, informed, and public-spirited citizenry. However, unlike the progressive critics, the Framers harbored no illusion that the necessary level of civic education and involvement could be imposed from above. Imagine a federal Department of Civic Engagement. Rather, such a vital task could only be performed locally because the task of citizenship can only be learned through practice. It is a muscle. It is strengthened and honed through exercise. Americans in 1788 had such skill, which had been learned over several generations of de facto self-government in the colonies-turned-states. But the framers of the Constitution did not take this knowledge for granted, and in their public and private statements they made clear that civic education, while not an appropriate task of a government department, was the shared responsibility of all citizens—and a special responsibility of public servants themselves.[102]

For most of us, such opportunities to exercise our civic responsibilities only exist nearby. For example, in their towns and counties citizens can serve on juries—indeed, they *must* serve, if chosen; it is not an option. Juries are the richest source of muscular citizenship since they require their members to deliberate among themselves about weighty matters: sending a person to prison—or setting the defendant free; judging discrimination claims; settling contract disputes. Such deep involvement sharpens civic abilities far more than mere voting or donating, the political acts to which most citizens are limited beyond their local community.[103] These smaller jurisdictions also provide many other rich civic opportunities—serving on the school board, the conservation committee, or the trustees of the library. Here again the state role is secondarily essential. Unlike states, local governments are not constitutionally protected. Therefore, it is up to the state to ensure that local political life is preserved and protected.

Federalism combines with other constitutional principles to check excessive central government power. The most fundamental method for checking power is dedication to rights, as we have already stated. Because rights are paramount, government cannot undermine them. Indeed, the scope of its authority is limited to their protection. This profound idea is simply stated in both the Declaration of Independence and the Bill of Rights, but those statements are too broad and vague to provide clear guidelines for governing. The Constitution assigns that task to Article I, which limits the legislative powers of government to those powers "herein granted." The article then proceeds to enumerate what those powers are—providing for the national defense, regulating interstate commerce, taxation, delivering the mail, and so on. Enumeration gives concrete meaning to the principle of limitation because it requires government to restrict its reach to the powers listed. If Article I does not enumerate it, government cannot do it! Indeed, some of the Framers justified their opposition to a bill of rights on the grounds that the constraints on the government's reach that Article I provided already offered an adequate protection of the people's rights. As discussed earlier, we believe that including a Bill of Rights did enhance liberty, but we would also agree that the enumeration that Article I provides is fundamental for ensuring that rights are protected—by making as clear as possible what the government may do, or what it must do, thereby making equally clear, by process of elimination, what it has no authority to do. Federalism enables these restrictions on the national government to operate because the police power allows the states to perform the wide range of essential tasks that Article I forbids the national government from undertaking. Providing this alternative prevents the most dangerous level of government—the one with the greatest means to oppress—from reaching too deeply into people's lives. *[handwritten: What about Article II?]*

The purpose of declaring rights is, in part, to restrict public deliberation about what they are intended to protect. This is true of those enumerated in the Bill of Rights. Indeed, the rights to free speech, press, assembly, and religious expression enrich the citizens' capacity to deliberate. However, even a good thing can be overdone, and this is so with the expansion of rights that began in a profound way with *Roe v. Wade*. As we discussed earlier, once something is declared to be a right, it is removed from full-fledged public deliberation. From the 1970s until 2022, the Supreme Court took it on itself to declare new rights that did indeed restrict public deliberation about such profound matters as abortion and homosexuality.

The rationale for declaring these new rights was first offered in the context of birth control. In 1965 the Court repealed a Connecticut statute that banned the dispensation of instruments of birth control. In overturning that statute the Court ruled that even though the Constitution did not contain a right to privacy, the Bill of Rights was enshrouded in a "penumbra" (a pervasive shadow) of a "right to privacy" and thus protected by the Fourteenth Amendment's Due Process Clause. The birth control ban, the majority argued, violated the right to privacy.[104] In 1973 the Court declared that women have a right to an abortion. In doing so it relied on the same doctrine of a right to privacy proffered in *Griswold*.[105] It likewise invoked a right to privacy granting rights to homosexuals. In 2003 it overturned a Texas law forbidding homosexual sex acts.[106] In 2015 it required the states to issue marriage licenses to homosexual couples.[107]

In 2022 the Court, for the first time in modern history, abolished a right.[108] In *Dobbs v. Jackson Women's Health Organization*, a 6–3 majority ruled that the Constitution does not contain the right to privacy asserted in *Griswold*, that there is no "penumbra" surrounding the Constitution, and that such an assertion can therefore not support a federal right to abortion. As of 2022 it is too soon to say whether the Court will use its denial of the penumbra principle to revoke other rights declared on a right to privacy. At a minimum, the Dobbs decision opens up public deliberation about abortion and ensures that this will take place in the appropriate deliberative forum: the state legislatures.

THE SENATE AND THE ELECTORAL COLLEGE AS OBSTACLES TO DEMOCRACY

The Senate and the Electoral College have, for the past century at any rate, stood as symbols of the "undemocratic" biases of the Constitution, and they remain a target of would-be constitutional reformers who search for ways around the fact that the Constitution says that the clause guaranteeing each state two senators is unamendable.[109] The antidemocratic nature of both institutions is clear. California has almost forty million people, whereas seven states have fewer than a million each, and yet each state, from the largest to the smallest, has the same number of senators. Thus, a Californian's vote for a member of the Senate is only one-fortieth the value of the vote of a citizen from one of these seven smaller states.

By giving each state two Senate seats, regardless of the state's population, a Senate "majority" can represent a collection of states whose combined population is far less than a majority of the American people. Furthermore, by giving each state two extra votes in the Electoral College beyond its number of congressional districts (which are proportioned to the state's population), presidential elections can be won by a candidate who has lost the popular vote. As we noted earlier, this is a rare outcome, happening only three times in the nineteenth century, and twice in the past twenty years, most often because of the presence of a popular third-party candidate. But it is a possibility the presidential campaigns must plan for, and has (it is claimed) an unfortunate effect on the way presidential campaigns are conducted. Instead of "campaigning everywhere," candidates must focus on those states they have a realistic chance of winning, but that polls indicate they could lose—the so-called swing states. Shrewd campaign advisors therefore urge the candidate to "shore up" their support in these critical states, paying far less attention to the states they are bound to win and those they are bound to lose. Indeed, it was by some reports Hillary Clinton's rejection of her advisors' recommendation to spend more time in the northern tier of midwestern states that had been carried by President Obama, but which looked "iffy" for her, that cost her an Electoral College victory in 2016—defeating Donald Trump in the popular vote by nearly three million votes but losing the Electoral College by seventy-seven votes.[110] She built up huge margins in several solidly Democratic states, like New York, Illinois, and California, but lost several states in the Midwest and the Upper Midwest that Obama had carried.

Circumstances such as these lie behind the efforts of contemporary critics of the Constitution to make dramatic changes in the constitutional design. One plan is to abolish the Electoral College, so that the winner of the popular vote would always become the president.[111] Another plan, which has nothing to do with elections, is to expand the size of the Supreme Court, with a Democratic Senate majority (with the vice president breaking the tie) confirming enough liberal justices to neutralize the current conservative majority of five.[112] Unlike the "court-packing" plan, the abolition of the Electoral College would require approval by two-thirds of both houses of Congress, and then ratification by three-fourths of the state legislatures—hurdles that are almost certainly insurmountable. There is a "work-around," however, making its way through the states: state laws requiring that the state's electoral votes be given to the winner of the popular vote in the national presidential election, regardless of how the state's own voters have voted.[113] The so-called National Popular Vote Bill had been passed by fifteen state legislatures and the District of Columbia as of April 2021. While this approach does not seem to violate the letter of the Constitution, it certainly violates the Constitution's intent. More to the point, however, it is likely to anger the voters in the states that voted for the loser of the popular vote—and then had their votes cancelled by their own state legislature. They might well retaliate by electing a different legislature at the first opportunity.

There is more than a little irony in these complaints, since both the Senate and the Electoral College, allegedly the most "undemocratic" elements in the Constitution, were grudging concessions by the Federalist faction at the Constitutional Convention to the more "democratic" faction, the Anti-Federalists. The first plan submitted to the convention when it convened in mid-May 1787—written largely by James Madison and known as the "Virginia Plan"—proposed that the House of Representatives would be chosen by the people in the several states, and that these members would in turn elect the members of the Senate from a list of candidates submitted by the state legislatures. The Congress would also choose the president and the members of the national judiciary. Congress would have the authority to veto any acts of the state legislatures that "[contravened] . . . the articles of the Union." And there would be a Council of Revision, composed of the president and members of the federal judiciary, who could veto any act of Congress before it could take effect, sending it back to the Congress to be "revised."[114]

This plan was immediately accused of being a scheme to "abolish the State Governments altogether," and from that moment on the most hotly contested matter was the role that the states were to play in this new Union. There was a substantial sentiment at the convention that the complete subordination of the states was a direct threat to popular (i.e., democratic) government—but an equally strong sentiment on the other side that the continued existence of the states as important parts of the political order was not only unnecessary, but a *danger* to republican government, so poorly had the states performed under the Articles of Confederation.[115]

It was this conflict that shaped subsequent debates on all of the major features of what became, by late September, the Constitution of the United States, including most importantly the election of the president, the size and powers of the Senate, how the Senate would be chosen, and what powers would remain in the hands of the states. Many of the features now charged with being "undemocratic" were insisted upon by what must be seen as the more "democratic" faction at the convention. What powers could the states retain, if the Congress could veto any state legislation thought (by the Congress) to be unconstitutional? That provision was therefore rejected. Who would choose the members of the Senate, if not the House of Representatives? By the end of June, the answer to that question was the *state legislatures*—and each state would be *equally* represented, regardless of its population (a concession to the fear of small-state representatives that the large states would dominate the government). Equal representation of the states in the Senate was the most contentious issue at the convention, and nearly brought it to a premature close: what is now known as the "Great Compromise" was agreed to in order to keep the convention from dissolving.[116]

Who would choose the president, if not the Congress? Here the answer was an Electoral College, whose members would be appointed by state legislatures, the number of their votes to be based *mostly* but not exclusively on their relative size (i.e., the number of House districts, plus two more for their members in the Senate). Gone was the power of Congress to veto acts of the state legislatures, and gone as well was the Council of Revision.[117]

It took all summer to resolve these conflicts through a series of compromises, and many decisions were postponed, changed more than once, or decided only at the last minute. But it is useful to imagine the government that would have resulted from a complete victory of the Virginia Plan. The president and his council could veto any act of Congress—and the president, though not eligible to reelection, would be in office for longer than four years; the Congress could veto any act of the state legislatures; the Senate would be chosen by the House, and not by the states or by the voters; and the president would also be chosen by the Congress rather than by the voters. Federalism as we have come to understand it would never have existed, and state and local politics, to the extent that there would be such a thing, would be dramatically weakened.

Although the result of a "Great Compromise," and one that few members of the convention were prepared to defend absolutely, the Senate was understood to possess some important virtues. The Senate's greatest virtue, perhaps, is that it balances the power that the House of Representatives bestows on the most populated states. To obtain a majority in the Senate, advocates must appeal to representatives from a wide variety of settings and regions, which is likely to empower a different set of interests and opinions, and encourage a reasonable compromise among opposing views. The small states fought for the Senate because they did not want to be overwhelmed by the larger states. Today the concern is much the same. If both houses were apportioned on the basis of population, the states with smaller populations would suffer the fate that the original small states successfully fought against at the Constitutional Convention.

Equal state representation in the Senate is one of only two *unamendable* provisions in the Constitution.[118] Despite the claim by a prominent political scientist that it represents "the worst example of gerrymandering," it is here to stay.[119] Therefore critics have focused on making its procedures as majoritarian as possible. The least democratic aspect of Senate procedure is the filibuster.[120] Until 1917 the Senate had no rules about ending debate. Then, in response to the abuse of the capacity of a single senator to stall a bill by continuing to talk, the upper house determined that debate could be ended by a two-thirds vote. The first time this rule was put to the test was in 1919, when the Senate used it to stop a filibuster aimed at preventing a vote on the Treaty of Versailles.[121] But successful clotures were few, and the filibuster was used mostly by southern Democrats to block civil rights legislation—until, finally, it was successfully invoked to end debate on the 1964 Civil Rights Act, which enabled the act to be passed. To further restrict the filibuster, the Senate voted to lower the threshold for cloture to three-fifths.[122] To avoid lengthy delay, if the leadership knows that forty-one senators will oppose cloture, they take the bill off the floor, which means that in practice passage of any reasonably controversial measure requires a three-fifths supermajority.

The change from two-thirds to three-fifths was salutary; it removed the southern stranglehold on civil rights bills. But a modest supermajority requiring only ten votes beyond a simple majority is not only reasonable but a positive check on impulsive democracy. Important statutory changes need to stand the test of time and embody, if not full-fledged popular consensus, at least a consensus consisting of well more than half the country. The fraction three-fifths is of course an arbitrary measure of sufficient consensus, but so is any other number above 50 percent. If a proposal is really sensible, surely, over time, either Senate turnover or the very reasonableness of the proposal will secure it the requisite sixty votes. There is no longer a retrograde "Solid South," and even if there were it could not mobilize forty-one votes.

In addition, the Electoral College and the Senate are bulwarks of federalism, because they connect the national legislative and executive branches to the states. The Electoral College turns the presidential election into fifty state elections. Having to win a sufficient number of state elections encourages a candidate to appreciate and respond to the main forms of diversity that the different states embody. The aspirant must put together a tapestry of victories. If the office could be won by a simple national popular majority, the president might be consistently chosen exclusively by voters in those metropoles with the largest, densest populations: the Atlantic Coast belt extending from the suburbs of Washington, D, through Philadelphia and New York to Boston; the Pacific Coast belt extending from Los Angeles to Seattle; and greater Chicago. Citizens of those places deserve to be heard, but they hardly constitute a microcosm of the entire American populace. Having to campaign in many other places allows many more diverse voices to be heard and appealed to. This attribute is especially valuable at a time when both economic and cultural power have become concentrated along the coasts. There can be found the institutions that shape our lives in so many ways—Wall Street, Hollywood, Google, Facebook, Amazon, the *New York Times*, NPR. The Electoral College deprives the coasts of a degree of political power equivalent to their power over the culture and the economy.

The most telling criticism of the Electoral College is that it causes the candidates to ignore so-called safe states—those they either have no reasonable chance of winning or no likelihood of losing. Therefore, citizens of those "safe" states may feel as if they are merely bystanders of the presidential contest. Of course, they are not bystanders. Their vote counts as much as anyone's; it's simply that their votes, or the votes of the state's majority, are *predictable*—not that they are irrelevant. Only in an almost impossibly rare instance, where the presidential contest hinges on the outcome in one state and the outcome in that state is determined by a single vote, does one's vote really "count" in the sense of being decisive. Nonetheless, voters' sense of political efficacy may diminish as a result of being passed over by all the hoopla surrounding a presidential election: incessant ads, candidate visits, and media scrutiny. This is indeed a loss.[123] Citizens who don't think they make a difference are likely to be less active than those who do. On the other hand, the political world gains from the intense competition that goes on in the dozen or so states where the partisan balance is close enough to earn them the moniker of "battlegrounds." The small margins of victory to be attained in those states attest to their heterogeneity. Far more than the coastal states that are safe for the Democrats and the Southern and Mountain states that are Republican strongholds, they contain a rich mix of the ethnic, religious, racial, ideological, and economic groups that comprise the nation as a whole. It is good to have the presidential contest decided by those political arenas that are the nearest to being microcosms of the nation.[124]

Sadly, a culture war besets the nation. A most telling indication of its political reach was Hillary Clinton's remark during the 2016 election campaign that "you could put half of Trump's supporters into what I call the basket of deplorables. They're racist, sexist, homophobic, xenophobic—Islamophobic —you name it."[125] Since Trump received almost sixty-three million votes in 2016 (and seventy-four million in 2020), Clinton was claiming that nearly thirty-seven million Americans are "deplorable." The absurdity of this claim does not refute the fact that far more than half of Trump's voters are far different from the coastal cosmopolitans that Clinton identified with. They go to church, run small businesses, serve in the military, own guns, hunt, and belong to the Kiwanis club, Knights of Columbus, Elks, or other fraternal organizations. Neither the Senate nor the Electoral College can call a truce to this culture war. However, these sustainers of federalism do work to ensure that neither side can claim a total victory in that war, and therefore they keep alive at least the *prospect* of an eventual truce. At a minimum, it will be a long time before a candidate for president dismisses so many millions of voters as deplorable—at least before they have had a chance to cast their ballots.

As progressives recognize, the Senate's staggered six-year terms determine that only one-third of the body is elected at each national election.[126] Thus, the popular majority, having won the House, might still find itself thwarted if an insufficient number of Senate seats change hands in its direction. This restraint on majority rule represents mitigated democracy at work. The Framers ensured that one house of the legislature, the House of Representatives, would be highly responsive to majority sentiment because its members each represent the same number of voters and they face reelection every two years. The upper house was intended to ensure that public sentiment stood the test of a reasonable length of time. If the sentiment was durable, the majority, failing to win enough Senate elections at one time, is very likely to do so in the subsequent election, and therefore its waiting time is only four years. In the unlikely event that even a subsequent national election also failed to produce a Senate majority, the waiting time would be six years. If an entire six-year cycle does not result in victory, it is fair to say that no durable majority ever existed and that the staggered terms prevented impulsive and unpopular action.

The Supreme Court is obviously the least democratic aspect of the constitutional order: a fact recognized at the Founding, and a reason some Americans opposed ratification. Progressives are *ambivalent* about the Court, however, because its undemocratic nature has at times served progressive ends. In the 1950s, when Southerners dominated Congress, the Supreme Court ordered that the public schools be desegregated—a policy unlikely to have found favor with a majority of the Senate of that time. In the early 1970s the Court legalized abortion at a time when a slim majority of Americans opposed it. From the 1950s through the early 1980s the Supreme Court issued a series of decisions regarding the rights of criminal defendants, apportionment of state legislatures, and other matters supported by progressives, about which the public had not registered strong views, but which would not have passed Congress.

However, because in recent decades Republican presidents have had more opportunity to appoint Supreme Court justices than have Democrats, the Court has taken on a conservative cast. Hoping to eventually recover a majority, progressives have not proposed amending the Constitution to reduce its power. Instead, they propose changes in how long justices serve and in the number of serving justices. To put limits on judicial terms would require a constitutional amendment and is therefore extremely unlikely to be achieved. However, the president could choose to only appoint justices who promised to step down after ten, twelve, or eighteen years, the most common term lengths proposed, and/or the Senate could choose to confirm only nominees who agreed to make such a pledge.[127] On the other hand, the very fact that the president and the Senate majority have chosen someone who reflects their ideological outlook makes it very unlikely that they would choose to limit that justice's tenure.

Another option is expanding the Court when possible with jurists more sympathetic to the views of the majority party in the Senate at the time of appointment. As we will discuss in more detail below, this was President Franklin Roosevelt's plan, but under the circumstances of 1937, it was impossible to get the idea even debated in Congress. We are living in different times now, and the reception of such a plan is likely to be more favorable; indeed, as we write, Democrats in Congress have submitted a bill to increase the size of the Supreme Court by four justices.[128] *Another option: change jurisdiction*

Yet in their eagerness to keep the Court from undermining the progressive agenda, contemporary court-packing advocates are prepared to sacrifice the Court's independence. Curiously, toward that end they threaten to damage their own cause. Over the long haul, the nation is likely to elect, from time to time, conservative presidents who enjoy Senate majorities. If progressive presidents pack the court, conservative presidents will undoubtedly emulate them. Not only will this make the size of the court unwieldy, but it will exacerbate the problem that already exists of the court frequently splitting along partisan lines.

As the court-packing example indicates, the Constitution is more than the sum of its parts. It embodies a certain spirit. We speak of a person as having a "constitution," meaning that the person's specific physical, emotional, and mental attributes add up to a particular way of living. Likewise, the particulars of the American Constitution add up to a particular way of life, a free life. The American people are free to make their own decisions about how and where to live, how or whether to raise a family, what jobs to seek, how to or whether to worship, and what opinions to express. This is not a recipe for anarchy. The laws of the land will impinge on these choices, but the government *except abortion* will not dictate them. "Private" does not mean selfish. But it does imply that government must, on the whole, stay very much in the background as individuals determine the quality and character of their moral, social, economic, and spiritual lives. That, after all, is what it means to be free, and freedom, as the Declaration of Independence proclaims, is one of the natural rights that governments exist to protect.

CONSTITUTIONAL FEDERALISM AND THE
ELECTORAL SYSTEM

More ambitious than ending the filibuster or adding seats to the Supreme Court have been the Biden administration's efforts to make major changes in election law, changes that passed the House on March 3, 2021, as H.R.1.[129] Supporters of this bill claimed that it would make elections more democratic, but its real purpose was to ensure Democratic dominance at all levels of national government. Even though it did not pass (it was filibustered by Senate Republicans)—and the Supreme Court might well declare many of its provisions unconstitutional if it passes in the future—it is worth paying attention to, because it received the votes of every Democratic member of the House, the Democratic caucus in the Senate, and was endorsed by President Biden.[130] Should the Democrats gain a safe majority in the Senate in 2024, while maintaining control of the White House, H.R.1 might well get a second chance.

The Constitution has two crucial clauses regarding federal elections. Article I, Section 4, Clause 1 states: "The Times, Places and Manner of holding Elections for Senators and Representatives, shall be prescribed in each State by the Legislature thereof; but the Congress may at any time by Law make or alter such Regulations, except as to the Places of [choosing] Senators." Thus, the Constitution does not clearly define the relative roles of the states and the federal government in formulating congressional election law, except to make state authority the rule, rather than the exception. The Supreme Court has interfered with federal laws regarding voting age, voter registration, and other state practices that involve exclusion on the basis of race, but it has never undermined the primacy of state control. The most important statutory basis for federal involvement is the landmark Civil Rights Act of 1965 that bans racial discrimination in voting or voter registration. But as we discuss later, the Supreme Court has recently refused to overturn state laws that the plaintiffs claimed violated the Voting Rights Act and/or the Constitution, thus reinforcing the principle of state primacy.

The Constitution accords no role for the Congress or the Executive in presidential elections, because those being elected should not control the rules by which they will be chosen. Article II, Section 1 states that "Each State shall appoint, in such Manner as the Legislature thereof may direct, a Number of Electors, equal to the whole Number of Senators and Representatives to which the State may be entitled in the Congress: but no Senator or Representative, or Person holding an Office of Trust or Profit under the United States, shall be appointed an Elector." As the convention debates demonstrate, the exclusion of Congress from involvement in presidential elections was based on the delegates' commitment to avoiding presidential dependence on Congress for position and authority.[131]

Yet H.R.1 was so comprehensive that it amounted to a full-fledged nationalization of the conduct of elections, and it is doubtful that it would survive a constitutional challenge were it to pass. It requires the states to enact a number of laws that are described as "making voting easier": online registration; automatic voter registration through agencies such as the state departments of motor vehicles, social service providers, or public universities; address changes at the polls on election day; same-day registration; mandatory voting for felons; mandatory use of paper ballots exclusively; "no excuse" absentee voting by mail; mandatory early voting at least two weeks before election day; provisional ballots for voters whose eligibility cannot be determined on election day. The law also forbids certain practices currently used by many states, both Democratic and Republican: photo IDs for voting; electronic voting machines; and any efforts designed to purge the voting rolls of people who have died, or who have moved out of the precinct or even the state (by comparing registration records with neighboring states); and "voter caging," the practice of sending mail to registered voters and noting which mail is returned as "addressee unknown."

In addition to usurping state power, the law tilts the balance between easy voting and secure voting in favor of easy—and in the process increases the *evidence?* opportunity for vote fraud and voter intimidation, and risks exposing all elections to the kinds of cheating accusations that marred the 2020 presidential race. This is evident both in what the law requires and what it forbids. Banning voter ID makes it too easy to cheat. Simply requiring a signature is insufficient to verify who a voter really is, because poll workers are not handwriting experts, and even handwriting experts get stumped—which is why some states have decided to require a partial Social Security number, or some other checkable form of ID, in place of a signature.[132] In 2020, some 228 million Americans held a drivers' license.[133] It would take some effort to ensure that voters without driver's licenses or passports could all be issued a picture ID, but the task is not herculean, and a number of states have already achieved it.[134]

Although it purports to suppress voter intimidation, the proposed legislation actually promotes intimidation by enabling "ballot harvesting." Ballot harvesting involves the collection of absentee ballots by agents of a candidate or party who then take them to the polls en masse.[135] Because the proposed law forbids any limits on absentee ballots and makes no effort to restrain ballot harvesting, it greatly encourages the practice. It offers no defense against someone coming to your door, instructing you how to vote, and then taking possession of your ballot. And, it does not prevent the collector from learning how you have voted, and then, once taking possession of your ballot, tossing it in the trash if you voted the "wrong" way. This is precisely the type of voter intimidation the secret ballot was designed to prevent. The secret ballot was not imposed by federal law, yet some form of it has been voluntarily adopted by all fifty states.

True, the 2020 election did not reveal voter fraud sufficient to change the election outcome, but why should fraud be made easier in the future? And, since "ballot harvesting" is not defined as fraud, we have no idea how many voters were thus intimidated, or persuaded, since the practice is not policed. The 2020 election witnessed a record voter turnout and the election of a Democratic Senate and president. The House remained in Democratic hands, albeit by a reduced majority. So, it is hard to credit Democratic allegations of *massive voter suppression*—especially when the presidential vote total set a new record. In the absence of a crisis, it is incumbent on Congress to act deliberately to preserve the proper balance between federal and state control of elections, and to cope with voter intimidation via ballot harvesting.

This comprehensive constitutional defense naturally raises the question: Why, if it is so wise, has the Constitution been significantly undermined during the course of the twentieth and twenty-first centuries? In chapter 4 we attempt to answer this bedeviling question.

CHAPTER 4

Reform in the Constitutional Grain

Since the 1930s, the activities of the national government have expanded continually, so that they now touch every aspect of American life.[1] Naturally, those who made this transformation possible had every intention of doing good, and it is impossible to deny that the federal government does many useful things. Why, then, do so many Americans have such a negative view of it—a fact that public opinion polls have revealed consistently over a very long period of time? In 2021 Gallup asked whether Americans were satisfied with their government: 60 percent said "no"; only 8 percent said they trusted government "a great deal."[2] The Pew Research Center has been asking Americans since 1958 whether they "trust the government in Washington always or most of the time." The results are stark: in 1958, 73 percent of respondents answered "yes" to that question; by 1979 the yes response had dropped all the way to 28 percent, and in May 2022 the yes response was only 20 percent. Trust in the government showed a marked increase during the 1990s and reached a peak after the 9/11 attacks, but then returned to its historic postwar decline through the administrations of George W. Bush, Barack Obama, and Donald Trump, and has continued to decline well into Joe Biden's first term.[3]

There is some tendency for voters to trust the government a bit more when their own party is in power, but that trust erodes long before the administration has left office. For example, 69 percent of conservative Republicans trusted the government in October 2001—one month after the 9/11 attacks, and less than a year into George W. Bush's first term—but by October 2008 trust in the government among conservative Republicans had declined to only 28 percent. President Obama was no luckier: 42 percent of self-identified liberal Democrats trusted the government at the beginning of his first term, but that trust had dropped to 28 percent by October 2015. As of May 2022, trust in government among Democrats stood at 20 percent.[4]

Even so, and to make matters even more perplexing, American support for the federal government "doing more to help solve problems"—which had hovered in the mid-thirties since the question was first asked in 2010—has now gone up. The latest Gallup poll shows that as of 2019 (long before the pandemic, it should be pointed out) 42 percent of those polled were willing to say that the federal government should "take active steps in every area it can to try and improve the lives of its citizens."[5]

So while many Americans are willing to give the federal government more to do, most Americans continue to have very little faith or satisfaction in it, no matter which party is in office. What is going on?

The lack of satisfaction and trust comes from a deep-seated ambivalence about contemporary government. On the one hand, what James Q. Wilson called the legitimacy barrier has been breached.[6] The question asked in the face of new proposals for government action used to have two parts: Is this proposal a good idea, and if so, is it constitutional? Now the question has only one dimension: Is it a good idea? There is a growing presumption that, contrary to the clear language of the Constitution, the federal government is directly responsible for managing the social and economic lives of the citizenry, and should be responsive to majorities, however slim—even if this requires enormous budget deficits and greater federal intrusion into matters once off-limits to federal intervention.[7] On the other hand, there is a broad sense that much of what government is about in recent times ignores common sense. Furthermore, politics seems to be a game that only the rich, the clever, the lawyers, the famous, or the well-organized can play, and the results are frequently disappointing, insulting, or sometimes just puzzling.[8] In this way we have generated a crisis in representative government.

For example: Why is it that, while the Civil Rights Act forbids discrimination on the basis of race or gender, affirmative action programs in public and private institutions do just that all the time? Affirmative action may well be a good idea; but it is clear from the language of the relevant statutes that it is *illegal*, and yet even those members of Congress who are strong supporters of affirmative action have taken no steps to rewrite those laws, as if it made no difference what the laws actually say.[9] Or, for that matter, how did the federal government get the authority to tell high schools how to organize their bathrooms, or tell colleges what intercollegiate sports programs they are allowed to sponsor?[10] What all of these examples have in common is that they have no clear basis in law, and yet they are imposed anyway.

BREAKING THE LEGITIMACY BARRIER

The demand that the federal government do more, on a wide variety of subjects—even in the face of widespread public distrust of the government—stems from a change in the way public policy is understood. Over time, as the ambitions of the federal government have exceeded its ability to deliver concrete results, citizens have learned to hold two contrary thoughts in their minds at the same time, and do not want to jettison either: (1) The government is responsible for my social and economic well-being, and (2) the government is incompetent, unresponsive, or corrupt, and maybe all three at once.

We have come to this pass after a long journey, which began with the stock market crash of 1929. Over time, many Americans became convinced that they need not worry about the constitutionality of government action, and this of course made each subsequent expansion of government easier to accept. In turn, as more and more Americans became acclimated to receiving benefits from the federal government—everything from Social Security to discount medicine in their old age—the "legitimacy barrier" was broken.[11]

The "legitimacy barrier" defines what once had been a fairly solid line between the federal government and the states, or between governments in general and the private order. This line became blurred, and then it disappeared. As a result, expectations about what the federal government should do expanded, and reformers naturally took this as a sign to become even more ambitious. Not only would the government subsidize citizens, it would now attempt to fix whatever appeared to need fixing. As the government attempted ever more ambitious programs of reform, it increased the chances that it would fail. Hence, the growing distrust and disenchantment with the *results* of government, even as citizens continued to enjoy the fruits of the entitlement state.

This pattern, which began with the New Deal, has continued ever since, with only occasional interruption and much expansion into one realm after another. We will trace the pattern through the New Deal, the Great Society, and the emergence of "stealth government"—the sub-rosa government of courts, agencies, and interest groups.[12] That is, we are the heirs of a long tradition of progressive reform—in the 1930s, 1960s, and beyond—and these together have managed to produce a crisis of representative government. How?

To answer that question, we need to revisit these progressive moments. At the end of the journey we find a government that is notably unpopular, extraordinarily powerful, fiscally irresponsible, but only intermittently effective—and rarely, if ever, representative. Thus, the paradox: an increasingly busy and generous government that is also increasingly unpopular and irresponsible. And all of this because we have managed to transfer the responsibility for governing from a regime of parties, legislatures, and elected executives to a regime of courts and administrative agencies where much of what happens takes place out of sight of the voters.[13]

WORKING WITH THE GRAIN INSTEAD OF AGAINST IT

We acknowledge that this transformation was the result of efforts to solve very serious problems: economic paralysis in the 1930s; racial segregation, poverty, and environmental damage in the 1960s and beyond. But it is our contention that the results of these efforts at renewal would have been better had the federal government remained closer to the constitutional grain. As we explain in the introduction, the term "constitutional grain" is not a synonym for "constitutional." We are purposely choosing a metaphor from outside of politics, borrowing instead from another practical art: carpentry. Working *with* the grain rather than *against* it is a way to make the end result more durable and even more attractive. In constitutional terms, working *with* the grain of the Constitution is a way to deal with the problems of modern life that comports with our deepest political principles, with the way in which the constitutional regime was meant to operate—and the way citizens expect it to operate.

It's also a way to profit from an important lesson from the Founding era: when contemplating the pursuit of valuable public ends, it makes a great difference *how* those ends are to be accomplished. The Constitution established a structure designed to promote deliberation, consensus, public participation, and the preservation of liberty, without surrendering the values of stability, energy, and legitimacy—conceding, by the way, that such a government might sometimes be slow to act. Additionally, the Constitution supposes that there are some things a national government can do well, and some things that it cannot do well—and therefore should not attempt. Some things, that is, are best left to levels of government closer to the problems at hand. To use the simplest example of what the Framers meant, the federal government is better at sending a man to the moon than it is at improving math and reading scores in a local grade school.[13]

This chapter will discuss some of the most consequential political initiatives since the Great Depression—with a view to demonstrating the way in which working against the constitutional grain has produced unnecessary difficulties, often aggravating problems rather than solving them, while weakening the structure of the constitutional order and the public's confidence in the institutions of government—wasting vast sums of money, and piling up dangerously large debts, in the process. As earlier chapters have made clear, this was a gradual process, involving a long series of adaptations, each defended at the time as a necessary response to a crisis. For the most part, it has been a bipartisan effort as well. Taken together, however, this pattern has produced its own crisis, greater than any other: the undermining of representative government, the creation of a peacetime financial deficit larger than any in our history, and a dangerous loss of faith in the institutions of government by much of the voting public. *Prove the link?*

We will divide this transformation into three segments to see how we arrived at this critical juncture: the New Deal, the Great Society, and the subsequent emergence of "stealth government"—the largely invisible government of courts and administrative agencies.

It is well to remember that the American government can and must remain energetic, but it can do so while remaining within the constitutional grain. The difficulty develops when judicial and bureaucratic excesses and congressional inattention cause problems to be attacked with methods that distort constitutional forms and principles. As we have shown, not only do those distortions threaten our liberty, but they are often ineffective as well, and therefore sap government of its energy and the public confidence it needs in order to govern legitimately. To arrive at a balanced understanding of how energy and liberty are to be made compatible, we need to remind ourselves of those many policy arenas where government action is compatible with constitutional norms. We need not detail all that the federal government does, for example, to protect national security, deal with foreign nations, and control borders. But there is much more.

Because air and water cross state boundaries, ensuring environmental quality requires national action. The Interstate Commerce Clause (Article I, Sec. 8) readily justifies that. Likewise, major infrastructure projects—highways, dams, airports, and so on—have nationwide impact. The nation possesses national treasures in diverse forms including national parks, wilderness areas, and monuments; these are deserving of national protection. The public benefits from the government's myriad research and data gathering efforts as well.

We have been highly critical of treating income subsidies as *rights*. Properly construed, however, income support for those who are either temporarily or permanently disadvantaged is compatible with a sound constitutional order. The key is to abandon the metaphor of rights and adopt a different metaphor: the safety net. We cannot pretend to live in a world in which everybody can be relied upon to save sufficiently to weather job loss, illness, or even old age. Children are born to parents unable or unwilling to support them. Efforts to aid such people can be done without undermining their sense of personal responsibility. Obviously, the elderly and those with severe mental and physical handicaps cannot be expected to provide for themselves, and adequate provision should be made for them.[14] But with all other aid, recipients should be encouraged to climb up from the safety net and accept ever greater degrees of responsibility for themselves and their children.

The model for such well-conceived assistance is the 1996 welfare reform. Its official name denotes the key to its success—not "Assistance to Needy Families," but *Temporary* Assistance to Needy Families (TANF).[15] Lots of people need help, but making it temporary puts recipients under steady pressure to become self-sufficient. The law explicitly states that it "shall not be interpreted to entitle any individual or family to assistance." Thus poor, single-parent families do not enjoy support by right. The decision to give such aid is a policy decision, in other words, not something that can simply be demanded. TANF attempts to discourage dependency by requiring recipients to find work within two years and limits their eligibility to a total of five years. It also establishes a child-support-enforcement program designed to ensure that fathers of out-of-wedlock children help support them. So many of the programs we consider in this book have proved to be notably ineffective. TANF proved (for a while at least) to be an exception.[16] Welfare caseloads *and* poverty have both declined dramatically since its passage. As Robert Doar concludes:

> Few programs have generated such strong gains in poverty reduction and employment. The program's robust work requirement, accountability of state performance, and expanded administrative flexibility all helped raise the labor force participation of never-married mothers from 59.5 percent in 1995 to 73.8 percent in 2001 and reduce their poverty rate from 51 percent to 38.5 percent over the same time period. While a strong economy and the expanded Earned Income

Tax Credit certainly helped, studies that isolate the impact of welfare reform find that TANF itself also increased employment and earnings.[17]

Other safety net policies also encourage self-sufficiency. Time limits on unemployment compensation pressure those who lose their jobs to find new work even as they enjoy a decent period of time to perhaps find better jobs. Disability insurance likewise enables those who cannot work to survive even as, in theory at least, it requires them to return to work if they are able to recover. The Americans with Disabilities Act, by requiring that access to educational facilities, public buildings, and workplaces be provided for the physically handicapped, reduces their dependency and helps return them to the mainstream of economic and civic life. These programs only jump the grain if their aims are altered by judges and bureaucrats.

So how does that happen? To answer that question, we have to return to the beginning of the modern era of Big Government, the New Deal of the Roosevelt administration.

THE NEW DEAL

The great policy transformation of the New Deal had elements that remained in the constitutional grain as well as many elements that departed from it, sometimes dramatically.[18] Of course this dichotomy is overly simple, because, as we shall see later in the chapter, even policy reforms constitutionally defensible in themselves have often been construed, at a later date, as providing precedents for more far-reaching, constitutionally dubious initiatives. Examining key aspects of the New Deal enables us to better understand its complex constitutional legacy.

Since the early days of the republic the federal government had played a vital role in building infrastructure—the web of transportation, communications, and other physical improvements vital to the nation's development, prosperity, and well-being.[19] The New Deal followed in that grand tradition. The Tennessee River Basin is an instructive example. The basin includes parts of six states. The region was poor, lacking electricity, and subject to devastating floods. The New Deal Congress responded by creating the Tennessee Valley Authority (TVA) in order to build dams, electric generating stations, and power lines that brought flooding under much better control, and brought cheap electricity to the region.[20] Or consider the Grand Coulee Dam, the massive hydroelectric project that brought cheap electricity and irrigation to the Northwest.[21] As of the early 1930s, only 10 percent of rural America had electricity. In 1935 Congress established the Rural Electrification Administration, which succeeded in more than doubling that number in only four years. By 1945 almost 90 percent of American farms had electricity.[22]

Several attributes of these projects keep them securely in the constitutional grain. Because their benefits spilled over state lines, no single state would have fully undertaken them on its own and therefore they easily fit within the rubric of interstate commerce. The private sector had proven unwilling to adequately supply them, in large part because the cost of building transmission lines in remote areas would require electricity rates higher than farmers could afford.[23] In this case, the Rural Electrification Administration of the New Deal years proved to be an effective substitute. The great expansion of electrification and arable land that such projects made possible boosted private enterprise, providing all sorts of new opportunities for purveyors of consumer and agricultural products and for the establishment of new industries. And, they were within both the constitutional and practical competence of the federal government to accomplish. They clearly involved interstate commerce, and the physical engineering tasks involved were far simpler than the social engineering tasks we shall explore when we look at the 1960s and beyond. They passed the "man on the moon" test.

On the other hand, the New Deal's signature policy for coping with the implosion of the economy, the National Industrial Recovery Act,[24] was also among its most constitutionally dubious—and would have given the federal government the authority to do what the government could not possibly do effectively: run the American economy through a network of administrative committees. The hope appears to have been that the various actors would abide by the web of administrative restrictions (NRA "codes") voluntarily. There is no evidence that this elaborate scheme yielded any positive results whatsoever before being mercifully declared unconstitutional by the Supreme Court in 1935.[25]

But the outlook reflected in the NIRA had powerful support among such influential New Deal advisors as Rexford Tugwell, perhaps FDR's most important policy advisor in the early phase of the New Deal, and Alvin Hansen, a renowned and influential Harvard economist. Hansen termed his theory "the stagnation thesis."[26] It argued that as an economy "matures," opportunities for productive investment diminish and the economy's rate of growth decreases. Active government intervention is necessary to prop up the stagnating economy: thus the need, now, for "enlightened administration." This is fully in line with what progressives had learned from Edward Bellamy and Herbert Croly, among others, who were convinced that in modern times the market would have to give way to planners, making an already powerful national government more powerful than ever. In fact, the NIRA bore more than a fleeting resemblance to Bellamy's imagined "Industrial Army" from the world of the future.

"Enlightened administration" was not socialism.[27] Property would remain in private hands, but business conduct would be subject to strict regulation and supervision, tasks that could only be performed by administrators. As the NIRA demonstrated, enlightened administration was not content to punish businesses for misbehavior; it involved the far more ambitious goal of guiding, or perhaps dictating, resource allocation. The technical term for this is "cartelization." A cartel is any group of competitors that seeks to limit their competition by controlling supply and prices—that is, markets—as well as controlling the entrance of new competitors into existing markets. In the context of the NIRA, it meant running the entire economy through a network of industry-specific committees, armed with the power of the national government and supervised by administrators working for the government. The presumption, of course, was that administrators would possess sufficient knowledge and wisdom to act wisely—knowing exactly how many widgets the widget cartel must produce, for example, or what kinds of cars to market five years hence. Unfortunately, as we discussed in chapter 3, in a modern economy, information of this sort is the economic resource in scarcest supply, and therefore the data required to make "enlightened administrative decisions" is rarely obtainable. The analytic intelligence required to make sense of the data is in even shorter supply.

This hugely ambitious effort to cartelize the industrial economy and to substitute rule-making for markets was thwarted, at least temporarily, by the Supreme Court, but also by the resurgence of congressional conservatism, and by doubts raised among the voters by the more complex efforts of the New Deal to manage the country's economic life. The Court ruled the NIRA unconstitutional because it violated the separation of powers in its delegation of so much discretion to executive administrators in determining how the NRA codes would operate.[28] In the 1938 midterm elections Republicans gained seventy-two House seats and seven in the Senate—a sign of public dissatisfaction, not necessarily with President Roosevelt but with the puzzling manner in which the federal government was responding to the economic crisis. When combined with conservative Democrats, Republicans were now sufficiently numerous to block the further expansion of peacetime federal government administrative authority.

But the New Deal's experiment with "cartel capitalism" had much greater impact on a field of activity much older than the industrial system: American agriculture. Farm states were more important politically in the 1930s than they are today, and they were more closely divided between Democrats and Republicans. No administration could succeed without paying close attention to "the farm problem," as it was usually called. Cartelization of agriculture was the purpose of the Agricultural Adjustment Act of 1933—one of the first New Deal measures passed by the Congress. The "Triple-A" required farmers to reduce their acreage under cultivation, hoping to raise crop prices by reducing the quantity of crops placed on the market.[29] The Supreme Court rejected this plan in 1936 as outside the authority of the federal government, as the act of growing crops was purely local—as contrasted with selling them, an activity that clearly fell into the category of "interstate commerce" and thus was the jurisdiction of the federal government.[30]

Fearing that the Court would continue to block the New Deal, President Roosevelt determined to gain control of it before it was too late. Accordingly, he proposed a statute in 1937 that would allow him to nominate additional Supreme Court judges, up to a maximum of six, for every sitting judge over the age of seventy. Although not technically unconstitutional—the Constitution does not stipulate how many judges the Supreme Court should have—this proposal clearly went against the constitutional grain, specifically the principle of checks and balances and the separation of powers. For these reasons, the Senate balked, refusing even to report the "Court Packing" bill out of committee. Pushback from the Court, Congress, and the voters, in other words, curbed the New Deal's most radical effort to cut across the constitutional grain.[31]

But while FDR did not get to pack the Court, the Court itself retreated from much of its opposition to the expansion of federal power, even approving a new Agricultural Adjustment Act in 1938 that was nearly identical to the original version. Then, in 1942, the Court drastically expanded the definition of interstate commerce by ruling in *Wickard v. Filburn*[32] that if even the most marginal, indirect, relationship could be drawn between a congressional statute and interstate commerce, the Court would uphold its constitutionality—even if the act in question was simply a farmer feeding his own crops to his own livestock.

During the half-century after the New Deal, and despite often having a majority of judges appointed by Republicans, the Supreme Court did not declare a single act of Congress unconstitutional until *U.S. v. Lopez* in 1995—which overturned, as exceeding Congress's authority under the Interstate Commerce Clause, a federal law banning the possession of guns in local public schools.[33]

THE TRANSFORMATION OF RIGHTS

But the New Deal's most enduring legacy is the transformation of the idea of "rights"—and this is also its most constitutionally ambiguous legacy. As we described in chapter 1, the New Deal rested on previous progressive principles and expanded beyond them. In true progressive fashion it determined to use government as a means for social improvement, but it added a new dimension to that effort. It was not just about ushering in great social and economic change, but, harking back to the Framers, it claimed to be securing rights, which, in the Framers' understanding, is the essential purpose of government. But the new rights the New Deal sought to fulfill were profoundly different in kind from those enumerated in the Bill of Rights. Those older rights describe what government may not take away: freedom of speech, assembly, religion, and so on. By contrast, the New Deal sought to provide what Sidney Milkis has called "programmatic rights,"[34] the most notable being income security for the elderly—given by its creators the suggestive name "Social Security" rather than the simpler and more accurate label "old-age pension." That is, programs are set up to *give* tangible benefits to citizens. Instead of warding off incursions on liberty, fulfilling this new right required the government to subsidize the incomes of elderly persons, writing them monthly checks. In his Fireside Chat explaining Social Security, FDR gave the impression that the government was merely facilitating an insurance program, helping people to save for their old age.[35] But this is not true. Social Security does not operate on insurance principles, nor does it simply pay out to people money that they have saved and invested. It is not a 401k. Rather, it is funded through a payroll tax imposed on virtually all workers, the proceeds of which are then paid out to the currently eligible elderly recipients. Rather than an insurance program it is a form of entitlement in which taxpayers as a whole support the entitled elderly. Inconveniently, Americans are now living much longer than anyone in the Roosevelt administration imagined they would live. When Social Security was passed there were 7.8 million people aged sixty-five or older, constituting 6 percent of the population. As of 2019 there were 54.1 million people sixty-five or older, constituting 16 percent of the population.[36] Thus the Social Security program has become fiscally precarious.[37] And since most of those who pay are young, and most of those who receive are old, the Social Security program is an income transfer from one part of the population to another, disguised as a pension program.

The other right the New Deal established, labor's right to organize, is actually a hybrid of the earlier Bill of Rights understanding and the programmatic concept embodied in Social Security. Although the federal government does not itself provide unionization, protection of the right to organize involves a much greater degree of government intervention than the protection of other nonprogrammatic rights, such as freedom of speech or religion. By contrast, the Wagner Act, "Labor's Bill of Rights," established an elaborate governmental machinery to umpire disputes between labor and management that unionizing efforts inevitably entail.

No government bureaucracy exists for the explicit purpose of enforcing any of the rights protected by the Bill of Rights. Government self-restraint and the vigilant operations of courts and police forces are deemed sufficient to protect these rights. But the National Labor Relations Board (NLRB), which the Wagner Act created, is charged with creating rules and enforcement mechanisms designed to ensure that collective bargaining elections are conducted fairly and free of management intimidation, and that the two sides bargain "in good faith."[38] Inevitably government comes to serve as an arbiter of shop-floor and boardroom activities alike.

A strong case can be made that these two signal New Deal rights initiatives, though they represent major extensions of governmental ambition, nonetheless remain in the constitutional grain, at least marginally. As a result of vast improvements in nutrition, sanitation, and medical science, great numbers of people are living for many years after they have stopped working, becoming, at least potentially, burdensome to their families, if indeed they even have families. This had never happened before in human history and therefore could scarcely have been anticipated by the Framers. The tradition of private philanthropy, especially through churches, was already robust at the time of the founding, and the Framers might well have assumed that the practice of charity would continue to meet the needs of the old, infirm, or unemployed. Had they been able to foresee the conditions of the mid-to-late twentieth century, they might have had some doubts.

Social Security also passes the effectiveness test: the federal government is capable of doing it efficiently. For the most part, the Social Security Administration confines itself to the straightforward tasks of verifying eligibility and sending checks.[39] Like the development of infrastructure, it too passes the "man on the moon" test—although it would get higher grades if it were placed on a sounder financial footing.

Nor could the Framers have anticipated the kind of conflict that labor-management relations would feature in a highly industrialized nation facing a major economic depression. Even those who gave serious thought to the possibility of industry—Alexander Hamilton most prominently—did not foresee a total collapse of the economy. Nor did the Wagner Act force workers to organize or join existing unions—steps that would have been beyond the constitutional authority of the Congress—or force management to succumb to union demands. But it did seek to "constitutionalize" labor management relations—impossible under a long-standing common law principle that a union constituted a "conspiracy in restraint of trade"—enabling workers to vote for or against establishing a union, and to regularize the negotiating process.

Nonetheless, as subsequent developments demonstrate, these extensions of government largesse and authority were taken to be precedents for many additional "rights" claims and a welter of other government intrusions into the private sector that *do* deviate from the constitutional grain, sometimes substantially. This is the beginning of the breakdown of the legitimacy barrier. As the public is taught that a major purpose of government is to provide them with goods and services, to which they are entitled as a matter of right, the list of programmatic rights can only grow. As James Q. Wilson pointed out in 1979, each one becomes an argument for the next.[40]

Placing rights enforcement in the hands of federal bureaucrats has also given enormous discretion to administrative agencies. As we will discuss, every additional grant of authority to the bureaucracy becomes an argument in favor of the next grant, and very quickly private-sector organizations and actors learn they must act always with politically unaccountable administrators looking over their shoulders. Over time, this relationship passes through a learning curve. Groups learn to manipulate agencies; agencies learn to manipulate groups; rules are made and unmade; and the general public, thinking that "the government" means the president and the Congress, is kept in the dark.

Meanwhile, the explosion of economic growth after World War II gave the lie to the stagnation thesis (as did the postwar "baby boom"), and the government has never again attempted to control market forces as comprehensively and aggressively as it did with the NRA. But FDR's faith in enlightened administration lives on. It no longer so clearly rests on a belief that the economy has fully matured. However, the supposed scarcity of natural resources, and, more recently, fears about the impact of climate change, have emerged as the new rationales for anticipating the end of economic growth and the need for more government superintendence over the private sector. This chapter began by pointing to popular discontent with government intrusion. The following discussions of the Great Society and "stealth" government will show the complex and ever-expanding course that "enlightened administration" has taken, even in the absence of the economic emergency that allowed it to take hold in the first place.

THE GREAT SOCIETY

One way to understand the significance of working with rather than against the constitutional grain is by noting an important difference between the New Deal and the Great Society. Despite the fact that the New Deal led to profound changes in the way constitutional government is practiced, it inspired a pushback from both parties in Congress, the Supreme Court, and the voters—not, for the most part, because of its ends, but because of its choice of means. As noted, the pushback may actually have rescued the New Deal from the consequences of its most extravagant ambitions—the National Industrial Recovery Act being the most extravagant of all. The core of those ambitions was the administration's deep belief in the virtues of central planning—a core feature of progressivism since the days of Herbert Croly. The problem with central planning, however, is that the central planners will never have the kind of knowledge needed in order for the plans to succeed.[41] They therefore have to turn those decisions over to those who *do* have the knowledge: the most important participants in each sector of the economy. This results in the creation of industry cartels, which has the effect of freezing the economic order at a particular moment in time. This is what the Supreme Court saved us from by killing the National Industrial Recovery Act.

No Great Society program was declared unconstitutional by the Supreme Court, but the Great Society did generate opposition in Congress and among the voters. In the 1966 mid-term elections, Democrats lost forty-seven seats in the House, while still holding a majority in both the House and Senate.[42] But by then the Johnson administration had been able to enact the most ambitious program of centralized, top-down reform since the Great Depression. Unlike New Deal planners, however, the architects of the Great Society had their sights on more than the economy (which in the 1960s was doing pretty well without the assistance of the government). The secret is in the names. A "new deal" implies at most a fresh deck of cards, and perhaps a more "honest" deal (although the actual New Dealers had much grander ambitions, as we have seen). A "great society" implies something at once more ambitious and more mysterious. As we will see, the "mystery" was no mere trick meant to fool the voters, but a true reflection of the planners' confusion about what this new departure was meant to achieve.[43]

Some elements of the Great Society had appeared, provisionally at least, in the policy ideas of the Kennedy administration—a federal health-care program for the elderly, for example[44]—and so in the wake of the president's death, those ideas were likely to get a more favorable hearing than they might have received had Kennedy served a full term. It helped enormously that the new president, Lyndon Johnson, was a full-fledged devotee of the New Deal and a great admirer of Franklin Roosevelt—so much so that it was his deepest ambition to surpass his hero, just as a skilled batter wants to break the regnant home run record, or surpass Ted Williams's .406 season batting average. It also helped that Johnson could rely on solid majorities in both houses of Congress for the entire time he was in office.

But while the Great Society attacked a different set of problems than the New Deal, and used different methods, it is fully in the same tradition of American progressivism that gave us the New Deal—with one significant exception. Unlike the 1930s, the 1960s was a decade when the civil rights movement broke through the invisible wall between Black Americans and the agencies of the federal government. JFK, and then in a more vigorous way, LBJ, took seriously the commitment to fulfill the unfinished business of Reconstruction that had been idled for nearly a century.

Otherwise, however, the Great Society fully resonated with the progressive themes that were already shaping American public policy even before LBJ succeeded to the presidency. One of those themes was "community." As

Daniel Patrick Moynihan has shown in his recounting of the Great Society programs,[45] the theme of "community" was ubiquitous as early as the 1950s, when sociologists such as Robert Nisbet and Paul Goodman explored the "loss of community," and terms such as *alienation* and *anomie* became a shorthand explanation for social ills as varied as divorce, suicide, and juvenile delinquency.[46] This theme of "community" and its weakening in the postwar era took root and popped up in a surprising number of places, including both the *Port Huron Statement* of the Students for a Democratic Society (SDS) and the Ford Foundation's "Gray Areas" urban renewal efforts.[47]

An idea with such a varied and disjointed pedigree is bound to be somewhat malleable, and therefore somewhat confusing. The SDS version had a clear political meaning: in a massive modern state, run by huge corporations as well as huge bureaucracies (and universities could be found in each of these categories), people are likely to lose control of the communities in which they live, ceding ever more power to the powerful—doubly so if the communities are already disadvantaged by poverty or racial discrimination. What this "sense of community" had to do with the existing constitutional arrangements of federal, state, and local government was never entirely clear, and this lack of clarity would prove to be the idea's undoing, at least as a practical program— but not before generating much unnecessary conflict and confusion.

The other major impetus for the Great Society was the persistence of poverty, well past the moment when economic recovery had taken the American economy far beyond the trough of the Great Depression and the inevitable privations of the Second World War.[48] The fact that poverty disproportionately afflicted Black Americans was an additional outrage, and the Great Society programs increasingly became caught up in the effort to put an end to the exclusion of Black Americans from the American Dream—something that went beyond the protection of civil rights through judicial and executive enforcement. The War on Poverty and the promotion of civil rights became linked in the minds of both the architects of the Great Society and the public whose support Lyndon Johnson eagerly courted.

We will soon have occasion to criticize aspects of the Great Society; however, its initial victory, the Civil Rights Act of 1964, stayed well within the constitutional grain. It needed Johnson's powerful lobbying presence to win passage, but it was very much the result of an active and arduous congressional deliberation and thus a shining example of what a representative body can accomplish when it sets its mind to it. Indeed, the debate on the Civil Rights

Act of 1964 was the longest congressional deliberation in American history. Along with the Voting Rights Act of 1965, it breathed life into the antislavery amendments, which, apart from the actual abolition of slavery, had lain largely dormant since their adoption. It banned discrimination based on race, color, religion, sex, or national origin with regard to public accommodations, employment, education, and voting.[49]

Both its legislative history and its explicit language make clear that it is limited to addressing discrimination and does not endorse the compensatory schemes that bureaucrats and judges later devised and that Johnson himself championed. As Christopher Caldwell points out: "The debate leading up to the Civil Rights Act of 1964 is filled with outright mockery of those who warned of some hitherto unimaginable federal government infringement: not just the regulation of Mrs. Murphy's rooming house . . . but also mandatory school busing, public and private hiring quotas and immigration quotas."[50] For example, Senator Hugh Scott (R-PA) responded to the fear voiced by Florida senator George Smathers that bussing might be employed to achieve racial balance in schools. "Does the Senator not agree that there is nothing whatever in the bill which relates to the transportation of school children by bus from one district to another?"[51]

Affirmative action to redress past wrongs is mentioned in the law, but its application is limited to those cases where employers have been found guilty of discrimination. Thus the strict application of equal opportunity is only to be deviated from when it has been demonstrated that a business has been violating that principle or has done so in the past.[52]

Southern Democrat though Johnson was, and as willing as he no doubt was to make the messy compromises necessary to get to the top, once he was there he was determined to do what was, by his lights, "the right thing." His famous 1964 commencement address at the University of Michigan, in which he outlined the idea of the "Great Society," shows this very clearly.[53] The speech reveals also the unmistakable mark of the progressives in the Johnson administration, many of them holdovers from the Kennedy White House, who were uneasy working with LBJ but willing to take the risk. They believed that the New Deal had been unfortunately interrupted by the Second World War and the brief Republican resurgence that followed. But now that peace and prosperity were accomplished realities—and the Democrats were back in charge— it was time to turn the nation's attention to the unfinished business of reform, and if LBJ was the horse they had to ride, ride him they would.

At the very beginning of the Michigan speech, Johnson makes a revealing observation regarding the Declaration of Independence and its protection of "life, liberty, and the pursuit of happiness." "The purpose of protecting the *life* of our nation, and preserving the liberty of our citizens, is to pursue the happiness of our people [added emphasis]." The clear implication is that it will be the government that will "pursue the happiness of our people." Jefferson would be appalled. In his version of the Declaration, people have the right to pursue their own happiness, and the government is required only to recognize this right and stay out of the way. The premise of the Great Society could not be more different from the premise of the Declaration. And while we know many ways in which individuals can pursue their own happiness—not all of them effective, of course—it is hard to imagine how federal bureaucrats can pursue it for them.

The speech then makes two big points in its substantive part. The first is that America's material problems have now been solved; the nation is wealthy, and we must now devote this wealth to the purpose of improving the quality of American life. "The Great Society," Johnson rhapsodized, "is a place where every child can find knowledge to enrich his mind and to enlarge his talents. It is a place where leisure is a welcome chance to build and reflect, not a feared cause of boredom and restlessness. It is a place where the city of man serves not only the needs of the body and the demands of commerce but the desire for beauty and the hunger for community."

There is much that could be said about a paragraph such as this, which shares with many other commencement addresses the sin of "turgitude"—the condition of being "swollen" or "congested," in this case with pious sentiments. Yet it does capture a supremely important theme of the 1960s progressive revival: the belief that something is deeply, fundamentally wrong, not just with ordinary things like laws and court decisions but with the entire American social, economic, and political order. The Framers' view of American society was clear: Americans were not much better and not much worse than the general run of humanity, but they were more skilled in the arts of self-government, through long practice. As to their private morality, that would improve or degrade depending on the kind of education, both religious and secular, they would have available to them—but this was a matter over which the national government could have no direct control. But all of our early presidents spoke frequently about the importance of education, both moral and civic, and encouraged the states to make such education available in every possible way.

President Washington urged Congress to create a national university for the purpose of training a core of public servants suitable to the government of a republican people, although Congress declined to do so.[54] But the early Congress established "land grants" in the Northwest Territory, requiring each new state, before entering the Union, to use such grants to establish public universities and schools because "religion, morality and knowledge [are] necessary to good government and the happiness of mankind."[55] Private colleges, many of them religious, also proliferated throughout the western frontier.

From the perspective of the 1950s and 1960s, an observer might be inclined to say that the hopes of the Framers had been undermined by conditions of modern existence that were difficult if not impossible to predict in the eighteenth century. High rates of family breakdown, whether caused by economic crisis, racial oppression, or the frivolity of modern life, had apparently left many young people lost and bewildered, where they fell prey to the temptations of juvenile delinquency, serious crime, or alienation. The sign of this concern was the surprising focus, at the national level, on the problem of juvenile delinquency.[56]

The second big point is that in some way the great wealth that America has generated is responsible for the problems of anomie and alienation. "There are these timid souls," Johnson said, "who say this battle [for a Great Society] cannot be won; that we are condemned to a soulless wealth."[57] Echoing many a psychological manifesto from the 1950s, Johnson argued that America had somehow lost its soul—and this just twenty years after winning the greatest war against the greatest evil in modern times. The men in their gray flannel suits, living in their cookie-cutter suburban homes, working in the corporate world, graduating from "multiversities"—these lives have been deprived of meaning, and it will be the job of government to restore that meaning.[58] Just as FDR had resolved the material problem, the Great Society will now resolve the great American spiritual problem. For those of a certain age, this kind of rhetoric will sound familiar. Despite its unlikely source, these themes sound very much like SDS's *Port Huron Statement*, adopted at its formative meeting just two years earlier.[59]

One year later, President Johnson gave another commencement address, this one at the historically Black Howard University in Washington, DC.[60] In his Howard speech Johnson gave the federal government another ambitious civil rights goal: not just protecting the constitutional rights of Black Americans—that had also been an important theme in the Michigan speech—but guaranteeing their success through a policy of *affirmative* action. That is, the government would commit itself not just to *defending* equal *rights*, but to *achieving* equal *results.*

To put the spirit of the Howard speech into practice, three months later the president issued Executive Order 11246. It required all those seeking federal contracts, if they employed more than fifty-one people, to not only show that they did not discriminate on the basis of race or sex but that they had taken "affirmative action" to move toward equal employment. The term "equal employment" is not defined, but the specific requirements imposed by the executive order show that they are intended to achieve employment levels proportional to the percentage of "qualified minorities and women" in the broader population (for no stated reason, religion and national origin do not appear to require affirmative action). To comply with the order, a contractor must provide:

> an estimate of the number of qualified minorities available for employment in
> a given job group expressed as a percentage of all qualified persons available for
> employment in the job group. The purpose of the availability determination
> is to establish a benchmark against which the demographic composition of
> the contractor's incumbent workforce can be compared in order to determine
> whether barriers to equal employment opportunity may exist within particular
> job groups.[61]

The term "benchmark" is used, not "quota," but in this context it implies *quota* since it is the objective at which the affirmative action program must aim and is the standard used to measure the progress of the program—despite the absence of any such authorization in the Civil Rights Act. As we will see, the practice of issuing administrative guidelines with no clear foundation in any congressional statute would become much more common in the future.

By 1965 the civil rights movement was *the* topic of the day, constantly debated and reported on, most vividly in the TV coverage of civil rights demonstrations in the South. But the Howard speech broke new ground: it would not be enough to focus on protecting rights, because the exercise of equal rights, no matter how vigorously protected, could not erase the enormous deficit of America's racial past. Black Americans have, the president argued, been so damaged by racism—and this was especially true of the Black poor living in the nation's biggest cities—that "equal rights" would not be enough. Johnson offered as the most compelling evidence of this deficit the data on Black family decline in the postwar decades, the accelerating consequence, he argued, of racial discrimination in employment and housing. This claim—based apparently on research presented to the White House by Daniel Patrick Moynihan— would provoke a major (and revealing) controversy in a matter of just a few years, but at the time, the president was praised for putting the resources of the federal government to the great task of ending not just racial discrimination but also the family breakdown that appeared to be one of racism's most intractable legacies.[62]

To do battle against these evils, Johnson declared a "War on Poverty." Food stamps provided subsidized food to the poor. Medicaid matched state expenditures to provide health services to the poor.[63] Title I of the Elementary and Secondary Education Act of 1965 pumped money into the poorest school districts to raise pupil performance to the levels enjoyed by the middle-class suburbs.[64] While these policies appeared to be of a kind with the civil rights acts, they had a significant difference: they did not promise to defend a constitutional right, but rather to provide a private benefit at public expense, or to marshal the resources of the federal government in order to *fix something*: "underperforming" schools, or an "unrepresentative" local political structure.

As ambitious as LBJ was, he realized that the federal government lacked the personnel to achieve the Great Society on its own and that there would be enormous political resistance to bypassing the states when it came to spending large amounts of money. Therefore, a great part of the bold new initiatives that comprised the Great Society needed to be carried out by the states. The device for achieving this federal-state partnership was the federal grant-in-aid. As the Congressional Research Service explains, the vast expansion of the size and scope of these grants greatly changed federal-state relations.

> Previously, most federal grants to state and local governments supplemented
> existing state efforts and, generally, did not intrude on state and local
> government prerogatives. Most of the federal grants created during the 1960s,
> on the other hand, were designed purposively by Congress to encourage state
> and local governments to move into new policy areas, or to expand efforts in
> areas identified by Congress as national priorities, especially in environmental
> protection and water treatment, education, public assistance, and urban renewal.
> . . . Most of the new grants had relatively low, or no, matching requirements,
> to encourage state and local government participation. New incentive grants

encouraged states to move into new policy areas and to diversify eligible grant recipients, including individuals, nonprofit organizations, and specialized public institutions, such as universities.[65]

From 1960 to 1968 the number of federal grants to state and local government grew from 132 to 387 and grant expenditures almost tripled, increasing from $7 billion in 1960 to $20 billion in 1969. In just one year, 1965, Congress established 109 new federal grants.[66]

Although the War on Poverty was actually fought along all the various fronts mentioned above, LBJ sought to create a new engine of war, the Office of Economic Opportunity (OEO), directly answerable to the president, to administer a set of more precisely targeted antipoverty initiatives. These included Project Head Start, to provide early childhood education to poor children; the Neighborhood Youth Corps, to provide work for young unemployed poor men and women; the Job Corps, to provide residential work and training for at-risk young people; Volunteers in Service to America (VISTA), to recruit, train, and deploy volunteers to assist antipoverty efforts, and a number of lesser programs.[67] Taken individually, these programs seem unremarkable and easily derivable from New Deal precedents. What made the War on Poverty different was the principle of "maximum feasible participation" it established. To that end, the OEO authorized the creation of nonprofit agencies called Community Action Programs situated in poor neighborhoods to disburse and administer War on Poverty funds, thus bypassing the established state and local agencies that were the conventional conduits for federal subsidies. Initially the local boards created to do so were chosen in large measure by the residents of the neighborhoods themselves.[68] Thus a new institutional channel, divergent from ordinary federal-state relations, was opened up. The war would be waged by a joint force of federal officials and the poor themselves. But who would the war be waged *against*? Mayors soon learned, to their displeasure, that the War on Poverty would be waged against *them*.

What transpired was a nasty conflict between "antipoverty organizers" and city halls. Activists began disrupting city council meetings, threw rats on the desks of public officials, and generally sought ways to cause mayhem. These conflicts did nothing to combat poverty, but they seriously aggravated social and political tensions within major cities, and especially in the neighborhoods where the poor lived.[69] What made these conflicts even more striking was that they were fomented by a Democratic administration in Washington against mostly Democratic mayors—adding to the fractionalization of the Democratic Party.

But LBJ was not a champion of class warfare. Indeed, he was determined to show that the Great Society benefited the *middle class* as well as the poor. To that end, the Great Society initiated what has become the most expensive federal program since the New Deal: Medicare. It provides health insurance for the elderly regardless of wealth or income.[70] Like Social Security, it is an entitlement, and like its New Deal predecessor it has acquired the status of a right—a programmatic right—one that only government can provide, that is on increasingly precarious fiscal foundations, and that proves nearly impossible to reform.

Unfortunately, like the New Deal, the Great Society's generous ambitions had a powerful and in many ways destructive constitutional impact. Johnson's Howard University speech reinterpreted a *constitutional* principle, equal protection before the law, as a *moral* principle, *fairness*. Thus, even if everyone is enabled to run the race from the same starting point, those with worse track shoes, inferior diets, and poorer coaching do not enjoy a fair chance to win. Therefore, to make the race fair they must receive whatever forms of compensatory advantage will enable them to compete on an equal basis.

So far this sounds like nothing more than a fuller understanding of equal opportunity. However, in practice it is not. As Johnson's executive order implies, it is simply too difficult to judge whether training regimens, nutritional balance, and equipment quality are distributed equally, and so the actual measure of fairness, as interpreted by courts and federal agencies, turns out to be results. With regard to race this means ensuring that racial minorities get access to jobs, higher education, and the like roughly in proportion to their percentage of the population. If this is *not* happening, then employers, universities, and others are expected to act affirmatively, to take measures that result in hiring and admissions policies designed to establish a simple correlation between the percentage of various groups in the workplace to their percentage of the total population.

Affirmative action has had a checkered history, in part because the term has acquired more than one meaning.[71] Sometimes it is taken literally, as a command to try harder to search out qualified minority job applicants who might not otherwise have applied. This approach is consistent with the letter of the law, as well as with its spirit. In other cases, however, businesses and universities have tried to meet numerical quotas for Black applicants, even when their paper records would not make them competitive. The courts have repeatedly said that these kinds of racial quotas are unconstitutional, and yet firms and universities have been creative in developing "work-arounds" that allow the practice to continue.[72]

Undoubtedly, much good has resulted from such efforts. Minority candidates who score somewhat lower on SATs or have somewhat less job experience than their white rivals may well perform just as well in college or in their jobs as would a white counterpart.[73] Unfortunately, the constitutional costs of these quasi-legal efforts outweigh the benefits. Equality of result cuts against the constitutional grain especially if, as Lincoln taught us, the Declaration of Independence is the true preamble to the Constitution. "Pursuit of happiness" sounds like a fuzzy phrase, but as understood by Jefferson, and as it has entered American political culture, it stresses that results should not be preordained but should be commensurate with one's efforts. Thus, the pursuit of happiness implies inequality of result. Any athletic contest needs an umpire. But umpires remain in the constitutional grain when they are as unobtrusive as possible, limiting themselves to ensuring that everyone leaves the starting gate at the same time and that runners don't trip each other. If, as in Kurt Vonnegut's brilliant short story "Harrison Bergeron," umpires seek to ensure a pre-ordained result by putting hobbles on the swift and masks on the beautiful, then it is the umpires who are running the race, not the runners.[74]

An important policy like affirmative action not only produces substantive results—larger numbers of Black students at elite universities, more Black hires—it also constitutes a constitutional teaching about who we are as citizens and who we ought to be. Whatever its other merits, affirmative action teaches the wrong civics lesson. It encourages African Americans, regardless of their skills and talents, to see themselves as victims requiring and deserving special help. In a culture that so prizes dignity, affirmative action is an affront to dignity. Paradoxically, racial preferences also encourage whites to see *themselves* as victims, cheated out of educational and vocational opportunities. According to a poll conducted by National Public Radio, the Robert Wood Johnson Foundation, and Harvard University's T. H. Chan School of Public Health, more than half of white Americans (55 percent) believe there currently is discrimination against white people in the United States.[75] Whether or not this is an accurate perception, it shows how pervasive the perverse educational impact of affirmative action has been. It should also be noted that this result was entirely predictable.

The expansion of programmatic rights as embodied in Medicare also teaches the wrong lessons. When a "benefit" becomes a "right," there is apparently no longer any discretion in the hands of the giver. A right cannot be reduced, it cannot be modified, it cannot be cancelled. It can only be increased. Obviously, as more of the federal budget falls into this category of "benefits as rights," more of the budget escapes any semblance of democratic control, and this is perhaps the most important way in which the programs of the Great Society went against the constitutional grain. By creating what are, in effect, a collection of permanent but growing benefit programs, the Great Society has violated an unwritten principle of every constitutional order: namely, that the government may not spend itself and its citizens into bankruptcy. According to one estimate, the true costs just of the Medicare program—estimated at its inception at $500 million per year—were, from 1965 to 2005, $1.4 trillion.[76] According to a 2020 estimate published by the Congressional Research Service, Medicare will become insolvent in 2026.[77] When this sort of fiscal irresponsibility, on the part of the states, emerged in the 1780s it was a prime cause for the adoption of a strong federal constitution, for framing a government capable of paying its debts. Now that government is itself encouraging the very same irresponsible behavior.

Since programmatic rights resist modification, they diminish Congress's capacity to set priorities, to deliberate about how the government should allocate its always limited resources—and in this way the expansion of programmatic rights diminishes representative government. The Great Society's vast expansion of matching grants to the states had a similarly negative effect on deliberation. The crucial example is Medicaid, the federal-state partnership that provides health care for the poor. The federal government provides matching funds to states to help them fund their Medicaid programs. At a minimum, Washington provides fifty cents for every dollar a state spends. In poor states like Alabama and Kentucky the ratio is closer to seventy-five cents per dollar.[78] This federal largesse is largely responsible for Medicaid becoming the single largest item in state budgets, accounting for 29 percent of all state spending, far surpassing what is spent on transportation, education, corrections, or higher education.[79]

Perhaps state legislatures, in the absence of this federal subsidy, would still choose to spend such an overwhelming percentage of their budgets on health care for the poor, rather than on other useful tasks, but we will never know the answer to that question since these payments so drastically skew the nature of state deliberations. The widespread availability of "free money" from the feds encourages states to act irresponsibly.[80] Rather than acting as decision makers, performing their proper representative function by reconciling the needs of their constituents to the burdens imposed on them, they come to see themselves as entrepreneurs devising ever more ingenious means for extracting money from elsewhere. They become takers, not deciders. In turn, voters come to expect such behavior, seeing it as the norm, and tend to reward with their votes the politicians who can make the most attractive but irresponsible promises.

DEMOCRATIZING PRESIDENTIAL ELECTIONS

In addition to tackling poverty and urban decline, the progressive impulses set loose in the 1960s reanimated a much older ambition: "democratizing" presidential elections, which in practice meant taking nominations away from party organizations. Recall that this had been the aim of progressive reformers early in the twentieth century, following the lead of Theodore Roosevelt's 1912 "third-party" campaign for the presidency. That campaign crystallized an argument that had been simmering for a long time: parties exist, so the story went, in order to collect and distribute "graft" and "patronage" to the party faithful, and they are entirely uninterested in the question of who should govern or how.[81] This means that those who choose the candidates are beholden to "the interests"—a diverse collection of persons, corporations, and groups whose main interest is protecting the status quo, or at least their own little corner of the status quo, and whose principal means of doing so is their control of campaign money.

This is, of course, a caricature of the party system of the early twentieth century, but it is not so far from the truth as to be unconvincing to reformers. "Let the people choose the candidates" became the rallying cry of a reform movement that came miraculously back to life again in the aftermath of the 1968 Democratic Convention—which seemed to "prove" the reformers correct when the assembled delegates refused to nominate a "reformer" for president and chose instead Hubert Humphrey, loyal vice president to the (now) despised Lyndon B. Johnson.[82]

After 1968, as during the earlier progressive campaigns, the antidote to "boss control of conventions" was the direct primary, in which candidates for the nomination would go before the voters, who would then indicate (if not outright choose) their favored candidates. The most favored candidate would therefore enter the convention with enough popular support that the party professionals would have little choice but to accede to his nomination. That, at least, was the theory. Only since 1972, in the wake of the McGovern-Fraser Commission, which rewrote the rules for nominations in the Democratic Party (soon to be copied by the Republicans), has it been possible to test this theory in the real world.[83]

As noted earlier, the Framers of the Constitution were notably hostile to political parties, even while they were finding it necessary to form them: either to remove the hated Federalists, or to block the machinations of the hated Democratic-Republicans.[84] This looked at the time like an inauspicious beginning—there were frequent denunciations in the literature of the time of the "spirit of party" that was now taking over American politics. But the two-party system became a permanent feature of the constitutional order because there was no other means, in such a large country, of taming and channeling political energy and ambition in a way that would strengthen rather than undermine constitutional government. The two-party system can therefore be understood as a constitutional "add-on" that is entirely in keeping with the spirit of the Constitution itself.[85]

Recall the earlier discussion of the progressive case against political parties, a product of the late nineteenth-century and early twentieth-century reform movements. A major obstacle to genuine political reform was the party system, which, like the Constitution itself, erected barriers to impulsive action. Party leaders were used to doing business by making deals, putting together coalitions, and managing conflict. They were used to not getting their way all of the time, and they understood politics to be a practical business best managed by people who knew what they were doing. They therefore saw nothing wrong with the special role the party system gave them in the decisions about who would run for office. After all, they reasoned, someone has to stand behind the candidates and give them the political support they need in order to get elected. Why shouldn't those who perform this role have the most to say about who the candidates will be? A candidate, after all, is a candidate of a *party*; he is not running on his own behalf, but with the backing of a party label and a party organization. Without a major party endorsement, a candidate has no chance. Therefore, the party should be the one to choose the candidates; and in any case, who is better equipped to do this than the people who "do politics" for a living, that is, the pros?[86]

For much of the twentieth century, the contest between the "regulars" (i.e., professionals) and the "reformers" (also known as "goo-goos" for their support of "Good Government") was a feature of almost every political campaign. If you were a politician, you were either a regular or a reformer, a typology that dated as far back as the political conflicts of the so-called Gilded Age of the late nineteenth century.[87] Regulars liked the way that party nominations were conducted, because, being in the hands of professionals, the nomination was likely to either put the party's candidate in office (in which case many favors could be expected from the grateful office holder), or lead the party to a predictable but not catastrophic defeat.[88] No one sitting on the Cook County Democratic Committee, for example, expected Adlai Stevenson to defeat Dwight Eisenhower in the presidential races of 1952 or 1956, but they supported him anyway, while paying special attention to the candidates farther down the ticket, the ones that actually mattered more to the local party. After all, it matters who the president is, but in some presidential elections—ones that, like in 1952 and 1956, the party was certain to lose—it matters even more who gets onto the Cook County Board of Commissioners.

Reformers, by contrast, were more interested in "issues" than in candidates, and they were rarely, if ever, interested in the kinds of low-wage public jobs that were often the reward of loyal service to the party. The reformers resented the influence the regulars had over party nominations, and from the early 1900s on there was never a time when someone wasn't trying to reform the process for nominating presidential candidates. The first Progressive Party— the party of Teddy Roosevelt—was deeply hostile to parties, and it hoped to undermine them by promoting direct primaries for choosing presidential candidates. These and similar reforms came to little—until the late 1960s, a decade that saw the success of many reforms that had been dreamed of but never achieved for half a century at least. Specifically, the reformers' big moment was the Democratic National Convention that met in Chicago in 1968.

That convention was one of the most dramatic—and disorderly—conventions in modern times, and the disorder outside the convention hall was especially dramatic. Thousands of anti-war protestors and advocates of peaceful and not-so-peaceful revolution converged on downtown Chicago, attempting to prevent the Democratic Convention from conducting its business, and generally causing a full-scale ruckus. Meanwhile, the convention delegates, trying their best to ignore what was going on outside, proceeded to do what everyone expected them to do: nominate the sitting vice president, Hubert Humphrey, as their candidate for president. Humphrey went on to lose a very close election (43.4 percent for Nixon to 42.7 percent for Humphrey, with George Wallace getting 13.5 percent), but immediately the calls for reforming the nominating process grew louder, as a new generation of Democratic Party activists moved into the ranks of the party's leadership. As noted earlier, the McGovern-Fraser Commission proposed a set of rules changes that led, more quickly than most people expected, to the establishment of primary elections as the chief means for choosing presidential candidates. The number of primaries increased; the primary campaign became in some ways even more interesting than the actual presidential campaigns that followed; and party conventions, once the focus of intense excitement and dramatic turns of fortune, became little more than a carefully staged endorsement of what the primaries had already decided.

George McGovern, the chair of the reform commission, would be the first Democratic Party beneficiary of this new selection process—and went on to lose the election to Richard Nixon, carrying only the state of Massachusetts. Professional politicians who had been mocked by the reformers—and in some cases barred from the convention itself—probably took some satisfaction from this defeat, but their day was now over, and a new era of presidential politics was about to begin in earnest. But it would not be what the reformers of 1968 expected.[89]

Having taken the nominations away from the professionals, reformers inadvertently made the entire political process more expensive. More primaries meant more advertising, more expenses for grassroots organizing, travel, and larger staffs. The heightened need to raise money now focused the nation's attention on the subject of "campaign finance." If money is so important, won't this mean that the wealthy will have an additional advantage? What followed was a confusing series of efforts to make money *less* important—but without changing any of the factors that had suddenly made money more important than ever.[90]

Many things have converged, in other words, to create the modern system for nominating and electing presidents and other public officials. But the short version of the story is simply this: campaigns are now much longer, since they involve many more primary elections than in the past; for this reason, they are far more expensive than campaigns in the 1950s and 1960s; they involve far more use of television (and now the internet) than previous campaigns, one reason for their being so much more expensive; and party organizations have almost nothing to say about who "their" presidential candidate will be. We saw this for the first time when George McGovern, a candidate roundly disliked by the now-doomed "regulars," lost to Richard Nixon. We saw it again in 2016, when Donald Trump, who had only recently become a Republican, captured the nomination by winning more primary votes than any of the other dozen or so contenders, all of whom were longtime Republicans, many of them well known. And money—once upon a time a secondary consideration if a candidate had the enthusiastic backing of party organizations all over the nation—is now more important in politics than it has ever been, because campaigns are now more expensive than they have ever been before.[91]

Both parties have acclimated themselves to the new, post-1968 regimen of fundraising, media buys, and ground-level campaigning, and each side has been able to raise more and more money in each election cycle. The rise of cable television and the internet have simply meant new things to spend money on in order to win over voters. The well-intentioned effort to "get money out of politics" has backfired spectacularly—an important lesson about the unintended consequences of poorly-thought-out reforms that ignore the existing constitutional order in the hopes of making the political order more "democratic."[92]

FAILING THE MAN ON THE MOON TEST

The constitutional grain is further frayed when major government undertakings prove ineffective—when they fail the man on the moon test. The failure of the War on Poverty was one of the early causes of the loss of faith in the federal government that has grown so great over time. Johnson sought not only to put more money in the pockets of the poor, but to restore a sense of community, a laudable goal but one never before attempted by the federal government. By making the poor an integral part of the process of ameliorating poverty, the expectation was that it would end their isolation from civic life and enable them to turn their disadvantaged neighborhoods into vibrant functioning communities. As President Johnson articulated in his Great Society speech, the loss of community affected all Americans, not just the poor. The well-off also suffered from alienation and excessive individualism. But LBJ never produced a plan for alleviating this broader problem. The effort of government to engineer a richer public life through the device of maximum feasible participation was confined to the poor, where it failed miserably. Fraud was common.

Turnout in the Community Action Board elections was abysmally low.[93] Some community organizations were taken over by street gangs. Even if the diagnosis of alienation and disengagement as the sources of poverty was an accurate one, "maximum feasible participation" proved an ineffective treatment.

This is a judgment shared, it needs noting, by liberals and conservatives alike. To mark the fiftieth anniversary of the inauguration of the War on Poverty, in 2015, both the conservative Heritage Foundation and the liberal *Washington Post* came to virtually the same conclusion.

- The Heritage Foundation concluded: "In the 50 years since that time, U.S. taxpayers have spent over $22 trillion on anti-poverty programs. Adjusted for inflation, this spending (which does not include Social Security or Medicare) is three times the cost of all U.S. military wars since the American Revolution. Yet progress against poverty, as measured by the U.S. Census Bureau, has been minimal, and in terms of President Johnson's main goal of reducing the 'causes' rather than the mere 'consequences' of poverty, the War on Poverty has failed completely."[94]
- The *Washington Post* poined out that "according to the census, 15.9 percent of Americans lived in poverty in 2012, which is just a couple of points lower than where the Census estimates it stood in 1965."[95]

To spend $22 trillion to move the poverty rate "just a couple of points," when poverty had already been declining from 1947 to 1965—from nearly one-third of the population to one-fifth—is astonishing, and raises an obvious but embarrassing question: Why are we still enforcing policies that obviously are not working but that are enormously expensive?

A similar difficulty exists with the related effort to improve public education, especially in the nation's poorest schools, which were often the schools serving low-income African American children. Here the spending curves are as steep as the achievement measures are flat. Since passage of the Elementary and Secondary Education Act of 1965, the share of the gross domestic product (GDP) represented by federal support for local schools has grown from 3.9 percent of GDP to 6.3 percent of GDP in 2021.[96] Meanwhile, *local* school spending has also increased sharply. But measures of student performance on standardized tests show little to no improvement over the entire period from the mid-1970s through mid-2007.[97] The Brookings Institution had this grim conclusion in 2000: "Although poor children have made some progress in the interval, it is difficult to attribute their progress to Title I funding. . . . Unfortunately, little has been learned since 1965 about the conditions under which poor children make the most progress."[98] For the poorest Americans, the nation's public schools are as much of a failure now as they were at the dawn of the Great Society.[99]

In trying to engineer such complex and subtle solutions to the multifaceted problem of poverty, the federal government got in way over its head. As we have had many occasions to notice, the federal government is simply too far removed from the actual life of communities to make sensible judgments about how to improve them. It is no better at reviving decaying communities than it is at improving the performance of local schools.

The Emergence of Stealth Government

In the wake of the policy failures of the 1960s, the public grew disenchanted with the free-spending liberalism of the Great Society. From 1968 to the present (2021), Republicans have occupied the White House more frequently than Democrats. And while these Republican presidents were not Coolidge conservatives, they certainly did not share LBJ's grandiose progressive ambitions. And yet the reform impulse has remained in full force. The remarkable thing about the post–Great Society American government is how robust—and yet relatively quiet—progressive policy expansion has been, even in the absence of progressive majorities in Congress or among the voters. We refer to this phenomenon as "stealth government." Popular disenchantment as represented by the election of Nixon and Reagan did not lead to meaningful retrenchment; indeed, progressively oriented policies continued to expand. This expansion has occurred because its champions have found means to mask its true costs, and have made shrewd use of courts and agencies to keep potentially unpopular policy changes out of sight as long as possible.[100]

As Chris DeMuth has argued, the real price tag of expansionary American public policy is greatly understated by two forms of "taxation evasion"—regulation and deficit spending.[101] Because the public does not see the true cost of ever more expensive federal programs, it is all the more willing to ignore the breakdown of the legitimacy barrier. Regulation hides the true costs of programs by shifting the burden from the federal budget, and hence from the taxpayer, to the private sector and to state and local governments. Congress has been unwilling to increase taxes since the late 1960s but has pursued

Nixon did not oppose congressional efforts—in fact, he created the Environmental Protection Agency by executive order—Democrats did not trust a Republican president to enthusiastically pursue regulation of the environment, the workplace, and the consumer market. The continued success enjoyed by Republicans in capturing the White House deepened this mistrust, which was often shared by those agency officials not under direct White House control. As Shep Melnick points out: "The answer was to rely on courts to interpret and enforce the new laws, to increase courts' authority to supervise the administrative agencies that interpret and enforce the laws, or to use congressional hearings and investigations to insulate those agencies from White House control."[110] Melnick calls this "leapfrogging." Leapfrogging occurs when either a court or an agency takes an initiative, then the other branch adds to the regulation and sends it back to the first, which in turn makes the regulation a bit more demanding.[111]

Leapfrogging has outgrown its initial partisan purpose. It has become standard operating procedure during Democratic as well as Republican administrations, as agency officials have come to treasure it as a means for mandating policies that might well prove unpopular if they had to pass Congress, especially if one or both houses have Republican majorities. Thus, regulatory stealthiness is exacerbated by these successful efforts to avoid public scrutiny.

Consider bilingual education. Title VI of the 1964 Civil Rights Act states that "no person in the United States shall, on the ground of race, color, or national origin, be excluded from participation in, be denied the benefits of, or be subjected to discrimination under any program or activity receiving Federal financial assistance." In 1970 a federal agency, the Department of Education's Office of Civil Rights (OCR), issued a memo interpreting "national origin" to imply that "where inability to speak and understand the English language excludes national-origin minority group children from effective participation in the educational program offered by a school district, the district must take affirmative steps to rectify the language deficiency in order to open its instructional program to these students."[112]

Perhaps because the OCR was uncertain how much authority it had to impose this interpretation on local school districts, the agency did little to put it into effect at first. Then in 1974 the Supreme Court issued a ruling stating that despite the lack of any mention of bilingual education in the law, lack of such instruction constituted discrimination on the basis of national origin, and therefore the Civil Rights Act did indeed empower the OCR to require local schools to provide such programs. The Court did not specify *what* the OCR had to do to comply. Nonetheless, the OCR used the court decision as a justification for issuing stringent regulations with which local schools had to comply, or risk losing federal education funding. The agency now *required*:

> school systems with a significant number of English language learners to adopt a bilingual, bicultural approach in elementary school; established a methodology for classifying limited English proficiency students; required middle and high schools to institute classes that recognize the contribution of ethnic minorities; and strongly encouraged them to extend bilingual-bicultural education beyond the elementary level.[113]

With additional help from the courts the OCR obtained compliance from five hundred school systems, including most of the large ones. The results of these efforts were very disappointing (and very expensive), yet these agreements were not renegotiated, but continued as they were written. New York City sued to terminate the agreement, but lost.[114] Here we have a double leapfrog. A vague federal directive is upheld by the Court, and then the agency interprets the decision to enable it to issue far more ambitious and stringent impositions, which are likewise upheld by the courts. Meanwhile, the straightforward and sensible aim of teaching English to students who do not already speak it gets lost in the shuffle.

Intercollegiate athletics provides another example of government by courts and agencies, and once again we turn to our colleague Shep Melnick for a brief summary.[115] Title IX of the Secondary and Higher Education Act empowers the Department of Education to issue rules promoting equality in male and female sports programs at colleges and universities. The first set of rules was issued in 1975 and required that schools "provide equal athletic opportunity for members of both sexes" in college sports. "Equal," in turn, was to be measured in two ways: by comparing the amount of money spent, and the variety of sports offered. Although there was no requirement that colleges had to spend the same amount of money on sports for men and women, it was understood that colleges would need to "effectively accommodate the interests and abilities of members of both sexes." The considerable ambiguity of these regulations pushed colleges to demand more clarification of the rules, which arrived in the form of a 1979 memo outlining a "three-prong" test. The first prong required schools to provide athletic opportunities to men and women in ways that were "substantially proportionate to their respective enrollments." The second prong offered forgiveness to schools that did not meet the first test but were substantially on the way to doing so in the near future. The third prong let schools be held in compliance if they could show that the "interests and abilities" of female students had been "fully and effectively" met by the existing program—that is, if all the women who wanted to be on a team could find one, even if the money spent on female teams was below what was spent on the male teams. But it was relatively clear from this memo that "proportionality" was now the gold standard that schools would increasingly have to meet.

Then the federal courts became involved, ruling in a 1996 decision that Brown University could *not* spend less on female sports than on male sports simply on the grounds that women were less interested in college athletics than men. Even if it could be demonstrated through opinion surveys that this claim was in fact true, the Court reasoned that the apparent lack of interest by women was simply more evidence that the college had been discriminating against them by not offering more athletic opportunities. From that decision on, it became clear that if any college or university felt compelled to reduce its athletic budget, for any reason whatsoever, they would have to do so by cutting men's teams rather than women's teams. During the Obama administration, the Department of Education issued a "Dear Colleague" letter announcing that the elimination of any female sports team would be evidence that the program is not in compliance with Title IX. A "Dear Colleague" letter does not have the force of law—unlike an actual regulation, it does not have to comply with the terms of the Administrative Procedures Act. From the agency's perspective, this is an advantage. The letter makes it clear that while the agency is not *forcing* the recipient to comply, the message that it would be wise to do so comes through very clearly. It is, simply, a threat.

Melnick concludes: "This saga is indicative of the current state of affairs: so many tests, so many prongs, so much clarification and reinterpretation of the meaning of each prong, so little use of standard rulemaking procedures, so few opportunities for public participation, and so little forthright discussion of the purposes of federal regulation."[116]

Of course, Congress could at any time rein in this stealth behavior by clarifying the intent of the statutes that the collusion of courts and bureaucrats has distorted. But with rare exceptions Congress has refrained from doing so. The results of this reticence are especially glaring in the environmental realm.

The Clean Air Act, passed in 1970, lists six "criteria air pollutants" for which standards are to be set. CO_2, the chemical most implicated in the so-called greenhouse effect, was not among them.[117] When the Environmental Protection Agency (EPA) came under pressure to regulate CO_2, a source of climate change, it refused to do so on the grounds that CO_2 was not a criteria pollutant and therefore was not covered by the Clean Air Act.[118] There had been no discussion of climate change when the act was passed in 1970, or when it was amended in 1990. Congressional failure to clarify the meaning of "pollutant" enabled leapfrogging to take place. Congress could have weighed in, but it declined to do so. Instead, the courts and EPA made rules with respect to CO_2.

First the Supreme Court declared CO_2 to be a pollutant, and therefore demanded that the EPA regulate it with regard to auto emissions, which is what the plaintiffs, a number of states led by Massachusetts, had sued to accomplish. The decision confined itself to auto emission regulation.[119] In 2014 the EPA interpreted this Court decision to also give it authority to regulate coal-fired power plants, the *major* source of CO_2 emissions.[120] The limits it placed on those emissions were so stringent that they threated to force a very large number of existing coal-fired plants to shut down, thus depriving the coal industry of its major source of business, and putting thousands of miners out of work. While this decision was not unpopular nationwide, it enraged voters in coal-producing areas, leading to unprecedented majorities for Donald Trump in the 2016 election, based largely on his promise to repeal the EPA plan.

In 2019 the Trump administration repealed Obama's plan and substituted the Affordable Clean Energy Rule, giving states discretion to set standards and giving power plants considerable flexibility in complying with those standards. The Trump EPA ended the Obama plan because it went beyond the agency's authority to make policy beyond what the statute granted it.[121]

Whatever the merits of the plan as a method for combatting climate change, it is a clear violation of the spirit of representative government to place the authority to destroy an industry, vital to the economy of a number of states, in the hands of bureaucrats—especially when the statute itself does not compel such action. Surely a decision of this magnitude requires congressional deliberation—and arguably an amendment to the law. Note how far this outcome deviated from democratic deliberation. First the Court substituted itself for Congress in making a major change to the Clean Air Act, redefining the meaning of "pollutant." Then the EPA stretched the Court's ruling from auto emissions to a far wider realm of emissions. Finally, it issued a rule so far-reaching and stringent as to threaten the viability of a major American industry. Of course, it is highly possible that the coal industry would decline even without the EPA plan, but if so, then it is even less justifiable for unelected officials to serve as executioners.[122]

The Biden administration reinstituted the plan. However, in June 2022, in *West Virginia vs. EPA* the Supreme Court overruled the plan.[123] Because the Clean Air Act made no mention of CO_2 or climate change, the Court determined that a regulatory agency, the EPA, lacked the authority to do so on its own. In his majority opinion, Justice Roberts determined that the EPA's bold plan to reduce greenhouse gases by changing how an entire industry controlled its emissions violated the "major-questions" doctrine—the doctrine that if Congress wants to give an administrative agency the power to make "decisions of vast economic and political significance," it must say so clearly.[124]

Another major environmental statute, the Clean Water Act (1972), gives the government the authority to protect "navigable waters."[125] Such a grant is easily defensible on the basis of the Constitution's Interstate Commerce Clause, since such waterways either flow between states or at least feed into other waterways that do so. But the law did not define the extent of the causal chain affecting the quality of navigable waterways.[126] The water that ultimately flows into such rivers may originate in swampy areas, properly called wetlands, which themselves may be dry much or most of the time and are often little more than large puddles. Defenders of an aggressive regulatory approach argue that virtually any water source, however indirectly connected to navigable waters, may have some impact on the larger body and therefore should be regulated. Landowners should need to obtain a permit to drain or otherwise alter sources on their own property. Property-owner associations countered that regulations should only extend to significant water sources and only to wetlands that were continuously in contact with larger streams and rivers. "Science" cannot settle this dispute because the tools are not currently available to measure the impact of minor, indirect sources on the water quality of navigable waterways.

Nevertheless, in its 2015 regulation called "The Waters of the United States," the EPA chose an aggressive approach. It extended its regulatory reach to *all* wetlands and ponds within 100 feet of a protected waterway or within the 100-year floodplain, and even to streams that only ran after rainfalls. Thus, even if the wetland was more than 100 feet away but fell within an area that, statistically speaking, could spill into the larger waterway once every 100 years, or if a stretch of dry land only became a stream when it rained, land use was restricted. For example, farmers using land near these newly regulated streams and wetlands were restricted from doing certain kinds of plowing and from planting certain crops. They needed to obtain EPA permits in order to use chemical pesticides and fertilizers that could run off into those bodies of water. If landowners sought to dredge or fill such water sources, they had first to obtain a permit to do so. Such permits might require costly environmental testing and legal expense and could, at the discretion of bureaucrats, be turned down. The Trump administration significantly modified these regulations, but a Democratic administration would likely reinstate them, even in the absence of any guidance from Congress about how remote an interstate impact can be and still be brought under stringent federal control.[127]

In 1973, in the wake of fears that the nation's symbol, the bald eagle, was in danger of becoming extinct, Congress passed the Endangered Species Act (ESA). In its early years the act was deployed mainly to protect large mammals, the sorts of animals that evoke strong public sympathy. However, as written, the act was not restricted to the noble, cute, and cuddly. In 1978 environmental lawyers successfully sued the Tennessee Valley Authority to prevent completion of its multibillion-dollar Tellico Dam because the dam would endanger the snail darter, a small drab fish of the perch family.[128] Congress ultimately amended the law to exempt the dam, but it did not set standards for determining what sorts of species should be saved regardless of cost or of pain and suffering to landowners who would lose discretion about how to manage their property. If it contained habitat the government deemed vital to the well-being of an endangered species, then the government could regulate it.

In the absence of such a congressional effort, the Fish and Wildlife Service (FWS) chose to act on its own by extending its regulatory reach. It issued a rule that undermined the distinction the act had made between "endangered" and "threatened" species. Whereas an endangered species is "in danger of extinction throughout all or a significant portion of its range," a threatened species is one that is "likely to become an endangered species within the foreseeable future." In other words, the species might be in danger of becoming endangered at some point in the future but still has sufficient habitat. Ignoring this distinction, the Fish and Wildlife Service chose to impose most of the same limits on landowner discretion to properties containing *threatened* species that it applied to those containing *endangered* ones. The rule is slightly less stringent than the endangered species requirement, but only because it gives the FWS the authority to *exempt* properties on a case-by-case basis—thus widening the agency's discretionary authority even further.

Robert Gordon describes just how the Fish and Wildlife Service has decided to protect a threatened water snake:

> A farmer on his tractor could unwittingly plow a snake's burrow or could put his cow in a pasture where it steps on salamanders in a seasonal puddle. The law does not require the farmer to intend to hit the snake with his plow, or the rancher to intend for his cow to step on salamanders, to potentially become felons. It is enough under the [Endangered Species Act] for the rancher to know that he put his cow in the pasture, the farmer to know that he was driving his tractor, or even the homeowner to know that he was mowing his lawn. . . . For example, the U.S. FWS outlined a raft of extraordinary rules for homeowner's association members on a Lake Erie island to follow in order to make sure that they would not be prosecuted for accidentally "taking" a threatened water snake: Homeowners were not allowed to let their pet cats outside, they were forbidden from spraying poison ivy with weed killer if a snake was within 20 feet, they had to pay for government research and allow researchers to access their property (including the two artificial snake dens constructed on each property), and they could not mow certain portions of their lawns unless it is at least 60 degrees Fahrenheit.[129]

Jonathan Adler shows how in Riverside County, California, the Endangered Species Act even prevented private landowners from clearing firebreaks on their own land lest they disturb the habitat of the Stephens' kangaroo rat. In the ensuing fires, several homes burned, as did much of the rat habitat the law was supposed to protect.[130]

Since laws are written by humans and not gods, they are bound to have unintended negative consequences. That is why they often require revision. A phrase applied privately by landowners fearful of being deprived of the use of their land is "shoot, shovel, and shut up."[131] In order to avoid restrictions on the use of their property, the law as written gives them a strong incentive to kill specimens of a threatened or endangered species and destroy its habitat before the FWS discovers it. This incentive to destroy is among the reasons that the Endangered Species Act has such a poor success record. During the past three decades fewer than thirty of the more than one thousand listed endangered and threatened species have come off the list. It may well be that two celebrated success stories—the bald eagle and the brown pelican—were helped

more by the 1972 ban on DDT than by their ESA designations. Other de-
listings resulted from subsequent evidence showing that the listed species were
never endangered or threatened in the first place, so the meaningful delisting
number is less than thirty.

These disturbing results have been known for decades, and yet Congress
has taken no action to improve the law. As a result, a program designed to improve nature has not done so and has created unnecessary economic hardship
for many. Worst of all, it has encouraged many otherwise law-abiding persons
to become law breakers, subject to serious penalties and to the guilt a good
citizen suffers when she ceases to be one. Especially in a free country, this is a
dangerous conclusion for citizens to draw—all the more so if it turns out to
be true.

The Supreme Court's decision to overrule the EPA's nonstatutory-based
plan to reduce power-plant emissions of CO_2 is the most powerful blow dealt
to stealth government since the New Deal. Perhaps the Supreme Court will
go beyond it and revisit a whole range of regulatory actions, including those
discussed previously, that have no basis in statute. But the Supreme Court can
only go so far in reining in rambunctious regulation. Its role is purely negative,
overturning bureaucratic decisions that violate the separation of powers. Only
Congress can play the positive role of writing and revising statues to ensure
that their implementation hews to the constitutional grain.

As this chapter documents, much of modern government is conducted
without adequate public scrutiny and deliberative decision making. The shining example of congressional deliberation, the Civil Rights Act of 1964, has
been reinterpreted and distorted in clear contradiction to what those who
passed it said during the debates in Congress at the time.[132] A similar process
has taken place in a number of other policy realms resulting in policy outcomes that violate statutory intent and do not comport with a sound constitutional order. One might expect the courts to serve as guardians of that
order and to invalidate bureaucratic excess, but the opposite has proven to be
the case. Judges have enabled and even invited such excess. Many presidents
have so enjoyed the exercise of executive discretion and/or have become pris-
oners of their underlings that they too have failed to stem the stealth tide.
President Reagan famously said that "government is the problem," but once
in office he did little to rein it in.[133] President Trump stridently declared the
administrative state to be a "swamp." But his attacks were indiscriminate and
often ill-considered, and he was all too eager to invoke emergency powers of

his own—for example, to oppose the will of Congress in order to build his security wall along the border with Mexico.[134] His threats to use powers the president does not have—for example, to overrule COVID-19 decisions made by governors—further undermined his credibility as a restrainer of excessive government intrusion.

So it falls to Congress to bring stealth government into the light of day and curb it. This is appropriate since, as the Framers intended, Congress is the heart of representative government. It is the only place where serious policy disputes can be fully aired. It has many tools at its disposal for performing this vital function—from holding oversight hearings, to cutting appropriations, to rewriting statutes to clarify their meaning. Unlike their bureaucratic counterparts, if their constituents don't like what they have done they can boot them out.

Indeed, the House of Representatives has several times passed a bill that would be a step in the right direction. The Regulations from the Executive in Need of Scrutiny (REINS) Act would shift the way in which major regulations—those imposing costs of greater than $100 million a year—become law. Instead of issuing such rules, agencies would propose them to Congress. They would only go into effect if both houses of Congress approved them. Impositions of such magnitude more closely resemble laws than mere housekeeping. Therefore it is proper that they must be considered and passed (or defeated) by a representative body. Unfortunately the House has not passed a version of this bill since 2017, and the Senate has consistently refused to pass any version, so it remains on the drawing board.[135]

The inability to pass REINS exemplifies Congress's continued abdication of its duty as statutory guardian. Its members have become so enamored of proclaiming their partisan proclivities that they have neglected the hard work of framing statutes, debating their merits, and overseeing their implementation. The United States is a modern state. It will inevitably take on a wide variety of tasks, and those charged with performing those tasks will just as inevitably seek to maximize their discretion regarding how those tasks are carried out. Mindful of this proclivity, the Framers created a key countervailing power—the Congress—hoping that the ambition of its members would drive them to fight against executive aggrandizement. The future of the republic rests on the willingness of Congress to reassert that noble ambition.

The title of this book—*Keeping the Republic*—is meant to emphasize the obvious: that the republic will not keep itself. That is, the constitutional order is a framework for ordering the nation's political life that cannot work properly if those in office choose, repeatedly, to ignore it. It was not, in fact, intended by its authors to be a "machine that would go of itself"—to refer to an earlier reference.[136] It is true, of course, that the Framers intended that "ambition [would] counteract ambition," so that no single branch, or level, of government would overpower all the rest. And while the famous checks and balances of the Constitution have prevented any one branch from becoming permanently in the ascendance, they have not prevented the political class as a whole from transgressing the Constitution's limitations. This is a problem that we will turn to in our final chapter.

CHAPTER 5

Thinking Constitutionally

AMERICA AS A REGIME

A constitution "constitutes"—that is, it forms—a people in a particular way. It is possible to imagine a different constitution for the United States as of 1788. We might have abolished the states, or alternatively, we might have created a much looser confederation, just one step removed from the Articles. We might have chosen a president for life, as Alexander Hamilton proposed.[1] In other words, the Constitution as it emerged from the convention created a *particular* kind of political regime in preference to other possibilities. A *particular* regime requires a *particular* way of thinking about politics. Over time, if the constitutional order thrives, citizens will learn a certain kind of discipline, a certain way of thinking and talking about politics. They will learn how to think constitutionally.

So far, so good

How does the Constitution encourage the citizen to think about politics? This is a question that the Framers took seriously, because they knew that Americans were already skilled in the practices of local and state government. They were already politically active, sometimes in ways that put their passions ahead of their common sense. They would need to learn a somewhat novel political discipline, combining loyalty to the nation with loyalty to, and even affection for, their local states and communities. In other words, the Framers had a theory about American citizenship, one that was consistent with the nature of the constitutional order about to come into being.

First of all, the primary job of the citizen under the American Constitution would be *to choose*. They would choose members of Congress; they would choose state legislators, who would in turn choose members of the Senate, and electors to choose the Executive. They would elect governors and local officials. This is admittedly a narrower understanding of citizenship than what was found in the ancient republics, but those republics were very small, and their citizenship class was smaller still—and far more homogeneous than the population of a modern state. Because of the size and diversity of America, citizenship must begin in the towns, cities, and states, where, by constitutional

Second job?

design, most of the governing would take place. America in the twenty-first century would appear to be, obviously, a very different place from America in the eighteenth century. Much more government takes place at the national level, for reasons that we have discussed.

But it remains a fact that there is a great deal of local politics in the United States, and that most Americans live in towns and suburbs that are small enough to be comprehensible, enabling citizens who wish to participate to do so. As of the 2020 Census, slightly more than half the population lived in jurisdictions with fewer than 25,000 people.[2] At these lower levels, the scope of citizenship would expand in inverse proportion to size: the smaller the sphere, the more intense the experience of citizenship could be.

So, what is it that citizens need to learn in order to "act constitutionally"? The first and most bitter lesson of politics is that you can't always get what you want. Governments operate with budgets, and budgets decide which things citizens will get and which things they won't. Under the best of circumstances, towns can put before the citizens a set of choices about how to spend a fixed amount of money, for example, for local schools. If citizens really want a new elementary school, they have to decide whether they want it badly enough to swallow some increase in their local taxes—or decide what programs already running should be reduced or ended. Or if they want ten more police officers and ten more teachers, and then discover that there's not enough money in the budget, they will have to settle for something less, say, five of each.

The second important political lesson is that people not only have different *opinions*—this will come as no surprise to most people; they also have different *interests*, and their interests are just as "special" to them as yours are to you. For example, a town needs another sanitation facility, and nearly everyone agrees that this need must be met. But where should the new facility go? Wherever it goes, its neighbors will be exposed to some degree of hardship in the form of an ugly, noisy, probably smelly installation. Those who complain will be accused of being "selfish." But the wiser course—which can only be learned through experience—is to understand that opponents are *not* being selfish; they simply have different interests from those living far from the new facility, and this fact cannot be ignored in the name of a putative "public" good. The dump must go *somewhere*. The clash of interests must be resolved. That's what politics is for. But if the political order is to hold together, the "winners" must strive to mitigate the pain suffered by the "losers" and, as the political process winds forward, the losers must win sometimes too.

It's much harder to develop this sense of generosity when the losers are total strangers, as they inevitably will be when decisions are made at higher levels. This is why the Constitution delegates to the Congress a list of powers that does *not* include the exercise of what was known at the time as the "domestic police," or the "police power"—that is, the power to regulate such matters as local education, family law, public health, sanitation, law enforcement, and so on. The way these powers are exercised will define, for better or worse, the quality of local life, and therefore must be left in the hands of local citizens.

What these examples illustrate is that citizenship is not so much a status as it is a job. Citizenship requires a willingness to learn by doing, which means that it requires practice and careful thought. Rightly understood, citizenship is an *office*, because the citizen is called upon to help *govern*, and this means far more than merely making demands. The citizen is a chooser, not a demander. This is not the same thing as "altruism"; it does not mean abandoning one's own interests. But it does mean understanding where one's own interests and the interests of others clash, where they coincide, and where they can be combined through some sensible process of compromise.

When citizens shift gears from exercising the civic office locally to choosing their representatives nationally, they will have acquired the ability to recognize in others the deliberative qualities that they have taught themselves. They will then be capable of making what Publius referred to as an "honorable determination"[3]—that is, an honorable choice about who will exercise the kind of political responsibilities that citizens will not be able to exercise directly because of the huge scale of the country. They will have learned to understand politics well enough to choose those with the qualities they know to be necessary, and to reject those who lack those qualities. In this way, local politics is meant to be a kind of school where Americans will continue to practice the civic habits and skills that made it possible to establish a great republic in the first place.[4]

What is true of the citizens is also true of those they choose to serve them. Members of Congress, for example, are also meant to be "honorable determiners," who would put aside the urge to "virtue signal," or to demonize their opponents. Instead, they would do their duty by crafting constitutionally responsible statutes, revisiting those laws when they produce unanticipated negative consequences, and strictly oversee their enforcement.

As we have made clear in previous chapters, members of Congress are not currently acting as "honorable determiners," and haven't been doing so for quite some time. The legislature's abandonment of its constitutional responsibilities has cleared the way for the emergence of "stealth government" and the bloated administrative apparatus that it has birthed. From many different quarters, on both the left and the right, we hear that the constitutional order is broken. Many on the left say that the Constitution has never served the interests of anyone but the rich and the well-connected. Many on the right say that the constitutional order has been twisted out of shape by several generations of progressive government. In addition, some on the left say that the entire society is steeped in racism and must be thoroughly cleansed. Some on the right see an all-out assault on the nation's traditional institutions and values.

What does the Constitution have to do with all of this?

Recall Benjamin Franklin's remark about what kind of government the Convention had devised: "A republic, if you can keep it." The republic won't keep itself, despite the excellence of the constitutional design. The keeping is up to the citizens. Just as the Constitution could not end slavery, it cannot end poverty, homelessness, or environmental degradation. That is our job, the job of citizens acting within the framework that the Constitution established.

But, say the critics, the Constitution gets in the way of solving these problems. By placing so many obstacles in the path of the majority, it undermines popular rule and enables rule by elites. After all, the rich are a minority by definition, and when the majority is prevented from getting its way, the result is inevitably rule by the wealthy few rather than by the many.

Yet this argument cannot account for the many policies, adopted over decades of public debate, designed to confront the most difficult problems posed by modernity—and by the particular problems generated by the existence of slavery. Indeed, the Constitution has not prevented real progress on a variety of critical fronts, including life expectancy,[5] the employment status of women,[6] and the economic conditions of African Americans.[7] The air and water are cleaner.[8] Voter turnout in the 2020 presidential election was the highest since 1992.[9] Nor has the Constitution prevented the adoption of many policies that have clearly *failed*—as we demonstrated in our earlier discussion of the failure of education reforms sponsored by the federal government. That is why it is a mistake to think of the Constitution as an "owner's manual"; it is not simply a set of instructions on "how to govern" but a framework that encourages a particular way of governing, one that privileges deliberation, compromise, restraint, and respect for federalism and the separation of powers.

To the extent that compromise, restraint, and federalism have become "optional" to many politicians, the Constitution has been undermined, and our politics have suffered.

[handwritten annotation: If your argument is that those elected to Congress have erred, why the focus on Biden? It just looks partisan, or ideological]

The Biden administration provides the most recent examples of long-term disturbing trends whose development we traced in chapter 4. Despite enjoying a mere nine-vote majority in the House and no majority in the Senate, its initial legislative priorities, meant to be pushed through Congress in his first year in office, revealed a disturbing disregard for restraint, compromise, and respect for federalism. Its comprehensive voting reform bill, discussed in chapter 4, sought to destroy the delicate state-federal balance of authority regarding elections, in favor of centralized national control. In a similarly aggressive spirit, the administration introduced two related plans, labeled the American Jobs Plan and the American Families Plan, whose combined cost was in the neighborhood of $4 trillion, the largest domestic spending initiative since the New Deal, and far larger than what was spent by the War on Poverty.[10] In the face of strong opposition from a single Democratic senator, Joe Manchin of West Virginia, the Biden administration renamed the proposal "Build Back Better" and reduced its price tag to a "mere" $2.4 trillion .[11] This revision was geared not to compromise with Republicans, but simply to gain the support of the sole Democratic holdout, Manchin, and therefore does not represent any sort of bipartisan compromise.[12] There is simply no peacetime precedent for such a massive expenditure being passed by a closely divided Congress.

Manchin remained opposed to this trimmed version and only agreed to support the bill, renamed the Inflation Reduction Act, when the spending level was further reduced and, as the name implies, provisions were added that promised to reduce the deficit in the future.[13]

In a similar vein, President Biden issued a number of executive orders intended to deprive states and localities of authority. On his very first day in office, he issued an executive order forbidding them from preventing transgender use of bathrooms and locker rooms and enabling transgender individuals to join the athletic teams of what previously would have been considered the opposite sex.[14] As we discussed in chapter 4, the Trump administration revised the Obama administration's sexual harassment regulations in order to provide greater due process guarantees to those accused of sexual harassment, and to restore the principle of "innocent until proven guilty." In June 2022 the Biden administration rescinded that previous order and issued regulations that will once again violate due process of law and the presumption of innocence.[15]

What the members of the Constitutional Convention understood from their long experience in colonial and state politics is that democratic regimes tend to produce "mutable" laws—that is, laws that are constantly changing, so that no one could be sure, from one session to the next, what their rights or responsibilities might be.[16] In addition to making the law *confusing*, unmitigated democratic government can make the law *unpredictable*, which is even worse. Who can make sensible plans for the future when no one knows what the government will do next? Or what the next government will proceed to undo? For example, the Biden administration has recently pursued two opposite courses simultaneously. On the one hand, the administration has urged fossil-fuel companies to produce more oil, because of the war in Ukraine. On the other hand, the administration has committed itself to policies designed to wean consumers *away* from fossil fuels, looking ahead to their eventual extinction. If you were the CEO of Exxon, how would these conflicting signals affect your company's investment plans?

Looking ahead, what are the greatest challenges to constitutional government that must be faced by both representatives and the citizens who choose them? To answer that question, we need to understand what the constitutional order is expected to foster: liberty, justice, equality, prosperity, security, and civic comity.

LIBERTY

Liberty is a complicated idea. It doesn't mean simply the absence of constraints. Liberty means the absence of *unjust* or *unnatural* constraints, or constraints not chosen by those who they were meant to bind, or restraints that are unreasonable. The words "freedom" and "liberty" imply *self*-government; they are preeminently *political* words, not so much concerned with private behavior as with *public* life. Liberty, freedom—these are the watchwords of republican government, or as Lincoln put it, of a government not just "for" the people, but "of" the people and "by" the people as well.

But the defense of liberty means paying attention not only to what the *government* does but to what private actors do as well, especially when those actions threaten liberty. Private actors may violate the spirit of the Constitution even if they do not violate the law. Even when a business has the right to fire one of its employees—because the firing does not violate the civil rights laws—that firing might still violate the *spirit* of the Constitution. For example, firing an employee for expressing unpopular political opinions may not be illegal, depending on the circumstances, but it unquestionably undermines the spirit of liberty that the Constitution exists to protect. The Constitution, of course, is first of all a set of restraints on *public* actors, but it also holds up a standard to which all citizens should aspire—even if they are the presidents of major corporations or major universities. Liberty therefore does not mean simply that the government can't stop you from doing something; it also means that citizens are entitled to respect from the private order as well as the public for their own opinions, however unpopular they might in some circles.

JUSTICE

One of the oldest symbols of justice, dating to ancient Greece and Rome, is the familiar figure of Lady Justice, standing tall, wearing a blindfold, holding a balance-scale in one hand and a sword in another. The symbolism is as obvious as it is powerful. Justice is blindfolded so that no personal favoritism can enter her calculations, however innocently. The scale is a scientific instrument, suggesting the importance of arriving at a *correct* measure of the factors indicating guilt or innocence. The sword is the most obvious of all, perhaps: justice is useless if it cannot be enforced.

In the Anglo-American context most relevant for understanding the Constitution, justice is a goal to be achieved by a correct reading of the law—the task of a judge—and its effective enforcement—the task of the executive. Like Lady Justice, those who judge and enforce the law should be blind to the persons involved in legal disputes, because the law must not see the person but only the case. Evidence should be carefully weighed, and the judgment must be enforced, even if at the point of a sword.

Under the American Constitution, the pursuit of justice is a task divided between the national government, the states, and whatever municipal institutions the state has provided for. As with many aspects of American federalism, results may vary. No one should be surprised by this. The Constitution itself anticipates the possibility of a "worst case"—a breakdown of law and order in a state—and provides a remedy in Article IV, Section 4: "The United

States shall ... protect each [State] against invasion; and on Application of the Legislature, or of the Executive (when the Legislature cannot be convened), against domestic violence." Of course, where federal law is being opposed and its enforcement blocked, the national government has the authority to intervene, with force if necessary: for example, suppressing the Confederate States of America during the Civil War, or sending federal troops to Little Rock, Arkansas, to enforce a court order against the wishes of the state government and an unruly mob.

On the whole, however, the federal courts, and most state courts as well, have provided forums in which aggrieved citizens and contending parties could find some measure of justice without resorting to what Locke called the "appeal to heaven"—that is, rebellion. Justice is therefore more than "fairness"—it is the expectation that every honest citizen should be able to live without fear of either private or public persons, to conduct their business openly without undue interference, and to enjoy the fruits of their own labor, under a "government of laws, not of men."

EQUALITY

The Constitution's promise of justice implies *equal* justice—that every citizen coming before a court or a magistrate can expect to be treated in the same way as any other citizen presenting the same circumstances. The notion that citizens should *expect* to be "equal before the law" is one of the oldest promises of the common-law tradition. When the law is enforced differently against one citizen than against another we understand instinctively that an injustice has been committed.

But "equal before the law" does not exhaust the meaning of equality; as Alexis de Tocqueville observed, the doctrine of equality inspires both healthy and unhealthy desires—on the one hand, the desire to "raise everyone up" as far as they can go, and, on the other, the desire to drag everyone down to the same common level.[17] An example of the first would be a publicly supported school system that guarantees a good education to students from all backgrounds, rich and poor. An example of the second would be an insistence that no student in such a school should ever be embarrassed by getting poor grades or by being punished for disruptive behavior. As is obvious, these two understandings of equality are incompatible—and Tocqueville worried that in a democratic society, the second version might be more powerful, ultimately, than the first. Who would now insist that he was wrong?

Still, equality before the law opens the door to opportunities that would otherwise be closed to those without superior social resources—money, reputation, connections. Legal equality creates more than merely a "level playing field." Legal equality multiplies the opportunities for success by removing artificial barriers to achievement. The eighteenth century dreamed of a society "open to talents"—understanding that talent might exist in unexpected places. What Europeans coming to America experienced early in the nation's history was a powerful sense of openness and possibility, and indeed this is a quality that continues to draw immigrants to the United States from around the world—even though immigrants have *never* faced a level playing field upon arrival. And yet still they come.

Of course, some will be more successful than others. Some of the people toiling in their garages back in the 1970s invented Microsoft and Apple, while others invented nothing, or at least nothing nearly so lucrative. But throughout American history, the toilers have understood that if they succeeded they would prosper, because the law would protect what they invented and allow them to profit from its usefulness. Equality of opportunity—the ability to succeed based only on your abilities and not your social status—will lead, inevitably, to *unequal* outcomes. These two factors cannot be separated. Some people will be rich, and some people will not—and while we can, as a society, seek to eliminate *poverty*, we cannot eliminate income inequality without undermining the equality of opportunity, which is its natural parent.

[handwritten marginal note: but strive to eliminate those elements of it that reflect unfair advantage, such as resources distributed equally before the law]

PROSPERITY

As we have said from the beginning, a good constitutional order must comport with human nature—humans as they are, not as we might long for them to be, for the simple reason that reality does not care about what we long for. From Athens onward and even before, people have sought to make themselves materially better off. Only those with the deepest commitments to otherworldliness—monastic orders, Hindu mystics—have chosen voluntary poverty. There is something magnificent about such self-denial—but note what an infinitesimal percentage of humanity chooses it. For millennia, material well-being was considered to be, in large measure, a zero-sum game. I could only improve *my* lot by taking from you. The great change in outlook, but not in human nature, occurred as a result of the advent of capitalism. The free exchange of goods could make everybody better off by making goods more plentiful. This success spurred, and was itself accelerated by, industrialism, which brought previously unimaginable productivity gains. Now that it is possible for everyone to be better off, people have come to expect, indeed to demand, prosperity. Presidents who preside over even mild recessions are defeated unless the country emerges from such setbacks before they run for reelection. Thus, the promotion of prosperity has become an expectation the constitutional order must fulfill. Fortunately, it has proven capable of doing so, in part because it was designed to make prosperity possible. Its twin underpinnings of private property and free markets have enabled most Americans to live well. Other nations, with different constitutional orders, have also accomplished this—but they are all small and homogeneous by American standards. None faces America's challenge of enabling an enormous and diverse population to prosper. And like America, all of them are essentially capitalist. With a population of more than 300 million, the United States has the highest per capita income of any nation with a population of more than nine million people.[18] Of course, the market is imperfect, and some fall into poverty, or fail to emerge from poverty as they hit adulthood. A well-crafted safety net is a necessary complement to a free economy.

But no form of capitalism can sustain itself without good government. In the absence of the rule of law, it pays to cheat. Reasonable people can differ about the right mix of law, taxation, and regulation necessary to keep the economy humming, but achieving prosperity demands that taxation not be so confiscatory or so trivial, nor regulation so burdensome or so ineffective, as to threaten the economy's capacity to thrive.

Nor is prosperity synonymous with unbridled materialism and greed. Being a good parent, citizen, and friend are virtues that are compatible with economic success. Poverty is rarely elevating. Like citizenship itself, however, these virtues need to be cultivated. Unfortunately, as the framers recognized, the national government can play at best a minor role in such cultivation. No federal government program ever created a good father, mother, or neighbor. This is the responsibility of schools, religious congregations, extended families, voluntary associations, and other forms of civic and social life. A prosperous citizenry, whose prosperity is fostered by private property and free markets, disciplined by a sensible level of regulation, is in the best position to learn to curb its material appetites, and combine self-interest with self-control and generosity.

SECURITY

Chaos and fear are the enemies of all decent life. People expect their government to keep them safe. Governments fail to provide adequate security either because they are too weak or too foolish to do, or because their tyrannical aspirations impel them to keep their citizens fearful and insecure. Our constitutional order has survived riots in major cities—including the efforts in 2020 to burn down several downtown neighborhoods and police stations. It has survived domestic rebellion and foreign threats, and even an invasion of the Congress, without falling prey to despotism. Its federal form has proven effective in preserving liberty, because local governments, and not the nation's military, have the primary responsibility for providing security of life and property close to home.

Thus, in our depiction the word "order" is as pregnant with meaning as the word "constitutional." People crave order by fair means or foul. Only a constitutionally grounded republic, one that mitigates democracy, enables order without oppression. This is especially critical because the dynamism, diversity, and scale that modernity brings is inherently disorderly. Such disorder accomplishes much that is good. However, left unconstrained it will spill over into intolerable levels of disorder—a Hobbesian world of "all against all." Being intolerable, this condition will indeed not be tolerated. It will be disciplined by one or another form of tyranny: if not the harsh physical and ideational oppression of authoritarian despotism, then a soporific and doctrinal "soft" despotism enforced by the Mandarinate that even now controls much of our mass media, and our educational and cultural institutions. The Mandarins have gone to the best schools, from first grade through graduate school; they dominate more and more of the professions, beginning with academia and the law, and now, according to one report, even medicine.[19]

This explains, we think, the "surprising" rebellion against masks, and especially against mask *mandates* during the COVID-19 crisis. Masks are a good idea, and so are vaccinations; but being a good idea is not enough. Those in power have to remember what kind of public they are talking to. Mandarins love mandates; they love to be obeyed. But the people to be mandated frequently see things differently and will often resent being "told what to do," even when it is for their own good. This is a political problem. We put "surprising" in quotes above because no one should have been surprised by this resistance. This is a country where many people don't like to be told what to do. This is not news. It has always been this way. It is one of the few things about American politics that *hasn't* changed in two hundred years. That public officials *were* surprised tells us something important and discouraging about *them*: those who govern have lost touch with those they are governing. They no longer understand them and often hold them in contempt. Which reminds us of the old gag: "Sire," says the lackey, "the peasants are revolting." "Of course, they're revolting," replies the king; "they're peasants."

National security presents a different problem from domestic policy concerns, such as public health. The level of preparedness required is not a matter of choice but is dictated by the level of threat posed by the nation's foes. Because the United States does indeed have dangerous enemies, it commits more resources and engages in greater surveillance than a free people might wish for. The letter of the Constitution alone cannot maintain the balance between security and freedom. That requires commitment to the constitutional order on the part of those well placed to disrupt it—the president and the generals. For this reason, they both take a similar oath: "that I will preserve, support, and defend the Constitution of the United States." Notice: they swear to defend the *Constitution*, not the country, implying that to do one is to do the other.

So far, no president has exploited his commander-in-chief powers to become a despot. The generals have not staged coups or even threatened to do so. The United States is not Argentina. But if the broader population treats the constitutional order with less reverence, why should those with the power to disrupt it not also weaken their commitment to it? Cynicism of that sort, which this book has identified and lamented, is not only misplaced; it is dangerous.

CIVIC COMITY

Recall the earlier discussion of the challenges posed by the modern state: enormous scale; huge populations displaying great diversity with respect to social class, race, religion, ethnicity, political affiliation, and many other markers thought by citizens to be important. The kind of mutual respect that makes self-government possible is not easily achieved in such a society—which makes its achievement all the more important.

Forbearance is a republican virtue. Its literal meaning is "the action of refraining from exercising a legal right."[20] We might, for example, have the legal right to say that all members of the "X" party are morons, or racists, or (to borrow a now infamous term) "deplorables." But for what should be obvious reasons, our legal right is not the same thing as our moral right, or what prudence would recommend as a course of action. Or perhaps the reasons are *not* so obvious; perhaps we have gotten so used to inflammatory political rhetoric that we take it for granted, or assume it has no serious consequences. Yet we know that one of the consequences of such rhetoric is to divide the populace in ways that are unhealthy—that undermine the disciplines needed to make republican government work properly. More and more Americans cannot engage in a political conversation with someone from "across the aisle" because the aisle has become a chasm—and this appears to be the case in the Congress as well as among the public. On the eve of the 2016 presidential election, according to the Pew Research Center, 70 percent of Democrats said that Republicans were more "closed-minded" than other Americans; not surprisingly, Republicans returned the compliment, with 52 percent saying Democrats were more "closed-minded" than other Americans—and that Democrats were also "more dishonest," "more immoral," and "lazier" than other Americans.[21] A more recent poll found that 62 percent of Americans say they have political views that they are afraid to share.[22]

If one of the tasks of political leaders is to set a good example, here would be a good place for them to start—the sooner the better.

Notes

INTRODUCTION

1. Ryan D. Doerfler and Samuel Moyn, "The Constitution Is Broken and Should Not Be Reclaimed," *New York Times*, August 19, 2022.

2. Trenchant critiques of the Constitution include Robert Dahl, *How Democratic Is the American Constitution?* (New Haven, CT: Yale University Press, 2001); Sanford Levinson, *Our Undemocratic Constitution* (New York: Oxford University Press, 2006); and William Howell and Terry Moe, *Relic* (New York: Basic Books, 2016). These critiques, as well as other important arguments by legal scholars, will be presented in chapter 2, which traces the evolution of anticonstitutional thought in America. See also Daniel Lazare, *The Frozen Republic: How the Constitution Is Paralyzing Democracy* (New York: Houghton Mifflin, 1996). Important contemporary defenders of the constitutional order include George Will, *The Conservative Sensibility* (New York: Hachette Books, 2019); James W. Ceaser, *Designing a Polity: America's Constitution in Theory and Practice* (Lanham, MD: Rowman & Littlefield, 2011); Harvey C. Mansfield Jr.'s collection of constitutional essays, *America's Constitutional Soul* (Baltimore: Johns Hopkins University Press, 1991); and John Agresto, *Rediscovering America* (Los Angeles: Asahina & Wallace, 2015). A fuller collection of references can be found in the bibliography

3. On the impact of climate see Charles de Montesquieu, *Spirit of the Laws* (Cambridge: Cambridge University Press, 2002): 231–263.

4. Alexis De Tocqueville, *Democracy in America*, vol. 1, (Chicago: University of Chicago Press, 2000), 3–18.

5. Tocqueville stresses the novelty of the "free voting of taxes" by the citizens of New England towns. *Democracy in America*, 39.

6. Powerful discussions of the political implications of modernity are to be found in Bertrand de Jouvenel, *Sovereignty: An Inquiry into the Political Good* (Carmel, IN: Liberty Fund, 1998), especially the chapter called "Prisoner of the Corollaries"; and Stephen Toulmin, *Cosmopolis: The Hidden Agenda of Modernity* (Chicago: University of Chicago Press, 1992). For a comparison of the French and American Revolutions see Gertrude Himmelfarb, *The Roads to Enlightenment* (New York: Vintage, 2005), 147–226. See also Karl Polanyi, *The Great Transformation* (New York: Farrar, 1944).

7. For a brilliant discussion of the compatibility of social, technological, and economic modernization with America's "Tudor Polity" see Samuel P. Huntington, "Political Modernization: America vs. Europe," *World Politics* 18, no. 3 (April 1966): 378–414.

8. We do not mean to imply that Hobbes was the sole inventor of modern politics. We are aware of the influence of Francis Bacon, Niccolò Machiavelli, and others in breaking with traditional ideas of science, politics, and religion. That is why, following Devin Stauffer, we stress that Hobbes was the first to *systematically* do so. See Devin Stauffer, *Hobbes' Kingdom*

of Light (Chicago: University of Chicago Press, 2018). The following discussion is heavily indebted to Stauffer's profound and insightful elaboration of Hobbes's system.

9. Aristotle, *Politics*, book 1, ch. 2, trans. Ernest Barker (Oxford: Oxford University Press, 1995).

10. Stauffer, *Hobbes' Kingdom of Light*, 18, citing the Latin edition of *De Civ*, ed. Howard Warrender (Oxford: Oxford University Press, 1983).

11. As Stauffer persuasively argues, Hobbes does not demonstrate that the passion for peace and security is the paramount passion, surpassing such other passions as the desire for honor and glory or spiritual fulfillment; he merely asserts it. Stauffer, *Hobbes' Kingdom*, 206.

12. The Leviathan appears in the Books of Job and Isaiah, and also in the Psalms, as a fearsome creature of the sea, "the gliding serpent, . . . the coiling serpent" (Isaiah 27:1). Job 3:8 warns against "those who are ready to rouse Leviathan." Job also asks, "Who can penetrate its double coat of armor? Who dares open the doors of its mouth, ringed about with fearsome teeth. Its back has rows of shields tightly sealed together" (Job 41: 12–15). It is not difficult to conclude that, for Hobbes, the most important quality of the modern state is that it can, when necessary, inspire fear.

13. Thomas Hobbes, *Leviathan*, ed. Edwin Curley (Indianapolis: Hackett, 1994), 13.14, 14.8, 15.4. See also Stauffer, *Hobbes' Kingdom*, 236.

14. Hobbes, *Leviathan*, 46.15.

15. Part of this argument, of course, would have seemed puzzling to many English subjects, who were not aware that they had consented to anything. As we will see, John Locke provided a solution to this puzzle.

16. Athens had a population estimated at 400,000 in the fifth century B.C., but only about 10 percent of the residents were citizens entitled to participate in the city's government. A. H. M. Jones, *Athenian Democracy* (Baltimore: Johns Hopkins University Press, 1957), 76–77 See also John Rothchild, *Introduction to Athenian Democracy of the Fourth and Fifth Century B.C.E.*, Wayne State University Law School Research Paper no. 07–32.

17. "Hobbes's new doctrine holds that the sovereign derives his authority from below. . . . Even if the sovereign is an absolute monarch . . . his authority is a human creation flowing from a democratic source." Stauffer, *Hobbes' Kingdom*, 246.

18. "It has been calculated that 100,000 soldiers and civilians died in the course of the conflict, and that a larger portion of the population perished than in the Great War of 1914–18. It has therefore justly been described as the bloodiest war in English history." Peter Ackroyd, *Civil War: The History of England*, vol. 3 (London: Pan Macmillan, 2014), 302.

19. See, among others, Robert N. Bellah, *The Broken Covenant: American Civil Religion in a Time of Trial* (New York: Seabury Press, 1975) See also Jacob Wolf, "Harmonizing Heaven and Earth: Democratization and Individualism in American Religion" (PhD diss., Boston College, 2020).

20. See especially Tocqueville, *Democracy*, 403–478.

21. For an illuminating consideration of the problems of how the Constitution confronts the challenge of reconciling liberty and equality see Marvin Meyers, "Liberty, Equality and Constitutional Self-Government," in John Agresto, ed., *Liberty and Equality under*

the Constitution (Washington, DC: American Historical Association, 1983), 1–24. See also Tocqueville, *Democracy*, 479–482.

22. John Locke, *The Second Treatise of Government*, ed. C. B. Macpherson (Indianapolis: Hackett, 1980), 11. Locke wrote his two treatises in the mid-1680s before being forced into exile in Holland. The works were published anonymously, and Locke never acknowledged his authorship during his lifetime.

23. When men live without a civil state to protect them, they live in "continual fear and danger of violent death, and the life of man, solitary, poor, nasty, brutish, and short." Hobbes, *Leviathan*, 13.9.

24. "It" is the appropriate pronoun here, since (as the illustration used as the frontispiece of *Leviathan* demonstrates) the "king" is really a composite of the separate bodies of the subjects. On the ambiguous meaning of this illustration, see Stauffer, *Hobbes' Kingdom*, 272–274.

25. Those contemporaries who criticized Locke's writings often did so because of the resemblance they bore to Hobbes. On this point, see Thomas L. Pangle, *The Spirit of Modern Republicanism* (Chicago: University of Chicago Press, 1988), n. 8, 303–304, and n. 11, 305–306. Locke at first makes this transition seem little more than a sensible adjustment, but he concedes as the argument progresses that men would have been "quickly driven into society."

26. Locke, *Second Treatise*, 8.

27. Locke, *Second Treatise*, 8.

28. "Thus in the beginning all the world was America, and more so than that is now." Locke, *Second Treatise*, 66.

29. Locke, *Second Treatise*, 28.

30. Locke, *Second Treatise*, 54.

31. Although the *Second Treatise* begins with an observation about "reason" and "scripture" agreeing, reason remains, but scripture drops out of the discussion pretty quickly.

32. In this context, the word "estate" refers to tangible property. Thus, the phrase "life, liberty, and estate" includes everything the commonwealth is created to protect. Locke's understanding of "natural rights" appears in the Declaration of Independence, which also borrows "the pursuit of happiness" from Locke's *An Essay Concerning Human Understanding*, vol. 1, book 2, ch. 21 (New York: Everyman's Library, 1961), 219–220.

33. Locke, *Second Treatise*, 72.

34. Himmelfarb, *The Roads to Enlightenment*, 161.

35. Ceremonial, or symbolic, links between the state and the church continue to exist in some modern states. The British monarch, for example, has the official title of "Defender of the Faith and Supreme Governor of the Church of England." The only genuine theocracies are now in the Muslim world, and even there they are much rarer than they once were.

36. The only great twentieth-century exception to this rule appears to be Russia, but that only goes to show that the USSR was really an empire and not, as it claimed, a union.

37. Locke, *Second Treatise*, 26.

38. Since World War II, Western European states have not had to face this reality because the United States has placed them under its nuclear umbrella. This is a rare exception to the rule that a state must be as strong as its most dangerous rival—a fact that the

Russian invasion of Ukraine has brought home to many governments that had previously ignored it.

39. https://www.brainyquote.com/quotes/samuel_gompers_205273.

40. Thus, revolutionary France's ambassador to the United States—born Edmond-Charles Genêt—became simply "Citizen Genêt."

41. Himmelfarb, *The Roads to Enlightenment*, 185.

42. Statistica.com, https://www.statista.com/statistics/1009279/total-population-france-1700–2020 (accessed August 1, 2022). Donald Greer, *Incidence of Terror* (Cambridge, MA: Harvard University Press, 1966 [1935]), 38–70.

43. There were not many such feudal remnants, but two were of special importance: *primogeniture* (a rule *requiring* that property descend entirely to the oldest son), and *entail* (a rule requiring that property inherited by a married daughter return to *her* family after her death, rather than remain with her husband or her husband's family). These laws did not prevail everywhere in the colonies, but their disappearance meant an even wider distribution of property, including land, than before. On the significance of property and inheritance laws, see Tocqueville, *Democracy in America*, vol. 1, 46–53.

44. Alexander Hamilton, John Jay, and James Madison, *The Federalist: A Commentary on the Constitution of the United States*, ed. Robert Scigliano (New York: Modern Library, 2000), 330–335.

45. See Samuel Beer's illuminating discussion of "government by discussion," in his *To Make a Nation: The Rediscovery of American Federalism*, 3rd ed. (Cambridge, MA: Harvard University Press, 1997). See also Garry Mucciaroni and Paul J. Quirk, "Deliberative Choices: Debating Public Policy in Congress," *Political Science Quarterly* 122, no. 1 (March 2007): 152–154; and the discussion of deliberation in Marc Landy, Marc Roberts, and Steve Thomas, *The Environmental Protection Agency: Asking the Wrong Questions* (Oxford: Oxford University Press, 1994), 13–15.

46. See Sean M. Theriault, *Party Polarization in Congress: The War Over Two Social Contracts* (Cambridge: Cambridge University Press, 2019); and B. Dan Wood, Soren Jordan, and David Hopkins, *Red Fighting Blue: How Geography and Electoral Rules Polarize American Politics* (Cambridge: Cambridge University Press, 2017).

47. See especially Richard Hofstadter, *The Idea of a Party System: The Rise of Legitimate Opposition in the United States, 1780–1840* (Berkeley: University of California Press, 1970); James Ceaser, *Presidential Selection: Theory and Development* (Princeton, NJ: Princeton University Press, 1979); and Joel Silbey, *The Partisan Imperative: The Dynamics of American Politics before the Civil War* (Oxford: Oxford University Press, 1987).

48. 123helpme.com, https://www.123helpme.com/essay/Americas-Constitution-Dbq-3FE6AC04295C5EBE (accessed August 1, 2023).

49. See chapter 3 for a further discussion of these proposals.

50. Sidney M. Milkis, "The Presidency, Policy Reform, and the Rise of Administrative Politics," in Richard Harris and Sidney Milkis, eds., *Remaking American Politics* (Boulder, CO: Westview Press, 1989), 146–187.

51. James Q. Wilson, *American Politics, Then and Now* (Washington, DC: AEI Press, 2010).

52. A transcript of the National Labor Relations Act can be found at https://www.our documents.gov/doc.php?flash=false&doc=67&page=transcript. The Affordable Care Act can be found at http://housedocs.house.gov/energycommerce/ppacacon.pdf (accessed July 15, 2022).

53. Christopher DeMuth, "The Bucks Start Here," *Claremont Review of Books* 13, no. 3 (Summer 2013).

54. This number is usually around 40–43 percent, although it was a surprisingly high 61 percent in 2020 because of various factors associated with the pandemic. See the report by the Brookings Institution Tax Policy Center at https://www.taxpolicycenter.org/taxvox /covid-19-pandemic-drove-huge-temporary-increase-households-did-not-pay-federal-in come-tax?utm_medium=twitter& utm_source=tpc social (accessed August 15, 2022).

55. Government Accountability Office, Financial Audit: Bureau of the Fiscal Service's FY 2020 and FY 2019 Schedules of Federal Debt, November 9, 2020, https://www.gao.gov /products/gao-21-124.

56. R. Shep Melnick, "The Odd Evolution of the Civil Rights State," *Harvard Journal of Law and Public Policy* 37, no. 1 (2014): 124.

57. A variety of cogent explanations for Congress's decline, by contemporary experts on Congress, are contained in William Connelly Jr., John Pitney Jr., and Gary Schmitt, eds., *Is Congress Broken?* (Washington, DC: Brookings Institution, 2017).

58. *Federalist* 39.

59. Anonymous (later revealed to be Miles Taylor), *A Warning* (New York: Twelve, 2019).

60. See chapter 4.

61. Arthur Schlesinger Jr., *The Imperial Presidency* (Boston: Houghton Mifflin, 1973).

62. *New York Times*, https://www.nytimes.com/interactive/2019/08/14/magazine/black -history-american-democracy.html (accessed August 2, 2023). This quote serves as the headline for Hannah-Jones's article introducing the project. It was printed in very large type, filling an entire page. It does not appear in the subsequent book version. In that version the word "enshrine" was removed and "shroud" replaced "hide" (New York: New York Times Company, 2021); see page 19. We leave it the reader to judge whether the original version that went free to the *Times*'s 7.6 million readers made more of an impact than the book version that can be purchased on Amazon for $22.80. There is much to be learned from the book. It provides many very important facts about the history of American racism. Nonetheless, it suffers the fate of all single-factor analyses of major historic developments in that its presentation of American history is far too schematic.

63. There are a number of important writings that argue that pervasive racism dominates contemporary American life. For example, see Ta-Nehisi Coates, "The Case for Reparations," *Atlantic*, June 2014, https://www.theatlantic.com/magazine/archive/2014/06 /the-case-for-reparations/361631 (accessed August 4, 2023). See also Ibram X. Kendi, *Stamped from the Beginning: The Definitive History of Racist Ideas in America* (New York: Nation Books, 2016); and Kimberlé Crenshaw, Neil T. Gotanda, Gary Peller, and Kendall Thomas, eds., *Critical Race Theory: The Key Writings That Formed the Movement* (New York: New Press, 1996).

64. *Federalist* 49. For a nuanced discussion of Madison's views on veneration, see Jeremy

Bailey, "Should We Venerate That Which We Cannot Love? James Madison on Constitutional Imperfection," *Political Research Quarterly* 65, no. 4 (December 2012): 732–744.

CHAPTER 1: AMERICA AS A MODERN STATE

1. State centralization preceded Hobbes but later gained its justification and credibility from the incorporation of Hobbesian principles, all the more so once the monarch was deposed or demoted in the wake of the French Revolution. For a profound depiction of the rise of the modern state in France see Alexis de Tocqueville, *The Old Regime and the French Revolution*, trans. Stuart Gilbert (New York: Anchor Books, 1955).

2. Liah Greenfeld does a masterful job of tracing the rise of nationalism in Britain, France, Germany, Russia, and America. See her *Nationalism: Five Roads to Modernity* (Cambridge, MA: Harvard University Press, 1992). See also Benedict Anderson, *Imagined Communities: Reflections on the Origin and Spread of Nationalism*, rev. ed. (London: Verso, 2006), as well as the classic account of nationalism: Hans Kohn, *Nationalism: Its Meaning and History* (Princeton, NJ: Princeton University Press, 1955).

3. For the struggle to overcome linguistic diversity in France, see Graham Robb, *The Discovery of France: A Historical Geography* (New York: W. W. Norton, 2008), 50–70.

4. On Locke's influence see Claire Rydell Arcenas, *America's Philosopher: John Locke in American Intellectual Life* (Chicago: University of Chicago Press, 2022).

5. The authors of the Constitution were acutely aware of the shortcomings of their fellow citizens, from observing them during the Revolutionary War (when local farmers would sell food to the British rather than take the lower prices the army could offer). See Ron Chernow, *Washington: A Life* (New York: Penguin Press, 2010), 323–337.

6. Gertrude Himmelfarb, *The Roads to Enlightenment* (New York: Vintage, 2005). See also Ralph Lerner, *The Thinking Revolutionary: Principle and Practice in the New Republic* (Ithaca, NY: Cornell University Press, 1987).

7. This claim is elaborated in chapter 2. For an incisive discussion see James Ceaser, *Progressivism and the Doctrine of Natural Rights*, published online by Cambridge University Press, July 17, 2012, https://www.cambridge.org/core/jouls/social-philosophy-and-policy/article/abs/progressivism-and-the-doctrine-of-natural-rights/15B10C725F9EE12B394FFE5B5CA0ED4D (accessed August 4, 2023). This view is also central to Marxism: "To build communism it is necessary, simultaneous with the new material foundations, to build the new man and woman." Quoted in Che Guevara, *Socialism and Man in Cuba* (Atlanta, GA: Pathfinder Press, 2009).

8. Aristotle, *Politics*, book 1, ch. 2, trans. Ernest Barker (Oxford: Oxford University Press, 1995).

9. David Epstein, *The Political Theory of the Federalist* (Chicago: University of Chicago Press, 1984), 24–25.

10. For a brilliant consideration of these matters see Wilson C. McWilliams, *The Idea of Fraternity in America* (Berkeley: University of California Press, 1973).

11. The chapter on "The Forms of Government" in *The Second Treatise* (ch. 10), at two

paragraphs, is the shortest in the book, as if to say, the question of the "forms of government" is not really a very useful or interesting question. John Locke, *Second Treatise of Government*, ed. C. B. Macpherson (Indianapolis: Hackett, 1980), 186–187.

12. We do not claim that Aristotle and the Framers had the same understanding of man as a political animal, only that the Framers understood human nature to be permanent, and to have a political dimension, as did Aristotle.

13. *Federalist 72*.

14. Epstein, *Political Theory of The Federalist*, 6.

15. Epstein, *Political Theory*, 5.

16. Epstein, *Political Theory*, 7.

17. Epstein, *Political Theory*, 124.

18. See Louis Hartz, *The Liberal Tradition in America: An Interpretation of American Political Thought* (New York: Harcourt, Brace, 1955). The "equality of conditions" is central to Tocqueville's analysis of American democracy. See especially the introduction to vol. 1, along with ch. 3 of the same volume.

19. As were, in theory, former slaves living in the northern states—although Tocqueville learned that African Americans, even when free, and even when legally franchised, were often prevented from voting—even in Pennsylvania, a state founded by antislavery Quakers. Alexis De Tocqueville, *Democracy in America*, vol. 1, trans. Harvey C. Mansfield Jr. and Delba Winthrop (Chicago: University of Chicago Press, 2000), 241, n. 4.

20. Historians estimate that from 16 percent to 30 percent of colonial Americans—as many as half a million people—were Tory in their sympathies and considered the revolution to be either a drastic mistake or a crime against the King. See Rick Atkinson, *The British Are Coming: The War for America* (New York: Holt Paperbacks, 2020), 311.

21. A brilliant depiction of this revolutionary process is in Francois Furet, *The French Revolution: 1770–1814* (Oxford: Oxford University Press, 1996). See also Hippolyte A. Taine, *The Origins of Contemporary France*, vol. 6, *The French Revolution* (Gloucester, MA: Peter Smith, 1962 [1876]), especially ch. 3, 63–66.

22. See Samuel Beer, *British Politics in the Collectivist Age* (New York: Knopf, 1965).

23. Daniel Shays was a Massachusetts farmer who, like many farmers, had incurred debts to local banks and merchants during the relatively prosperous years following the revolution, and then fell behind when the economy slumped. In August 1786 he led a group of armed veterans in an attack on several county courthouses in order to stop foreclosure hearings. The violence did not end until the following January, when Shays and his troops attempted, unsuccessfully, to occupy the armory in Springfield. Several were arrested, tried for treason, sentenced to death, and then pardoned by President Washington.

24. Stanley Elkins and Eric McKitrick, *The Age of Federalism: The Early American Republic, 1788–1800* (New York: Oxford University Press, 1993).

25. Jack P. Greene, *Interpreting Colonial America* (Charlottesville: University of Virginia Press, 1996), and *The Intellectual Construction of America: Exceptionalism and Identity from 1492 to 1800* (Chapel Hill: University of North Carolina Press, 1997).

26. For the impact of that war on Americans see Fred Anderson, *Crucible of War: The*

Seven Years' War and the Fate of Empire in British North America, 1754–1766 (New York: Vintage, 2001).

27. James Stoner, *Common Law Liberty: Rethinking American Constitutionalism* (Lawrence: University Press of Kansas, 2003), 11.

28. Stoner, *Common Law Liberty*, 12.

29. Stoner, *Common Law Liberty*, 12.

30. For example, it was an English judge (Lord Mansfield) who ruled that since slavery was not "allowed or approved by the law of England," no one could be held in slavery on English soil. Somerset v. Stewart (1772), 98 ER499.

31. The exception is Louisiana, whose state law is based on the civil code left from the time Louisiana was governed by the Spanish and the French.

32. Stoner, *Common Law Liberty*, 11–12.

33. Tocqueville, *Democracy in America*, 260.

34. See David Potter, *People of Plenty: Economic Abundance and the American Character* (Chicago: University of Chicago Press, 1954).

35. Freakonomics.com, https://freakonomics.com/2011/09/were-colonial-americans -more-literate-than-americans-today/ (accessed August 4, 2023).

36. See Gordon Wood, *Creation of the American Republic, 1776–1787* (Chapel Hill: University of North Carolina Press, 1969).

37. *Federalist* 9, 47.

38. *Federalist* 9, 47.

39. *Federalist* 9, 51.

40. Bertrand de Jouvenel, *On Power* (Boston: Beacon Press, 1962).

41. Bertrand de Jouvenel, "The Chairman's Problem," *American Political Science Review* 55, no. 2 (June 1961): 368–372.

42. *Federalist* 10. See also Nancy Schwartz, *The Blue Guitar: Political Representation and Community* (Chicago: University of Chicago Press, 1988); and Hannah Pitkin, *The Concept of Representation* (Berkeley: University of California Press, 1972).

43. Population estimates are taken from A. H. M. Jones, *Athenian Democracy* (Baltimore: Johns Hopkins University Press, 1957), 76–77. To give a contemporary (and local) perspective on the public spaces in ancient Athens, the Boston College football stadium can accommodate 44,500 fans. The public space in Athens could accommodate roughly half that number.

44. US Census Bureau, 2020 Census Apportionment Results, https://www.census.gov /data/tables/2020/dec/2020-apportionment-data.html.

45. Yet the US Congress is still *relatively* small, as modern legislatures go—especially considering that the United States is the third-largest country in the world. The British Parliament has 650 members; the German Bundestag has 709. The US Congress does not even make the top twenty. It is not a coincidence, perhaps, that the world's largest "democratic" legislature is that of Communist China, with 3,000 members. See Patrick H. O'Neil, Karl Fields, and Don Share, *Comparative Politics*, 7th ed. (New York: W. W. Norton, 2021), 57, 246, 427.

46. On the art of deliberation see Joseph Tussman, *Obligation and the Body Politic* (New York: Oxford University Press, 1960).

47. *Federalist* 10, 58–59.

48. Epstein, *The Political Theory of the Federalist*, 68–80.

49. There is more to be said on the topic of the national debt, which we will save for chapter 4.

50. Founders Online, National Archives, https://founders.archives.gov/documents /Adams/99-02-02-3102.

51. Tocqueville, *Democracy in America*, 500–503.

52. Michael Kammen, *A Machine That Would Go of Itself: The Constitution in American Culture* (New York: Knopf, 1986).

53. *Federalist* 10, 57.

54. *Federalist* 51, 331.

55. Chernow, *Washington: A Life*, 463.

56. Chernow, *Washington: A Life*, 463.

57. *Federalist* 1, 3.

58. George Washington, "Farewell Address," 1796, in Scott J. Hammond et al., eds., *Classics of American Political and Constitutional Thought* (Indianapolis: Hackett, 2007), 651–658.

59. For a contrary view—that the authors of the Constitution neglected the problem of civic virtue—see Patrick J. Deneen, *Why Liberalism Failed* (New Haven, CT: Yale University Press, 2018).

60. This discussion owes much to an unpublished paper by Stephen J. Lange, "Civic Virtue and the American Republic: Federalism and the Formation of Citizen Character," presented at a federalism symposium sponsored by Morehead University, held in Lexington, Kentucky, June 27, 2013.

61. The Supreme Court has reasserted the importance of the states' police power. See United States v. Alfonso D. Lopez, Jr., 514 U.S. 549 (1995); and United States v. Morrison, 529 U.S. 598 (2000).

62. *Federalist* 9, 52. It is true, however, that Hamilton was among the skeptics of federalism, believing that a better arrangement might be to turn the states into what would amount to administrative districts of the national government. But he never urged this idea on his colleagues because such an arrangement could never have been approved by the state ratifying conventions. See Hamilton's long speech at the Constitutional Convention for June 18, 1787. On the "police power"—that is, the power of states to regulate the "health, morals, and welfare of the people"—see the entry for "Police Powers" at the Cornell Legal Information Institute website, https://www.law.cornell.edu/wex/police_powers.

63. Lange, "Civic Virtue and the American Republic," 2.

64. Lange, "Civic Virtue," 20, 21.

65. John Dinan, *The American State Constitutional Tradition* (Lawrence: University Press of Kansas, 2006), 224.

66. Dinan, *The American State Constitutional Tradition*, 23.

67. Land Ordinance of 1785, May 18, 1785, as published by the State Historical Society

of Iowa, https://iowaculture.gov/sites/default/files/history-education-pss-shapes-landordi nance-transcription.b.pdf.

68. Northwest Ordinance, Articles 3, 6ff.

69. See *Federalist* 84; and James Madison, "Letter to Thomas Jefferson, October 17, 1788," https://founders.archives.gov/documents/Madison/01–11–02–0218. See also Jack N. Rakove, "James Madison and the Bill of Rights: A Broader Context," *Presidential Studies Quarterly* 22, no. 4 (Fall 1992): 667–677.

70. The passage of the Bill of Rights was largely the result of the pressure exerted by the Anti-Federalists in the ratification debates. See Herbert Storing, *What the Anti-Federalists Were For* (Chicago: University of Chicago Press, 1981); and Pauline Maier, *Ratification: The People Debate the Constitution, 1787–1788* (New York: Simon & Schuster, 2010).

71. Colonial Maryland was unusual in the extent of its religious diversity, with America's largest Catholic population, along with the usual mix of high- and low-church Protestants, and a small Jewish community. For this reason, its legislature enacted a law criminalizing the use of religious epithets, such as "heritick, Scismatick, Idolator, puritan, . . . Jusuite, . . . Calvanist, Roundhead . . . or any other such name or terme in a reproachfull manner." *An Act Concerning Religion* (1649). The long list of such epithets suggests the gravity of the problem Americans were trying to avoid. The act can be found at https:// teachingamericanhistory.org/document/maryland-act-concerning-religion/ (accessed August 4, 2023).

72. See, for example, President Washington's justly famous letter to the Hebrew Congregation in Newport, Rhode Island (https://founders.archives.gov/documents/Washing ton/05–06–02–0135, accessed August 4, 2023); and President Jefferson's letter to the Baptists (https://www.loc.gov/loc/lcib/9806/danpre.html, accessed August 4, 2023).

73. Such protection did not extend to the individual states, which, prior to the incorporation of the First Amendment into the protections offered by the Fourteenth, could favor the state's dominant religion—although the states had voluntarily abandoned church establishments by the 1830s. Here again we see how mobility served the interest of liberty, since if one was being hampered in one's free exercise of religion one could move to a different state where such oppression, at least against one's own religion, was not being exercised. The clearest example of this is the movement of Mormons, persecuted in the settled states, to the territory of Utah. Richard E. Bennett, *We'll Find the Place: The Mormon Exodus, 1846–1848* (Norman: University of Oklahoma Press, 2009).

74. Ron Chernow gives a lively account of these events in *Washington: A Life*, 684–700.

75. Constitution, Article II, Section 1, Clause 1; and Article II, Section 3.

76. Although three presidents have been impeached (one of them twice), none has been convicted. However, Richard Nixon resigned when he became convinced that he was about to be impeached, and in all likelihood convicted, and so his departure is the only really meaningful invocation of the impeachment power.

77. Richard J. Ellis, ed., *Founding the American Presidency* (Lanham, MD: Rowman & Littlefield, 1999), 116–124.

78. See especially Sidney Milkis, *Political Parties and Constitutional Government* (Baltimore: Johns Hopkins University Press, 1999), 13–41. See also Wilson C. McWilliams, "Parties

as Civic Associations," in Patrick Deneen and Susan McWilliams, *Redeeming American Democracy* (Lawrence: University Press of Kansas, 2011).

79. *Federalist* 72, 463.

80. See especially V. O. Key with Milton C. Cumming Jr., *The Responsible Electorate* (Cambridge, MA, Harvard University Press, 1966).

81. *Federalist* 72, 464.

82. Susan Hennessy and Benjamin Wittes, *Unmaking the Presidency: Donald Trump's War on the World's Most Powerful Office* (New York: Farrar, Straus & Giroux, 2020). See especially ch. 1.

83. Hennessey and Wittes, *Unmaking the Presidency*, 57–79, 164–225.

84. The best statement of the need to endure a potentially dangerous executive is by Harvey Mansfield Jr., *Taming the Prince: The Ambivalence of Modern Executive Power* (New York: Free Press, 1989). See also William Howell, *Power without Persuasion: The Politics of Direct Presidential Action* (Princeton, NJ: Princeton University Press, 2003).

85. Anthony Cordesman, "From Competition to Confrontation with China: The Major Shift in U.S. Policy," Center for Strategic and International Studies, Johns Hopkins University, August 3, 2020, https://www.csis.org/analysis/competition-confrontation-china-major-shift-us-policy (accessed August 4, 2023).

86. Michael Lind, "In Defense of Mandarins," *Prospect Magazine*, October 2005, https://www.prospectmagazine.co.uk/magazine/indefenceofmandarins (accessed August 4, 2023).

87. Various forms of scientific groupthink are explored in David Allen and James Howell, eds., *Scientific Groupthink: Greed, Pathological Altruism, Ideology, Competition, and Culture* (Cham, Switzerland: Springer Nature, 2020). The term was originally coined by Irving Janis, *Victims of Groupthink: A Psychological Study of Policy Decisions and Fiascoes*, 2nd ed. (Boston: Wadsworth, 1983). The term was coined in the first edition, 1972.

88. William Nordhaus, *A Question of Balance: Weighing the Options on Global Warming Policies* (New Haven, CT: Yale University Press, 2008). See also Steven Koonin, *Unsettled: What Climate Science Tells Us, What It Doesn't, and Why It Matters* (New York: Penguin Random House, 2021).

89. The classic study of the administrative state is by Dwight Waldo, *The Administrative State: A Study of the Political Theory of American Public Administration* (London: Routledge, 1948). For an important recent study of this phenomenon see Brian Cook, *The Fourth Branch: Reconstructing the Administrative State for the Commercial Republic* (Lawrence: University Press of Kansas, 2021).

90. Joel Aberbach and Joel Rockman, "Mandates or Mandarina? Control and Discretion in the Modern Administrative States," *Public Administration Review* 48, no. 2 (March-April 1988): 606–612.

91. Historical Federal Workforce Tables: Executive Branch Civilian Employment since 1940, https://www.opm.gov/policy-data-oversight/data-analysis-documentation/federal-employment-reports/historical-tables/executive-branch-civilian-employment-since-1940/ (accessed August 4, 2023).

92. For more on the problem posed by the administrative state see Brian Cook, *The Fourth Branch*; Cass Sunstein and Adrian Vermuele, *Law and Leviathan: Redeeming the*

Administrative State (Cambridge, MA: Belknap Press of Harvard University Press, 2020); and John Rohr, *To Run a Constitution: The Legitimacy of the Administrative State* (Lawrence: University Press of Kansas, 1986).

93. *Federalist* 68, 438.

94. A sign of how much disagreement this idea provoked is that the removal power was affirmed only when Vice President John Adams cast the deciding vote to break a tie in the Senate. See Aziz Huq, "Removal as a Political Question," *Stanford Law Review* 65, no. 1 (2013): 1–76.

95. Tenure of Office Act, March 2, 1867, 14 Stat. 430, Ch. 154; Myers v. United States, 272 U.S. 52 (1926).

96. US Constitution, Article I, Section 9.

97. "The last few centuries have seen us banish starvation and famine from a large part of the Earth. In the most successful countries, the average citizen now enjoys a material standard of living that would have made the greatest king of two hundred years ago turn green with envy." John V. C. Nye, "Standards of Living and Modern Economic Growth," *Library of Economics and Liberty*, https://www.econlib.org/library/Enc/StandardsofLiving andModernEconomicGrowth.html (accessed August 4, 2023).

98. See especially Drew R. McCoy, *The Elusive Republic* (New York: W. W. Norton, 1980).

CHAPTER 2: THE CASE AGAINST THE CONSTITUTION

1. Elbridge Gerry of Massachusetts, in James Madison, *Notes on Debates in the Federal Convention of 1787* (New York: W. W. Norton, 1987), 39.

2. The terms "Federalist" and "Anti-Federalist" are used now to designate two identifiable factions, based on arguments made on the floor of the Constitutional Convention, and in the many publications generated by the ratification debates. However, some who opposed the Constitution found much to approve of, and many who supported it found much to regret. The document was a compromise among politicians who were often, as we will see, far apart on certain fundamental questions raised by the failure of the Articles of Confederation.

3. The size of congressional districts was originally set at 40,000 but was reduced to 30,000 in the face of criticism that the districts were too large. George Washington's only speech at the convention was in favor of the smaller size district, on the convention's last day. See Madison, *Notes on Debates*, for September 17.

4. The critics were right about this. Only one Supreme Court justice has been impeached: Justice Samuel Chase, in 1804. He was acquitted by the Senate and remained on the bench until his death in 1811. See https://en.wikipedia.org/wiki/Samuel_Chase#:~:text =In%201804%2C%20Chase%20was%20impeached,to%20have%20ever%20been%20im peached (accessed August 1, 2023).

5. Concerns about the power of the chief executive almost certainly explain the fact that no president ever sought a third consecutive term until the administration of Franklin D. Roosevelt. The Twenty-Second Amendment, fixing the two-term limit, followed very

quickly, passed by the Congress in 1947 and ratified by three-fourths of the states by 1951. National Constitution Center: Two-Term Limit on Presidency, https://constitutioncenter. org/the-constitution/amendments/amendment-xxii (accessed August 1, 2023).

6. Thomas Paine, "Common Sense," in *Common Sense, The Rights of Man, and Other Essential Writings of Thomas Paine* (New York: New American Library, 1969), 26.

7. The literature on the early years of American constitutional government is vast. Some useful examples include Stanley Elkins and Eric McKitrick, *The Early American Republic, 1788–1800* (New York: Oxford University Press, 1993); and Gordon Wood, *Empire of Liberty: A History of the Early Republic, 1789–1815* (New York: Oxford University Press, 2009). Additional titles can be found in the bibliography.

8. The recent effort by Democrats in Congress to nationalize federal election law is a good example of this trend. Now that the Supreme Court has reversed *Roe v. Wade*, we will see a number of different abortion laws adopted by the states, as well as a probable effort on the part of Democrats in Congress to pass a federal law legalizing abortion everywhere. See chapter 3 for a discussion of the proposal to nationalize federal election laws.

9. Donald Ratcliffe, "The Right to Vote and the Rise of Democracy, 1787–1828," *Journal of the Early Republic* 33, no. 2 (Summer 2013): 219–254, citing the research of Robert J. Dinkin, *Voting in Revolutionary America* (Westport, CT: Praeger, 1982). Black voters in northern states that had abolished slavery were rarely able to vote, although Black men had the formal right to do so in a few states (Pennsylvania, New York, and New Jersey.) Yet even in those states, Blacks were illegally prevented from voting, and by the time of the Civil War all three states had repealed their enfranchisement of Black voters. When Tocqueville visited Philadelphia in 1831, he was told that Blacks, although they had the franchise, did not vote out of fear for their safety. Alexis de Tocqueville, *Democracy in America*, trans. Harvey C. Mansfield Jr. and Delba Winthrop (Chicago: University of Chicago Press, 2000), vol. 1, part II, ch. 7, 241n.

10. John A. Phillips and Charles Wetherell, "The Great Reform Act of 1832 and the Political Modernization of England," *American Historical Review* 100 (April 1995): 411–436.

11. Ballotpedia, "History of Initiative and Referendum in the U.S.," https://ballotpedia. org/History_of_initiative_and_referendum_in_the_U.S. (accessed August 1, 2023). See also Jon C. Teaford, *The Municipal Revolution in America: 1650–1825* (Chicago: University of Chicago Press, 1975).

12. Lincoln believed he did not have the authority to abolish slavery; the Emancipation Proclamation was limited to slaves living in states engaged in "rebellion against the United States." See the transcript at the National Archives website, https://www.archives.gov/exhib its/featured-documents/emancipation-proclamation/transcript.html.

13. See Eric Foner, *The Second Founding: How the Civil War and Reconstruction Remade the Constitution* (New York: W. W. Norton, 2019).

14. Abraham Lincoln, "Fragment on the Constitution," 1861, https://teachingamerican- history.org/document/fragment-on-the-constitution-and-union/.

15. Sean Wilentz labels contemporary critics of the Constitution for its slavery compromises "Neo-Garrisonians," in *No Property in Man* (Cambridge, MA: Harvard University Press, 2018). According to Wilentz the most influential statement of the Neo-Garrisonian

position is Paul Finkelman's "Slavery and the Constitution: Making a Covenant with Death," in Richard Beeman et al., *Beyond Confederation: Origins of the Constitution and American National Identity* (Chapel Hill: University of North Carolina Press, 1987). See also David Waldstreicher, *Slavery's Constitution: From Revolution to Ratification* (New York: Hill & Wang, 2009). The "Neo-Garrisonian" position can be found in many recent works on slavery and its role in American history: Nikole Hannah-Jones et al., *The 1619 Project*, first published by the New York Times Co. in August 2019; Ta-Nehisi Coates, "The Case for Reparations," *Atlantic*, June 14, 2014, 54–71; Ibram X. Kendi, *Stamped from the Beginning: The Definitive History of Racist Ideas in America* (New York: Nation Books, 2016); and Kimberlé Crenshaw et al., eds., *Critical Race Theory: The Key Writings That Formed the Movement* (New York: New Press, 1996).

16. Steven Mintz, "Historical Context: The Constitution and Slavery," History Resources, Gilder Lehrman Institute of American History, https://www.gilderlehrman.org/history-resources/teaching-resource/historical-context-constitution-and-slavery (accessed August 5, 2023).

17. George Washington left instructions in his will that his own slaves were to be freed after his death. See Ron Chernow, *Washington: A Life* (New York: Penguin, 2010), 800–803.

18. The New York law created a gradual process of manumission, which was not completed until 1827. See Craig Landy, "When Did Slavery End in New York?," Historical Society of the New York Courts (n.d.), https://history.nycourts.gov/when-did-slavery-end-in-new-york/ (accessed August 5, 2023).

19. Northwest Ordinance, 1787, https://ohiohistorycentral.org/w/Northwest_Ordinance (accessed August 5, 2023).

20. US Constitution, Article IV, Section 2. It is also true that not all such "persons" were slaves; some were free indentured servants (apprentices, for example, working off the cost of their passage from Europe to America). Such apprentices sometimes tried to evade the terms of these contracts by running off to another state. See Robert Dale Owen, "The Claims to Service or Labor," *Atlantic*, July 1863, 116–124.

21. Wilentz, *No Property in Man,* 210. See also his masterful discussion of the convention's deliberations on slavery, 58–114.

22. The history of the battle over slavery has generated an entire library of books. We can mention a few here. William Lee Miller, *Arguing about Slavery: The Great Battle in the United States Congress* (New York: Knopf, 1995); William W. Freehling, *The Road to Disunion: Secessionists at Bay, 1776–1854* (Oxford: Oxford University Press, 1990); Kenneth M. Stamp, *America in 1857: A Nation on the Brink* (Oxford: Oxford University Press, 1990); Harry Jaffa, *The Crisis of the House Divided: An Interpretation of the Issues in the Lincoln-Douglas Debates* (Chicago: University of Chicago Press, 2009 [1959]).

23. This incident is discussed in Ronald Osborn, "William Lloyd Garrison and the United States Constitution: The Political Evolution of an American Radical," *Journal of Law and Religion* 24, no. 1 (2008/2009): 65–88.

24. Massachusetts Historical Society, "No Union with Slaveholders," masshist.org (accessed August 1, 2023).

25. It became increasingly difficult for authorities to enforce the act in the decade before

the Civil War, in part because jurors refused to convict those who interfered with the law, no matter how clear the prosecution's evidence. For example, in 1851 a mob stormed the courthouse in Boston to rescue an escaped slave who had been hauled into court by a federal agent. The fugitive slave escaped to Canada, but several members of the mob were captured and charged. But when a jury refused to convict the first two defendants, the government dropped all charges against the others. See Dennis Hale, *The Jury in America: Triumph and Decline* (Lawrence: University Press of Kanas, 2016), 124–129.

26. The relation between John Brown and the Concord transcendentalists (in particular, Henry David Thoreau and Ralph Waldo Emerson) is discussed in Gilman M. Ostrander, "Emerson, Thoreau, and John Brown," *Mississippi Valley Historical Review* 39, no. 4 (March 1953): 713–726.

27. This essay has come to be known simply as "Civil Disobedience."

28. The Mexican War (1846–1848) began as a dispute over the boundary between Texas and Mexico but escalated into a conflict over control of what is now the American Southwest, including parts of California. The American victory added new territory that would have to be divided into states, and this fact immediately generated a conflict over whether the new states would forbid, or permit, slavery. See Douglas V. Meed, *The Mexican War: 1846–1848* (Oxfordshire, UK: Routledge, 2005).

29. Henry David Thoreau, "Disobedience to Civil Government" (aka "Civil Disobedience"), in Kenneth Dolbeare and Michael S. Cummings, eds., *American Political Thought* (Washington, DC: CQ Press, 2010), 223.

30. Thoreau, "Civil Disobedience," 224. "Washing your hands of it" was a phrase that would certainly have called to mind (for this Biblically literate audience) Pontius Pilate, and is for this reason an oddly appropriate (if self-incriminating) admission on Thoreau's part.

31. Henry David Thoreau, "Slavery in Massachusetts," in Scott J. Hammond, Kevin R. Hardwick, and Howard L. Lubert, eds., *Classics of American Political and Constitutional Thought*, vol. 1 (Indianapolis: Hackett, 2007), 1024–1030.

32. See the essay by George H. Smith, "The Abolitionists on the Right of Secession," https://www.libertarianism.org/columns/abolitionists-right-secession (accessed August 3, 2023). Some of those who welcomed secession changed their minds after the bombing of Fort Sumpter; others supported the right to secession on what would now be called "libertarian" grounds. Just as the United States had, in effect, "seceded" from the British Empire, the South would now secede from the United States. Significantly, Thoreau did not acknowledge the South's right to secede, and he supported the effort to put down the rebellion. He died in 1862.

33. Frederick Douglass, *Narrative of the Life of Frederick Douglass, An American Slave* (New York: Penguin Classics, 2014).

34. Frederick Douglass, "Country, Conscience, and the Anti-Slavery Cause: An Address Delivered in New York, New York, May 11, 1847," in *The Frederick Douglass Papers: Series One—Speeches, Debates, and Interviews*, vol. 2 (New Haven, CT: Yale University Press, 1979), 54.

35. "Speech on the Kansas-Nebraska Act at Peoria, Illinois (1854)," in Abraham Lincoln, *Lincoln: Speeches, Letters, Miscellaneous Writings, The Lincoln-Douglas Debates* (New York: Library of America, 1989), 338.

36. Frederick Douglass, "What to the Slave Is the Fourth of July?" (1852), in Hammond et al., *Classics*, 1012–1020.

37. BlackPast, https://www.blackpast.org/global-african-history/1860-frederick-doug lass-constitution-united-states-it-pro-slavery-or-anti-slavery/ (accessed August 1, 2023).

38. Douglass, "Pro-slavery or anti-slavery." Douglass refers here to remarks in the convention on August 28 and August 29, 1787. On August 28, Charles Pinckney and Pierce Butler, delegates from South Carolina, proposed a clause "to require fugitive slaves and servants to be delivered up like criminals." Roger Sherman from Connecticut replied that he "saw no more propriety in the public seizing and surrendering of a slave or servant, than a horse." Butler then withdrew his motion "in order that some particular provision might be made apart from" the article then under discussion. We can probably assume some off-the-record discussion outside the convention hall, for the next day the language of what became Article IV, Section 2, Clause 3 was approved unanimously, without debate, and without using the term "slave." See Madison, *Notes of Debates* for August 28 and 29.

39. In the late-life correspondence of John Adams and Thomas Jefferson, Jefferson conceded that Adams had been right about the French Revolution, and he wrong, at least in part. "Let me ask you, very seriously my friend," Adams wrote, "where are now . . . the perfection and perfectibility of human nature? Where is now, the progress of the human mind? Where is the amelioration of society?" (Adams to Jefferson, July 15, 1813). In his reply, Jefferson argued that "the world will recover from the panic of the first catastrophe. Science is progressive, and talents and enterprise on the alert" (Jefferson to Adams, October 18, 1813). See Merrill D. Peterson, *Adams and Jefferson: A Revolutionary Dialogue* (Atlanta: University of Georgia Press, 1976), ch. 4.

40. Tocqueville, *Democracy*, vol. 2, part 2, ch. 12, 510.

41. A notable example of this phenomenon is Brook Farm, the utopian farming community established in what was then suburban Boston. Nathaniel Hawthorne was a founding member of this community, but he became disenchanted by the apparent impossibility of resolving the conflict between the needs of the community and the continuing, and presumptively selfish, needs of the individuals living on the farm. Hawthorne explored these problems in *The Blithedale Romance*, published in 1852.

42. For example, in her acceptance speech at the 2020 Democratic National Convention, vice presidential nominee Kamala Harris promised that she and Joe Biden would "build that beloved community" if they were elected—a promise that could have been made by many reformers in the early nineteenth century, albeit not by the candidate of a major political party. To take another example, the protest movement calling itself "Occupy Wall Street" conducted group decision-making meetings during its two-month occupation of a downtown park near the New York Stock Exchange in 2011, with elaborate procedures for deciding who would speak and for how long, and using hand signals to indicate agreement or disagreement, and making decisions on the basis of consensus rather than voting. For Harris's remarks, see the CNN transcript at https://www.cnn.com/2020/08/19/politics/ka mala-harris-speech-transcript/index.html.

43. Bertrand de Jouvenel, "Utopia for Practical Purposes," *Daedalus* 94 (Spring 1965): 437–453.

44. Edward Bellamy, *Looking Backward: 2000–1887* (Las Vegas: Digibooks, 2021 [1881]), 41.

45. Bellamy, *Looking Backward*, 84.

46. Bellamy, *Looking Backward*, 97.

47. On the history of statewide initiatives and referenda, see Steven L. Piott, *Giving Voters a Choice: The Origins of the Statewide Initiative and Referendum in the United States* (Columbia: University of Missouri Press, 2003).

48. See Sidney M. Milkis, *Theodore Roosevelt, the Progressive Party, and the Transformation of American Democracy* (Lawrence: University Press of Kansas 2009), 217.

49. It *has* been possible, however, to *imagine* not having elections. The Democratic governor of North Carolina, Beverly Perdue, proposed in 2011 that congressional elections be suspended to give Congress the time to deal with the country's problems without having to worry about losing their seats. See Yuval Levin, "What Is Constitutional Conservatism?," *National Review*, November 28, 2011.

50. US Census Bureau. See also Robert E. Gallman, "Commodity Output, 1839–1899," National Bureau of Economic Research, 1960, 15. By contrast, the six decades from 1950 to 2010, which we normally think of as a time of "profound change," saw the economy grow by a factor of 6.4, while the population only doubled. GDP data from Federal Reserve Bank of St. Louis, Economic Research, "Real Gross Domestic Product," 1950–2019, https://fred.stlouisfed.org/series/GDPC1.

51. "Real Gross Domestic Product," 26.

52. Bellamy, *Looking Backward*, 365.

53. The history of the American party system has been extensively documented and discussed. Some helpful examples include V. O. Key, *Politics, Parties, and Pressure Groups*, 5th ed. (New York: Thomas Y. Crowell, 1964); Walter Dean Burnham, *Critical Elections and the Mainsprings of American Politics* (New York: W. W. Norton, 1971); A. James Reichley, *The Life of the Parties* (Lanham, MD: Rowan & Littlefield, 2000); E. E. Schattschneider, *Party Government* (New York: Holt, Rinehart & Winston, 2000); and William Nisbet Chambers and Walter Dean Burnham, *The American Party Systems: States of Political Development* (New York: Oxford University Press, 1975).

54. Milkis, *Theodore Roosevelt*, 217.

55. See, for example, Mary Putnam Jacobi, "'Common Sense' Applied to Woman Suffrage" (1894): "We do believe that this special relation of women to children, in which the heart of the world has always felt there was something sacred, serves to impress upon women certain tendencies, to endow them with certain virtues which not only contribute to the charm which their anxious friends fear might be destroyed, but which will render them of special value in public affairs." Hammond et al., *Classics*, vol. 2, 59.

56. William L. Riordan, *Plunkitt of Tammany Hall: A Series of Very Plan Talks on Very Practical Politics* (New York: Bedford Books/St. Martin's Press, 1993 [1905]).

57. We will have more to say about the consequences of "party reform" in chapter 4.

58. This is also the claim of the various strains of "socialism" that made their first appearance during the French Revolution, and which spread in both Europe and America throughout the nineteenth century. Most progressives were not socialists—but as we will

see, they were concerned about the extreme inequality of incomes represented by those who Franklin D. Roosevelt would later call "the malefactors of great wealth," and by the control that large corporations seemed to have over the economy as a whole.

59. The federal government imposed a progressive income tax (with only two rates, 3 percent and 5 percent) during the Civil War, repealing the tax in 1872. Congress adopted a new income tax law in 1894, with a single 2 percent rate on those earning more than $4,000 per year (roughly 1 percent of the population). This act was declared unconstitutional by the Supreme Court in *Pollock* v. *Farmer's Loan and Trust Co.* (157 U.S. 429), prompting Congress to submit a constitutional amendment to the states in 1909. The amendment sailed through the Congress (no senator voted against it, and only fourteen members of the House voted against). The amendment then went to the states and was ratified by early 1913. The central argument in favor of the amendment was that it would remove the burden of excise taxes, which fell on the wealthy and the poor alike, and shift it to the wealthy exclusively. See "The Income Tax Amendment: Most Thought It Was a Great Idea in 1913," Constitutional Rights Foundation, 2011, https://www.crf-usa.org/bill-of-rights-in-action /bria-11-3-b-the-income-tax-amendment-most-thought-it-was-a-great-idea-in-1913.html.

60. Herbert Croly, *The Promise of American Life* (New York: MacMillan, 1910).

61. Croly, *Promise*, 5.

62. Croly, *Promise*, 22. The idea that wealth is somehow "distributed" rather than "earned" is an important but little-noticed contribution of the early progressives to the modern vernacular. It is an important contribution, however, because if income is being "distributed," why not distribute it equally?

63. Woodrow Wilson, *Congressional Government* (Camp Road, UK: Wentworth Press, 2016), 199.

64. Wilson, *Congressional Government*, 206.

65. Wilson, *Congressional Government*, 215.

66. Woodrow Wilson, *The New Freedom* (New York: Doubleday, Page, 1913), 45–46. This is a curious charge, because there is no such reliance on "Newtonian theory" in the *Federalist's* defense of separation of powers—which (though it uses the term "orbits" to refer to the jurisdiction of each branch), relies entirely on an understanding the psychology of *ambition*, and in particular the ambition of those who would seek to rule.

67. Wilson, *New Freedom*, 51–52.

68. Wilson, *New Freedom*. When Wilson wrote this, the French Third Republic (a curious model for a successful constitutional regime) had recently adopted a modest national pension plan and had undertaken an ambitious program to bring the modern world to its many rural villages: "republican" schools, universal military conscription, and access to rail lines. He was apparently thinking of these reforms as suitable models for Americans. Canada, meanwhile, was following a policy of high tariffs to promote the development of local industries (as was the United States at the time, since the Sixteenth Amendment allowing an income tax would not be adopted until the following year), and had just completed the Canadian Pacific Railway, at the time the longest single rail line in the world.

69. "To understand the Great Depression is the Holy Grail of macro-economics." This is the opening sentence in Ben Bernanke's *Essays on the Great Depression* (Princeton, NJ:

Princeton University Press, 2004). Bernanke was chair of the Federal Reserve from 2006 to 2014.

70. "On Moving Forward to Greater Freedom and Greater Security," Radio Address of the President, September 30, 1934, http://docs.fdrlibrary.marist.edu/093034.html.

71. Crop prices had been unstable since the end of World War I, in part because farmers harvested more crops when prices fell to make up the difference, which only increased supply relative to demand—thus driving prices down even further. The Hoover administration had tried to deal with this problem by encouraging crop reductions, which farmers resisted. The export market was limited because of "anti-dumping" laws adopted by other countries, whose own farmers complained about the effect of American exports on prices they could charge for their own crops. These problems predated the Depression, but the fall in incomes along with rapidly declining prices for crops and livestock, which followed the stock market crash, turned a chronic problem into a crisis. The New Deal's response to this problem was to place limits on the volume of products that could be brought to market—or even used by the farmer who produced them. Limit the supply, and prices will go up—that, at least, was the theory. However, the Supreme Court declared the policy of taxing food processors and giving the proceeds to farmers in return for restricting output to be unconstitutional, in *United States v. Butler* (297 U.S. 1, 1936), on the grounds that regulation of agriculture was a state function outside the authority of Congress. The Congress tried again with the Soil Conservation and Domestic Allotment Act of 1936, which paid farmers to let part of their acreage lie fallow in order to restore the health of the land. On the tangled history of New Deal farm policy, see George Selgin, "The New Deal and Recovery, Part 9: The AAA," *Cato at Liberty*, January 11, 2021, https://www .cato.org/blog/new-deal-recovery-part-9-aaa. This second effort at raising prices by restricting output was also challenged in court, but was ruled a constitutional use of the congressional authority to regulate interstate commerce, in *Wickard v. Filburn* (317 U.S. 111, 1942).

72. Barbara J. Alexander, "Failed Cooperation under the NRA," *Journal of Economic History* 57, no. 2 (June 1997): 327. See also Amity Schlaes, *The Forgotten Man: A New History of the Great Depression* (New York: Harper Collins, 2007), 151.

73. *National Recovery Administration (NRA) and the New Deal: A Resource Guide*, Library of Congress Research Guides, https://guides.loc.gov/national-recovery-administration /history.

74. Franklin D. Roosevelt, *The Commonwealth Club Address*, https://images2.american progress.org/campus/email/FDRCommonwealthClubAddress.pdf.

75. "All our histories recognize, of course, the existence from the very beginning of our national career of two different and, in some respects, antagonistic groups of political ideas—the ideas which were represented by Jefferson, and the ideas which were represented by Hamilton." Croly, *Promise of American Life*, 28.

76. Commonwealth Club address. We will refrain here from extensive comment on FDR's view of Hamilton, except to note that Hamilton's *Federalist* contributions offer no support for it—nor does his voluminous correspondence, or the various reports he wrote as secretary of the treasury. Hamilton was *worried* about popular government, to be sure— because of its sorry record in the states—but he was not an *opponent* of popular government, so long as that government could also be both stable and energetic.

77. Roosevelt, Commonwealth Club address.

78. Roosevelt, Commonwealth Club address.

79. Roosevelt, Commonwealth Club address.

80. Roosevelt, Commonwealth Club address.

81. Statista, "Annual Gross Domestic Product and real GDP in the United States from 1929 to 2020" (accessed August 1, 2023).

82. The architects of the Social Security system had not counted on population growth, and constructed an old-age pension system under the belief that neither the ratio of retired to working Americans nor the average life span would change significantly. Both of these assumptions turned out to be spectacularly wrong, with grave implications for the health of the pension system, as the Social Security Board of Trustees acknowledged in 2003; https://www.ssa.gov/pressoffice/pr/trustee03-pr.htm.

83. *The Port Huron Statement* is available at https://www.americanyawp.com/reader /27-the-sixties/the-port-huron-statement-1962/ Manifestos/SDS_Port_Huron.html.

84. On this last point, see Amity Schlaes, *Great Society: A New History* (New York: Harper Collins, 2019), 56–92.

85. ATT and its network of regional phone companies was sued by a new company, MCI Communications, in 1974, which led to an FCC investigation and a Justice Department ruling effectively ending ATT's control of the nation's phone service. For an account of these events, see Steve Coll, *The Deal of the Century: The Breakup of AT&T* (New York: Simon & Schuster, 1988).

86. On the New Left, see Mitchell Cohen and Dennis Hale, eds., *The New Student Left: An Anthology* (Boston: Beacon Press, 1966); Greg Calvert and Carol Neiman, eds., *The New Left* (Ann Arbor, MI: Radical Education Project, 1969); and William L. O'Neill, *The New Left: A History* (Hoboken, NJ: Wiley-Blackwell, 2001). For a very early effort to understand the pull of identity politics, see Dennis Hale, "Mr. Dooley on Hate," *Commonweal*, December 22, 1972, 279–280. Amity Schlaes has a useful history of the early SDS in *Great Society*, 56–92.

87. This is the argument of The 1619 Project.

88. Robert Dahl, *How Democratic Is the American Constitution?* (New Haven, CT: Yale University Press, 2001), 38.

89. Dahl, *How Democratic*, 92.

90. Dahl, *How Democratic*, 2. Since both the authors of this book are old, we will venture a snarky comment: sooner or later, everyone is "long since dead and mostly forgotten." No constitution, therefore, can be "approved" by a majority that has any hope of lasting. See the discussion of Madison's argument with Jefferson on precisely this point in chapter 3.

91. Dahl, *How Democratic*, 41, 94.

92. Dahl, *How Democratic*, 134.

93. Dahl, *How Democratic*, 54.

94. Dahl, *How Democratic*, 55.

95. Sanford Levinson, *Our Undemocratic Constitution* (New York: Oxford University Press, 2006), 5.

96. Sanford Levinson, *Framed: America's Fifty-One Constitutions and the Crisis of Governance* (New York: Oxford University Press, 2012), 75–98.

97. Levinson, *Our Undemocratic Constitution*, 49–62.

98. Levinson, *Our Undemocratic Constitution*, 81–101.

99. Levinson, *Our Undemocratic Constitution*, 38–49, 63–64.

100. Levinson, *Framed*, 216–219.

101. Levinson, *Framed*, 11.

102. Levinson, *Undemocratic Constitution*, 6–7, 11.

103. Levinson, *Framed*, 391. For a compelling critique of the constitutional convention idea see Mark Graber, "Is Dysfunction an Illusion? Belling the Partisan Cats: Preliminary Thoughts on Identifying and Mending a Dysfunction Constitutional Order," *Boston University Law Review* 94, 3 (May 2014): 611–648.

104. Levinson, *Undemocratic Constitution*, 16–24.

105. Levinson, *Undemocratic Constitution*, 16.

106. Levinson, *Undemocratic Constitution*, 18.

107. Levinson, *Undemocratic Constitution*, 20.

108. Stephen Griffin, *Broken Trust* (Lawrence: University Press of Kansas, 2015).

109. This is a concern we share; see chapter 4.

110. Griffin, *Broken Trust*, 36.

111. Griffin, *Broken Trust*, 57–58. For a different interpretation of the failed response to and recovery from Hurricane Katrina see Marc Landy, "Mega-Disasters and Federalism," *Public Administration Review* 68, no. 1 (December 2008): 186–198.

112. Griffin, *Broken Trust*, 141.

113. At the moment, several states do indeed treat the redrawing of congressional districts as a matter for expert commissions, but this is a decision that must be made by state legislatures.

114. Griffin, *Broken Trust*, 144.

115. Griffin, *Broken Trust*, 146. Notwithstanding his emphasis on nonpartisan reform, Griffin shares both Levinson's mistrust of representative government and the impulse to expand direct democracy. But he does not propose any specific constitutional changes to bring this about. See pp. 149–156.

116. Joseph Fishkin and William E. Forbath, *The Anti-Oligarchy Constitution: Reconstructing the Economic Foundations of American Democracy* (Cambridge, MA: Harvard University Press, 2022), 419.

117. Fishkin and Forbath, *Anti-Oligarchy Constitution*, 430–431.

118. Fishkin and Forbath, *Anti-Oligarchy*, 438–440.

119. This echoes the late nineteenth- and early twentieth-century hopes for a "general strike" of all wage earners against all owners—a hope that was never fulfilled.

120. Fishkin and Forbath, *Anti-Oligarchy Constitution*, 451, 476.

121. Fishkin and Forbath, *Anti-Oligarchy Constitution*, 461, 471, 484.

122. As confident as they are of obtaining congressional majorities, they appear equally pessimistic of gaining control of the Court.

123. See our discussion of FDR and court packing in chapter 4.

124. Fishkin and Forbath, *Anti-Oligarchy Constitution*, 431.

CHAPTER 3: THE CASE AGAINST THE CONSTITUTION,
RECONSIDERED

1. In addition to the other critical works discussed in the introduction and chapter 1, see Patrick J. Deneen, *Why Liberalism Failed* (New Haven, CT: Yale University Press, 2018); Sanford Levinson and Cynthia Levinson, *The Framers, Their Fights, and the Flaws That Affect Us Today* (Atlanta: Peachtree Publishers, 2017); and "The Democracy Constitution Symposium," in *Democracy: A Journal of Ideas* 61 (Summer 2019), https://democracyjour nal.org/magazine/61/an-audacious-idea-whose-time-has-come/ (accessed August 2, 2023).

2. Joseph Bessette, ed., *Toward a More Perfect Union: Writings of Herbert J. Storing*, (Washington, DC: AEI Press, 1995), 396. See also John O. McGinnis and Michael B. Rappaport, "Supermajority Rules as a Constitutional Solution," *William and Mary Law Review* 40, no. 2 (February 1998-1999): 395–469.

3. "In Pew Research Center polling in 2004, Americans opposed same-sex marriage by a margin of 60 percent to 31 percent." The reversal in opinion did not show up in polling until 2010. Pew Research Center, "Attitudes on Same-Sex Marriage," Pew Research Center, https://www.pewforum.org/fact-sheet/changing-attitudes-on-gay-marriage/ (accessed August 2, 2023).

4. Peter Moore, "The First Amendment Is the Most Widely Known Amendment in the Bill of Rights, and the Most Appreciated," YouGov America, April 12, 2016, https://today .yougov.com/topics/politics/articles-reports/2016/04/12/bill-rights.

5. See District of Columbia v. Heller (554 U.S. 570, 2008); and McDonald v. Chicago (561 U.S. 742, 2010), which applied the Heller ruling to the states and cities. Most recently, the Court overturned a New York law that strictly limited permits for carrying a concealed handgun. New York State Rifle & Pistol Association, Inc., et al., v. Bruen, Superintendent of New York State Police, et. al., No. 20–843. Argued November 3, 2021, and decided June 23, 2022.

6. *Federalist* 84, in Alexander Hamilton, John Jay, and James Madison, *The Federalist: A Commentary on the Constitution of the United States*, ed. Robert Scigliano (New York: Modern Library, 2000), 551.

7. This idea, as expressed by Thomas Jefferson in a letter to James Madison, apparently moved Madison to take a more positive view of the Bill of Rights—which he had agreed to support only as a compromise with those who were suspicious of the Constitution's ability to protect the rights of American citizens, given the power of the new national government. See Michael Zuckert, "James Madison's Consistency on the Bill of Rights," *National Affairs* (Spring 2021): 154–164. See also Akhil Amar, *The Bill of Rights: Creation and Reconstruction* (New Haven, CT: Yale University Press, 1998).

8. Pauline Maier, *Ratification: The People Debate the Constitution 1787–1788* (New York: Simon & Schuster, 2010).

9. See the informative essays in Robert A. Goldwin and William A. Schambra, eds., *How Capitalistic Is the Constitution?* (Washington, DC: American Enterprise Institute, 1982).

10. The precise meaning of this guarantee has come into question in modern times. Does it only refer to a government's need to construct a public building (for example, a city hall,

public school, or public hospital) on already occupied land? Or can the government take your house, and then sell it to a developer who wants to build a privately owned shopping mall? Maybe. See Kelo v. City of New London, 545 U.S. 469 (2005), decided by a 5–4 vote.

11. For a recent critique of how American politics and government foster pervasive inequality see George Packer, *Last Best Hope* (New York: Macmillan, 2021).

12. A Pew Research poll published January 9, 2020, found that 61 percent of American adults agree that "there is too much economic inequality in the United States," although they rank inequality as a less important concern than affordable health care, terrorism, gun violence, and climate change; see https://www.pewresearch.org/social-trends/2020/01/09 /most-americans-say-there-is-too-much-economic-inequality-in-the-u-s-but-fewer-than -half-call-it-a-top-priority/ (accessed August 5, 2023).

13. For a recent reassertion of this hallowed notion see Noam Chomsky and Marv Waterstone, *Consequences of Capitalism: Manufacturing Discontent and Resistance* (Chicago: Haymarket Books, 2021).

14. Commonwealth Club address, September 23, 1932, https://www.americanrhetoric .com/speeches/fdrcommonwealth.htm (accessed August 5, 2023).

15. Statista, *Annual Gross Domestic Product and Real GDP in the United States from 1930 to 2020*, https://www.statista.com/statistics/1031678/gdp-and-real-gdp-united-states -1930–2019/ (accessed August 2, 2023).

16. The coronavirus pandemic that devastated the economy in 2020 did not change this fundamental reality. By the summer of 2021 the economy has recovered much of what it had lost during the height of the shutdown, and the unemployment rate, which was 14.8 percent in April 2020, had declined to 5.8 percent by May 2021. *Unemployment Rates during the Covid-19 Pandemic*, US Bureau of Labor Statistics, June 15, 2021; and *TED: The Economics Daily*, US Bureau of Labor Statistics, June 29, 2021. Fuel and food shortages brought on by the war in Ukraine are largely to blame for the drastic inflation that began in the spring of 2022. See the interview with Mark Zandi, chief economist at Moody's Analytics, in Christine Miu, "Top Economist Mark Zandi Says Forget Biden's Stimulus—Putin's War in Ukraine Is by Far the Biggest Driver of Inflation," *Fortune*, June 13, 2022, https://fortune.com/2022/06/13 /mark-zandi-moodys-chief-economist-inflation-russia-invasion-ukraine/.

17. For example, 97 percent of Americans own cell phones (Pew Research Center, Mobile Fact Sheet, April 2021), and 80 percent of the poor have access to a car (Caroline Cournoyer, "More Poorer Residents Are Driving Cars, Presenting New Issues for Transit Agencies," *Governing Magazine*, April 6, 2018, https://www.governing.com/archive/gov-car-ownership-poverty.html. See also Christopher Howard, *The Hidden Welfare State: Tax Expenditures and Social Policy in the United States* (Princeton, NJ: Princeton University Press, 1997).

18. Peter Baldwin, *The Narcissism of Minor Differences: How America and Europe Are Alike* (New York: Oxford University Press, 2009), 185, 193.

19. See especially Nicholas Eberstadt, "The Future of the Work Ethic," *Claremont Review of Books* 19, no. 4 (Fall 2019).

20. Fareed Zakaria, "Bernie Sanders's Scandinavian Fantasy," *Washington Post*, February 27, 2020, https://www.washingtonpost.com/opinions/bernie-sanderss-scandinavian-fantasy /2020/02/27/ee894d6e-599f-11ea-9b35-def5a027d470_story.html.

21. Sweden's billionaires mostly live outside the country so as to avoid taxes. Baldwin includes them in his comparative analysis in *The Narcissism of Minor Differences*, 188–189. See Christopher DeMuth, "Welfare and Debt: A Moynihan Assessment," *The American Interest*, April 23, 2019, https://www.the-american-interest.com/2019/04/23/welfare-and-debt-a-moynihan-assessment/. See also Zakaria, "Scandinavian Fantasy."

22. Adam Ozimek, "Lessons on School Choice from Sweden," *Forbes*, December 3, 2012, https://www.forbes.com/sites/modeledbehavior/2012/12/03/lessons-on-school-choice-from-sweden/?sh=5338387727fc.

23. 2021 Index of Economic Freedom—Sweden, https://www.heritage.org/index/country/sweden (accessed August 2, 2023).

24. 2021 Index of Economic Freedom—Sweden.

25. Kelly McDonald, "Scandinavia Isn't a Socialist Paradise," *The Federalist*, August 11, 2015, https://thefederalist.com/2015/08/11/scandinavia-isnt-a-socialist-paradise/.

26. Dylan Matthews, "America's Taxes Are the Most Progressive in the World," *Washington Post*, April 5, 2013. See also Scott Hodge, "News to Obama: The OECD Says the United States Has the Most Progressive Tax System," Tax Foundation, https://taxfoundation.org/news-obama-oecd-says-united-states-has-most-progressive-tax-system/ (accessed August 2, 2023).

27. Hodge, "News to Obama." Recent changes in the tax laws have apparently not changed this finding. See Alex Muresianu, "Yes, the U.S. Tax Code Is Progressive," Tax Foundation, September 17, 2021, https://taxfoundation.org/us-tax-system-progressive/.

28. See, for example, Robert Reich, *The System: Who Rigged It and How to Fix It* (New York: Vintage, 2021); Alana Semuels, "The Founding Fathers Weren't Concerned with Inequality," *Atlantic*, April 15, 2016; Richard Kreiter, "The Constitution Requires Inequality," *Boston Globe*, December 13, 2015; Ganesh Sitaraman, "Our Constitution Wasn't Built for This," *New York Time Sunday Review*, September 16, 2017.

29. *The U.S. Income Distribution: Trends and Issues*, Congressional Research Service, January 13, 2021, https://fas.org/sgp/crs/misc/R44705.pdf.

30. "Summary of the Latest Federal Income Tax Data, 2021 Update," Tax Foundation, February 3, 2021, https://taxfoundation.org/federal-income-tax-data-2021/.

31. "Federal Income Tax Data, 2021 Update."

32. Perhaps the most distinguished voice linking inequality and lack of economic growth is by Joseph Stiglitz, "Inequality and Economic Growth," *Political Quarterly* 86, no. S1 (December 2015): 134–155. This causal relationship is disputed by another equally distinguished economist, Robert Barro, who concedes that inequality hampers economic growth in poor countries but denies that it does so in rich ones. Robert Barro, "Inequality, Growth, and Investment," NBER Working Paper 7038, National Bureau of Economic Research, https://www.nber.org/papers/w7038.

33. The classic statement of this principle is by Simon Kuznets, "Economic Growth and Inequality," *American Economic Review* 45, no. 1 (March 1955): 1–28. See also B. Keith Payne, Jazmin L. Brown-Iannuzzi, and Jason W. Hannay, "Economic Inequality Increases Risk-Taking," *Proceedings of the National Academy of Sciences*, April 17, 2017, https://doi.org/10.1073/pnas.1616453114. Our discussion is not meant to imply that the current rate

of taxation of the rich is precisely right. Perhaps it could go higher, as long as it does not threaten to destroy the high propensity for risk found among America's wealthiest citizens. For a contrary view, see Heather Boushey, *Unbound: How Inequality Constricts Our Economy and What We Can Do About It* (Cambridge, MA: Harvard University Press, 2019).

34. Harry McCracken, "How Government Did (and Didn't) Invent the Internet," Time.com, July 25, 2012, https://techland.time.com/2012/07/25/how-government-did-and-didnt-invent-the-internet/.

35. Makada Henry-Nickle, Kwadwo Frimpong, and Hao Sunm, *Trends in the Information Technology Sector*, Brookings Institution, March 2019, https://www.brookings.edu/research/trends-in-the-information-technology-sector/.

36. "Although the US produces about 22 percent of the global GDP and accounts for 4 percent of the world's population, it accounts for 44 percent of global biomedical R&D expenditures and its domestic pharmaceutical market to about 40 percent of the global market." "Biopharmaceutical Innovation: Which Countries Rank the Best?," https://www.dcatvci.org/250-biopharmaceutical-innovation-which-countries-rank-the-best (accessed August 2, 2023).

37. Paula D. Johnson, *Global Philanthropy Report*, Harvard Kennedy School, Hauser Center for Civil Society (April 2018): 10. See also Christopher Howard, *The Hidden Welfare State: Tax Expenditures and Social Policy in the United States* (Princeton, NJ: Princeton University Press, 1997).

38. Baldwin, *The Narcissism of Minor Differences*, 153.

39. "Earned Income Tax Credit Overview," National Council of State Legislatures, https://www.ncsl.org/research/labor-and-employment/earned-income-tax-credits-for-working-families.aspx (accessed August 2, 2023).

40. Christopher Howard, *The Welfare State Nobody Knows: Debunking Myths about U.S. Social Policy* (Princeton, NJ: Princeton University Press, 2007), 13–27.

41. Rainer Zitelmann, "Why Inheritance Is Mostly Overrated as a Reason for Wealth," *Forbes*, June 24, 2019, https://www.forbes.com/sites/rainerzitelmann/2019/06/24/amazing-facts-that-prove-inheritance-is-mostly-overrated-as-a-reason-for-wealth/#4f32f0df1eca.

42. The most discerning discussion of this very thorny issue is by Bertrand de Jouvenel, in *The Ethics of Redistribution* (Indianapolis: Liberty Fund, 1990). Also, we cannot be the only ones who have noticed the odd mixture in the *New Yorker* of attacks on the indecent rich and ads for Gucci, Armani, etc.

43. Jouvenel, *Ethics of Redistribution*.

44. See, among others, *The Book of Genesis*.

45. Estimates of Vladimir Putin's wealth vary, but an internet search by the authors found no credible estimate below $40 billion. See "What Is Vladimir Putin's Net Worth? Kremlin Claims Russian President Earns $140,000 a Year—but Others Estimate His Net Worth at Over $200bn," *The Week*, May 31, 2022, https://www.theweek.co.uk/vladimir-putin/956928/what-is-vladimir-putins-net-worth.

46. See Breda Luthar, "Remembering Socialism: On Desire, Consumption, and Surveillance," *Journal of Consumer Culture*, July 2006, https://journals.sagepub.com/doi/10.1177/1469540506064745.

47. On this question see Alexis de Tocqueville, especially his discussion of the "equality of conditions" as the most important political consequence of the end of feudalism. *Democracy in America*, volume 1, introduction, 3–18, and part 1, ch. 2 and 3 (pp. 27–53). See also Peter Laslett, *The World We Have Lost* (Oxfordshire: Routledge, 1965).

48. For an argument that economic rights, those not stated in the Constitution, should nonetheless be protected by it see, Rotem Litinski, "Economic Rights: Are They Justiciable, and Should They Be?," *Human Rights Magazine* 44, no. 3 (November 30, 2019), https://www .americanbar.org/groups/crsj/publications/human_rights_magazine_home/economic -justice (accessed August 5, 2023).

49. "Democrats Roll Out $3.5 Trillion Budget to Fulfill Biden's Broad Agenda," *New York Times*, July 14, 2021.

50. The seminal discussion of the problems posed by rights expansion is Mary Ann Glendon, *Rights Talk: The Impoverishment of Political Discourse* (Detroit: Free Press, 1993).

51. To get some perspective on the size of our national debt, consider: As of 2021 the national debt stood at 102 percent of the size of the economy; it is projected by the Congressional Budget Office to be twice the size of the economy by 2051 (*Wall Street Journal*, March 4, 2021). This is a higher debt than the United States bore at the end of the Second World War. See also Eugene Steuerle, "This Is Not Your Grandfather's Debt Problem," *Washington Post*, May 27, 2020.

52. Daniel Lazare, *The Frozen Republic: How the Constitution Is Paralyzing Democracy* (New York: Houghton Mifflin, 1996). See also Richard Albert, "Time to Update the Language of the Constitution," UTNews, a publication of University of Texas Law School, July 6, 2020. See also the essays claiming constitutional obsolescence in Thomas Main, ed., *Is the Constitution Obsolete?* (Durham, NC: Carolina Academic Press, 2014).

53. Thomas Jefferson to James Madison, September 6, 1789, in *The Papers of Thomas Jefferson*, vol. 15 (Princeton, NJ: Princeton University Press, 1958), 392–398. The problem that Jefferson raised—that the most ambitious citizens will be reluctant to support a constitution they had no hand in making—was pondered by Abraham Lincoln in his "Lyceum Address," given in 1837. His subject was ambition, and men whose ambitions could never be satisfied by merely working a government invented by others. Such men belong "to the family of the lion, or the tribe of the eagle.... Towering genius disdains a beaten path." How then will the Constitution be preserved when all of those who were alive at the Founding have passed from the scene? "Address to the Young Men's Lyceum of Springfield, Illinois," January 27, 1838, in *Lincoln: Speeches, Letters, Miscellaneous Writings, the Lincoln-Douglas Debates* (New York: Library of America, 1989), 28–36.

54. Jefferson to Madison, September 6, 1789, *Jefferson Papers*.

55. Thomas Jefferson to John Wayles Eppes, June 24, 1813, https://founders.archives.gov /documents/Jefferson/03-06-02-0200 (accessed August 5, 2023).

56. Bertrand de Jouvenel has expressed this idea by comparing it to families. Each family receives a "waterfall of liberality" from its progenitors—a gift that expects no repayment (by the time we can repay our parents they are likely to be dead), but that is "repaid" with another waterfall of liberality showered on the next generation. *The Pure Theory of Politics* (New Haven, CT: Yale University Press, 1963), 49.

57. James Madison to Thomas Jefferson, February 4, 1790, Founders Online, https://founders.archives.gove/documents/Madison/01-13-02-0020 (accessed August 5, 2023).

58. Among the southern states, only Florida voted in favor of the poll tax amendment. Subsequent to its ratification, a number of states that had not voted on the Twenty-Fourth Amendment eventually signed on: Virginia, North Carolina, Alabama, and Texas. "The Twenty-fourth Amendment," US House of Representatives, History, Art, & Archives, August 27, 1962, https://history.house.gov/HistoricalHighlight/Detail/37045 (accessed August 2, 2023).

59. Seminal writings on the virtues of a two-party system include V. O. Key, *Southern Politics in State and Nation* (Knoxville, TN: University of Tennessee Press, 1949); James Sundquist, *Dynamics of the Party System* (Washington, DC: Brookings Institution, 1973); and Sidney Milkis, *Political Parties and Constitutional Government: Remaking American Democracy* (Baltimore: Johns Hopkins University Press, 1999).

60. Madison subsequently modified his opposition. See, among others, the essay entitled "Parties" in the *National Gazette* for January 23, 1792, https://founders.archives.gov/documents/Madison/01-14-02-0176 (accessed August 5, 2023).

61. *Federalist* 68, 435.

62. On the seminal election of 1800 see Noble Cunningham Jr., *The Jeffersonian Republicans: The Formation of Party Organization* (Chapel Hill: University of North Carolina Press, 1957). See also John Ferling, *Adams vs. Jefferson: The Tumultuous Election of 1800* (Oxford: Oxford University Press, 2004).

63. Joseph Charles, *Origins of the American Party System* (New York: Harper & Row, 1961). See also William Nisbet Chambers, *Political Parties in a New Nation: The American Experience* (New York: Oxford University Press, 1963).

64. On the development of the spoils system see Robert Remini, *The Life of Andrew Jackson* (New York: Harpers, 1988); and Leonard White, *The Jacksonians: A Study in Administrative History 1829–1861* (New York: Free Press, 1965).

65. Milton Rakove, *We Don't Want Nobody Nobody Sent: An Oral History of the Daley Years* (Bloomington: Indiana University Press, 1979).

66. The dean of writers on the significance of American political parties is Wilson C. McWilliams. See especially "Parties as Civic Associations" and "Democracy and the Citizen," in Patrick Deneen and Susan J. McWilliams, eds., *Redeeming American Democracy* (Lawrence: University Press of Kansas, 2011).

67. See John H. Aldrich, *Why Parties? A Second Look* (Chicago: University of Chicago Press, 2011).

68. "Israel's Parliament Approves New Government, Ousting Netanyahu," *New York Times*, Briefing, June 14, 2021, https://www.nytimes.com/live/2021/06/13/world/israel-knesset-bennett-lapid-netanyahu.

69. Tocqueville, *Democracy in America*, 169.

70. Karen Yourish, Larry Buchanan, and Denise Lu, "The 147 Republicans Who Voted to Overturn Election Results," *New York Times*, January 7, 2021.

71. "Congress Ratifies Bush Victory after Challenge," *New York Times*, January 7, 2005.

72. See, among many other news stories, "Mueller Finds No Trump-Russia Conspiracy,

but Stops Short on Exonerating the President on Obstruction," *New York Times,* March 24, 2019.

73. On the allegedly pernicious impact of federalism see Donald Kettl, *The Divided States of America: Why Federalism Doesn't Work* (Princeton, NJ: Princeton University Press, 2020). For a critique of the principle of limited government itself see Steven Kelman, "Limited Government: An Incoherent Concept," *Journal of Public Policy and Management* 3, no. 1 (Autumn 1983): 31–44.

74. Since this has become a contentious issue in recent years, this may be a good time to note that this outcome has only happened five times in the nation's history: three times in the nineteenth century and twice in the twenty-first century—and each time it has happened, there has been a third candidate with enough votes to deny a popular majority to either candidate. In recent elections, the main "spoilers" were Ralph Nader (2000) and Gary Johnson (2016).

75. The most discerning modern defender of federalism is Martin Diamond. See his collection of essays on the subject in William Schambra, ed., *As Far as Republican Principles Will Admit: Essays by Martin Diamond* (Washington, DC: American Enterprise Institute, 1992).

76. James Madison, *Notes on Debates in the Federal Convention of 1787* (New York: W. W. Norton, 1987), 129–139. Hamilton's speech is the only business recorded for that day.

77. Madison, *Notes on Debates*, 129–139.

78. For an exhaustive recent examination of the federalism debate in the convention, see Max Edling, *Perfecting the Union: National and State Authority in the U.S. Constitution* (New York: Oxford University Press, 2021).

79. *Federalist* 9, 52.

80. Is it a coincidence that the astounding growth of online communication networks has coincided with increasing levels of what we refer to these days as "polarization"—but that is often just a polite term for "hatred"? Could it be that more and more Americans have the opportunity to discover that the country is filled with people who don't think the way they do, and who for that reason deserve to be described in the most unflattering terms possible? We wonder if, prior to social media, the same kind of diversity existed, but most people were blissfully unaware of the fact.

81. Pietro Nivola, "Why Federalism Matters," Brookings Institution, October 1, 2005, https://www.brookings.edu/research/why-federalism-matters/.

82. New Hampshire Revised Statutes, Title XII, §159. See also Marc Landy, "Taking Federalism Seriously," *Real Clear Public Affairs*, February 17, 2021, https://www.realclearpublic affairs.com/articles/2021/02/17/taking_federalism_seriously_656952.html.

83. Committee for a Responsible Federal Budget, "COVID Money Tracker," April 20, 2020, http://www.crfb.org/blogs/covid-money-tracker-policies-enacted-to-date.

84. To take an extreme but illustrative example, on the day when New York State recorded 2,214 cases per 100,000 people, Maine recorded only 325 per 100,000 people. Obviously, the two states were facing very different problems. See Statista, "Rate of Coronavirus (COVID-19) Cases in the United States as of August 26, 2020, by State (per 100,000 people)," https://www.statista.com/statistics/1109004/coronavirus-covid19-cases-rate-us-americans -by-state/ (accessed August 5, 2023).

85. For example, some states (California was one of many) simply ordered houses of worship to close. Others (Massachusetts was one) recommended "capacity limits" for in-person attendance, and encouraged outdoor services—but did not order churches to close. On the California shutdowns, see "Newsom Orders Statewide Closures, Including Gyms and Churches in Monitored Counties," *Palm Springs Desert Sun*, July 13, 2020, https://www.usatoday.com/story/news/health/2020/07/13/newsom-orders-gyms-churches-closed-monitored-california-counties/5430110002/. On Massachusetts, see "MA Safety Standards: Places of Worship 2020," chrome-extension://efaidnbmnnnibpcajpcglclefindmkaj/https://www.mma.org/wp-content/uploads/2020/05/Places-of-Worship_Circular-Checklist_Eng.pdf (accessed August 5, 2023).

86. A tragic but illustrative example is the late-March 2020)order by Governor Andrew Cuomo of New York that nursing homes with empty beds be required to accept COVID-19 patients, resulting in the death from the virus of over 15,000 nursing home residents. The order was reversed in early May. The point here is not to beat up on the (now ex-) governor, but to point out how much worse it would have been if the Centers for Disease Control or some other federal agency had been authorized to issue a command binding on every nursing home and every hospital in the country. For differing opinions regarding COVID and federalism see "The Coronavirus Response Shows That Federalism Is Working," *National Review*, March 2020; and "Our System of Federalism Is a Huge Problem in Fighting Coronavirus," *New York Magazine*, March 2020, https://nymag.com/intelligencer/2020/03/u-s-federalism-creates-chaos-in-fighting-coronavirus.html.

87. Anke Kessler, "Communication in Federal Politics: Universalism, Policy Uniformity, and the Optimal Allocation of Fiscal Authority," *Journal of Political Economy* 122, no. 4 (August 2014).

88. On bureaucratic incentives, the seminal work is James Q. Wilson, *Bureaucracy: What Government Agencies Do and Why They Do It* (New York: Basic Books, 1991).

89. On this aspect of bureaucratic bias, see Steven Koonin, *Unsettled: What Climate Science Tells Us, What It Doesn't, and Why It Matters* (New York: Penguin Random House, 2021). Also, Marc Landy, Marc Roberts, and Steve Thomas, *The Environmental Protection Agency: Asking the Wrong Questions, from Nixon to Clinton* (Oxford: Oxford University Press, 1994).

90. The most important recent consideration of affirmative action is Melvin Urofsky, *The Affirmative Action Puzzle: A Living History from Reconstruction to Today* (New York: Pantheon Books, 2020). See also Barbara R. Bergmann, *In Defense of Affirmative Action* (New York: Basic Books, 1996). A further consideration of affirmative action appears in chapter 4.

91. Akhil Amar, *The Bill of Rights: Creation and Reconstruction* (New Haven, CT: Yale University Press, 1998).

92. Bryan D. Jones, Sean M. Theriault, and Michelle Whyman, *The Great Broadening: How the Vast Expansion of the Policymaking Agenda Transformed American Politics* (Chicago: Chicago University Press, 2019).

93. Energy Policy and Conservation Act of 1975 (Pub. L 94–163, 89 Stat. 871), enacted December 22, 1975.

94. The Constitution does not allow states to interfere with the movement of Americans from one state to another. The Framers envisioned a national community—the "people of the United States"—and not a collection of separate polities with impassable borders. This principle was reaffirmed in 1941, when the Supreme Court ruled that California could not arrest and deport "dust-bowl" migrants seeking jobs or public relief in the state during the Depression. Edwards v. California, 341 U.S. 160, 1941.

95. Manasa Reddigari, "States with the Lowest and Highest Taxes," MileIQ, April 15, 2019, https://www.microsoft.com/en-us/microsoft-365/growth-center/resources/states-lowest -highest-income-taxes.

96. *California Economy and Taxes*, Legislative Analyst's Office California Legislature, https://lao.ca.gov/laoecontax/article/detail/265 (accessed August 2, 2023); and Rice University William Fulton Kinder Institute for Urban Research, Research Institute, "It Seems Like All of California Is Moving to Texas. Is That True?," March 3, 2018, https:/kinder.rice.edu /urbanedge/2021/03/03/Californians-moving-to-texas-covid-migration.

97. The same phenomenon can be observed in New England, where many people who work in Massachusetts live in New Hampshire, which does not have a state income tax. Massachusetts has recently been making noises about getting around this "tax evasion," but it is unlikely to succeed. Rick Sobey, "Bay Staters Shipping up to the Granite State of New Hampshire Last Year," *Boston Herald*, December 25, 2019, https://www.bostonherald.com/2019/12/25 /bay-staters-shipping-up-to-the-granite-state/.

98. F. A. Hayek, "The Use of Knowledge in Society," *American Economic Review* 35, no. 4 (1945): 519–530.

99. See Larry Diamond, "Why Decentralize Power in a Democracy?," speech to the Conference on Fiscal and Administrative Decentralization, Baghdad, Iraq, February 12, 2004, published by Stanford University, https://diamond-democracy.stanford.edu/speaking /speeches/why-decentralize-power-democracy.

100. See Wilson C. McWilliams, "Democracy and the Citizen: Community, Dignity and the Crisis of Contemporary Politics in America," in Susan McWilliams and Patrick Deneen, eds., *Redeeming Democracy in America* (Lawrence: University Press of Kansas, 2011), 9–28.

101. A recent argument in this vein is Deneen, *Why Liberalism Failed.*

102. Lorraine Smith Pangle and Thomas L. Pangle, *The Learning of Liberty: The Educational Ideas of the American Founders* (Lawrence: University Press of Kansas, 1995).

103. Dennis Hale, *The Jury in America: Triumph and Decline* (Lawrence: University Press of Kansas, 2016).

104. Griswold v. Connecticut, 381 U.S. 479 (1965), https://supreme.justia.com/cases/fed eral/us/381/479/ (accessed August 5, 2023).

105. Roe v. Wade, 410 U.S. 113 (1973), https://supreme.justia.com/cases/federal/us/410/113 (accessed August 5, 2023).

106. Lawrence v. Texas, 539 U.S. 558 (2003), https://supreme.justia.com/cases/federal /us/539/558/ (accessed August 5, 2023).

107. Obergefell v. Hodges, 576 U.S. 644 (2015), https://supreme.justia.com/cases/federal /us/576/14–556/ (accessed August 5, 2023).

108. Dobbs v. Jackson Women's Health Organization, 597 U.S. ___ (2022), https://su preme.justia.com/cases/federal/us/576/14–556/ (accessed August 5, 2023).

109. Burt Neuborne, "Divide States to Democratize the Senate: A Constitutionally Sound Fix to a Vexing Political Problem," *Wall Street Journal*, November 19, 2018; Eric W. Orts, "The Path to Give California 12 Senators, and Vermont Just One: Maybe the Two-Senators-per-State Rule Isn't as Permanent as It Seems," *Atlantic*, January 2, 2019; Akhil Amar, "Philadelphia Revisited: Amending the Constitution Outside Article V," *University of Chicago Law Review* 55, no. 4 (Fall 1988): 1043–1104; Douglas Linder, "What in the Constitution Cannot Be Amended," *Arizona Law Review* 23 (1981): 717.

110. Ronald Browenstein, "How the Rustbelt Paved Trump's Road to Victory: The President-Elect Won by Locking in Support from Traditional 'Blue Wall' States Hillary Clinton Thought Were in Her Corner," *Atlantic*, November 10, 2016.

111. Darrell West, *It's Time to Abolish the Electoral College*, Brookings Institution Policy Brief, October 15, 2019, https://www.brookings.edu/policy2020/bigideas/its-time-to-abol ish-the-electoral-college/. See also the debate between Larry Sabato and George Edwards III regarding whether to radically change or abolish the Electoral College in Main, *Is the Constitution Obsolete?*. The US Senate considered a constitutional amendment in 1969 to abolish the Electoral College, in response to the election of Richard Nixon as president with a less than 1 percent majority of the popular vote—but a significantly lopsided victory in the Electoral College. The bill made it out of committee but was filibustered by a combination of Democratic and Republican conservatives, many from small states.

112. Stephen Feldman, *Pack the Court!: A Defense of Supreme Court Expansion* (Philadelphia: Temple University Press, 2021). On April 15, 2021, two prominent Democratic legislators—Sen. Edward Markey and Rep. Jerrold Nadler—submitted legislation for consideration of the Congress that would expand the size of the Supreme Court by adding four new seats—the nominees for these new seats would, presumably, be confirmed by the current Senate. However, Speaker of the House Nancy Pelosi quickly announced that she would not introduce the bill to the House.

113. Status of National Popular Vote Bill in Each State, https://www.nationalpopular vote.com/state-status (accessed August 2, 2023).

114. See Madison, *Notes on Debates*, 32 (the Council for revising legislation appears in Sec. 8 of the original Virginia Plan introduced on May 29).

115. This fear was expressed early in the Convention by Mr. Dickenson of Delaware, who argued that "to abolish the States altogether, would degrade the Councils of our Country, would be impracticable, would be ruinous." Madison, *Notes on Debates*, for June 7, 84.

116. See "About the Senate & the U.S. Constitution | Equal State Representation," US Senate, senate.gov/artandhistory/history/minute/A_Great_Compromise.htm (accessed August 2, 2023). Equal votes for the states in the Senate represented a defeat for the Federalist faction at the convention—one that they had not anticipated. See John Patrick Coby, "The Proportional Representation Debate at the Constitutional Convention: Why the Nationalists Lost," *American Political Thought* 7 (Spring 2018): 216–242.

117. Madison was so insistent on the Council of Revision that he introduced it again on two more occasions before finally giving up.

118. The other unamendable provision is the date after which the importation of slaves could be forbidden by the Congress. US Constitution, Article V.

119. Kay Schlozman, panel discussion of the early days of the Biden administration, Clough Center for Constitutional Democracy, Boston College, February 15, 2021.

120. *About Filibusters and Cloture/Historical Overview*, US Senate, https://www.senate.gov/about/powers-procedures/filibusters-cloture/overview.htm (accessed August 2, 2023).

121. *About Filibusters and Cloture.*

122. US Senate, "Cloture," https://www.senate.gov/artandhistory/history/common/generic/Origins_Cloture.htm#:~:text=In%201975%20the%20Senate%20reduced,by%20a%20simple%20majority%20vote (accessed August 2, 2023).

123. We concede that it is not *entirely* a loss, given the onslaught of objectionable campaign commercials that fill the broadcast networks and the internet, aimed at voters in the target states. Those who live in the "safe" states may understand "safe" as "safe *from.*" We understand.

124. See for example James Reinl, "Florida: America's 'Microcosm' State Is Make-or-Break in 2020 Vote," https://www.thenationalnews.com/world/the-americas/florida-america-s-microcosm-state-is-make-or-break-in-2020-vote-1.1103438 (accessed August 2, 2023).

125. Katie Reilly, "Read Hillary Clinton's 'Basket of Deplorables' Remarks About Donald Trump Supporters," *Time*, September 10, 2016, https://time.com/4486502/hillary-clinton-basket-of-deplorables-transcript.

126. M. Weston, "One Person, No Vote: Staggered Elections, Redistricting, and Disenfranchisement," *Yale Law Journal* 121, no. 7 (May 2012): 1584–2131.

127. In addition to the sources cited above, see "It's Time for Term Limits for Supreme Court Justices," Vox, June 27, 2018, https://www.vox.com/polyarchy/2018/6/27/17511030/supreme-court-term-limits-retirement.

128. "Democrats Unveil Long-Shot Plan to Expand Size of the Supreme Court," NPR, https://www.npr.org/2021/04/15/987723528/democrats-unveil-long-shot-plan-to-expand-size-of-supreme-court-from-9-to-13 (accessed August 5, 2023).

129. H.R.1-For the People Act of 2021, 117th Congress (2021–2022), https://www.congress.gov/bill/117th-congress/house-bill/1/text (accessed August 5, 2023).

130. Ballotpedia, "H.R.1, For the People Act of 2021," https://ballotpedia.org/HR1,_%22For_the_People_Act_of_2021%22 (accessed August 2, 2023).

131. Madison, *Notes on Debates*. The convention came to this decision somewhat grudgingly, however; it was still considering congressional election of the president in late August. The idea of electors appointed by the states choosing the president emerged in late July, was rejected, and then remerged in its final form on September 7. For an illustration of the problems raised by the selection of the chief executive, see the debates for July 24 to July 26.

132. We have some professional qualifications to weigh in on this debate, since we regularly struggle to read the handwriting of our students who do in-class exams on paper.

133. Mathilde Carlier, "Number of Licensed Drivers—United States 1990–2020, Statista, https://www.statista.com/statistics/191653/number-of-licensed-drivers-in-the-us-since

-1988/#:~:text=Around%20228%20million%20people%20held,female%20licensees%20 than%20male%20drivers (accessed August 2, 2023).

134. Currently, twenty states require a photo ID in order to vote. An additional fifteen states require a form of identification that does not have to include a photo. These rules apply to *voting* and are in addition to whatever identification requirements are required for *registering* to vote. Ballotpedia, "Voter Identification Laws by State," https://ballotpedia.org /Voter_identification_laws_by_state (accessed August 2, 2023).

135. See *The Conversation*, March 15, 2021, https://theconversation.com/is-ballot-collec tion-or-ballot-harvesting-good-for-democracy-we-asked-5-experts-156549 (accessed August 5, 2023).

CHAPTER 4: REFORM IN THE CONSTITUTIONAL GRAIN

1. As we discussed in chapter 3, the Supreme Courts' returning the issue of abortion to the states may prove to be the beginning of a trend to return power to the states. It is too soon to tell. Dobbs v. Jackson Women's Health Organization, 597 U.S. ___ (2022).

2. "Trust in Government," https://news.gallup.com/poll/5392/trust-government.aspx (accessed August 6, 2023).

3. Pew Research Center, "Public Trust in Government: 1958–2022," June 6, 2022, https:// www.pewresearch.org/politics/2022/06/06/public-trust-in-government-1958–2022/.

4. Pew Research Center, "Public Trust in Government."

5. "Preferred levels of government activity 2010–2019," https://news.gallup.com/poll /268295/support-government-inches-not-socialism.aspx (accessed August 6, 2023). This is, admittedly, a somewhat general question that might conceal many differences among those responding either yes or no.

6. James Q. Wilson, "American Politics, Then and Now," *Commentary*, February 1979, https://www.commentary.org/articles/james-wilson/american-politics-then-now/ (accessed August 6, 2023).

7. See the discussion of Dahl and Levinson in chapter 1.

8. For public dissatisfaction with government agencies, regulations, and policies, and with the undue influence of special interests, see https://news.gallup.com/poll/5392 /trust-government.aspx (accessed August 6, 2023).

9. The Civil Rights Act of 1964 is codified as Public Law 88–352-JULY 2, 1964, https:// www.govnfogov/content/pkg/STATUTE-78-Pg 241.pdf.

10. Joellen Kralik, "School Bathroom Access for Transgender Students," *National Council of State Legislators Policy Newsletter* 24, no. 26 (July 2016), https://www.ncsl.org /research/education/school-bathroom-access-for-transgender-students.aspx. See also Julie Hirschfeld Davis and Matt Apuzzo, "U.S. Directs Public Schools to Allow Transgender Access to Restrooms," *New York Times*, May 12, 2016. In July 2022 a federal judge issued a preliminary injunction barring the Biden administration from issuing new transgender bathroom regulations requiring local schools to permit students to choose their sex and

pick the bathroom they want. The Trump administration had rescinded a similar order imposed by the Obama administration. Brad Brooks, Reuters, "Judge Blocks Biden Administration's Directives on Transgender Athletes, Bathrooms," https://www.reuters.com/world /us/judge-blocks-biden-admin-directives-transgender-athletes-bathrooms-2022–07–16/. Jeremy W. Peters, Jo Becker, and Julie Hirschfeld Davis, *New York Times*, February 22, 2017. See also "Trump Rescinds Rules on Bathrooms for Transgender Students," *New York Times*, February 22, 2017, https://www.nytimes.com/2017/02/22/us/politics/devos-sessions-trans gender-students-rights.html.

11. James Q. Wilson, *American Politics, Then and Now* (Washington, DC: AEI Press, 2010). Wilson noted that "[once] the 'legitimacy barrier' has fallen, political conflict takes a very different form. New programs need not await the advent of a crisis or an extraordinary majority, because no program is any longer 'new'—it is seen, rather, as merely an extension, a modification, or an enlargement of something the government is already doing." We will see evidence of this argument in the remainder of this chapter.

12. We do not mean by the term "stealth government" what a number of scholars mean by the term "stealth democracy." The latter term was popularized by John R. Hibbing and Elizabeth Theiss-Morse in *Stealth Democracy: Americans' Beliefs About How Government Should Work* (New York: Cambridge University Press, 2002). Hibbing and Theiss-Morse argue that Americans show, in opinion polls, a preference for having decisions made by "experts" (including in some cases "business people") rather than by politicians. We don't for a moment doubt that people would rather have decisions made by those who know what they are doing rather than by amateurs—provided those decisions have a clear basis in the law. What we have in mind is a type of decision making that is deliberately opaque and that frequently pays no attention to the law.

13. On the difficulties in implementing policy see Jeffrey Pressman and Aaron Wildavsky, *Policy Implementation*, 3rd ed. (Berkeley: University of California Press, 1984). See also Martin Levin and Barbara Ferman, "The Political Hand: Policy Implementation and Youth Employment Programs," *Journal of Policy Analysis and Management* 5, no. 2 (1986): 311–325.

14. Helping the mentally ill is made all the more difficult because of judicial rulings that insist, essentially, that the mentally ill have a constitutionally protected "right" not to be helped. See Wyatt v. Stickney, 325 F. Supp. 781 (M.D. Ala. 1971), 334 F. Supp. 1341 (M.D. Ala. 1971, 344 F. Supp. 373 (M. D. Ala. 1971), sub nom Wyatt v. Aderholt, 503 F. 2d 10305 (5th Cir. 1974), https://mentalillnesspolicy.orfg/legal/wyatt-stickney-right-treatment.html. See also O'Connor v. Donaldson, 422 U.S. 563 (1975), Addington v. Texas, 441 U.S. 418 (1979). Read more at https://mentalillnesspolicy.org/legal/mental-illness-supreme-court .html. These cases call to mind the caustic observation by Anatole France: "The law, in its majestic equality, forbids rich and poor alike to sleep under bridges, to beg in the streets, and to steal their bread." It is a good example of how loose talk about "rights" can do more harm than good.

15. "What is TANF?," hhs.gov, https://hhs.gov/answers/programs-for-families-and-chil dren/what/is/tanf/index.html (accessed August 6, 2023).

16. There is evidence that weakening of the TANF law is undermining these salutary

developments. See Lawrence Mead, "Are Work Requirements Dead?," National Affairs 49 (Fall 2021), https://www.nationalaffairs.com/publications/detail/are-work-requirements -dead.

17. Robert Doar, "TANF Has Been a Success, Let's Make It Better," American Enterprise Institute, September 29, 2015, https://www.aei.org/articles/tanf-has-been-a-success-lets -make-it-better/.

18. The most influential study of the New Deal remains the second and third volumes of Arthur Schlesinger Jr., *Age of Roosevelt: The Coming of the New Deal* (Boston: Houghton Mifflin, 1958), and *The Politics of Upheaval* (Boston: Houghton Mifflin, 1960). See also William Leuchtenburg, *Franklin D. Roosevelt and the New Deal: 1932–1940* (New York: Harper & Row, 1963). The new standard narrative is considered to be David Kennedy's magisterial *Freedom from Fear: The American People in Depression and War, 1929–1945* (Oxford: Oxford University Press, 1999). For less hagiographic accounts see Alonzo Hamby, "The New Deal: Avenues for Reconsideration," *Polity* 31, no. 4 (Summer 1999): 665–681; and Amity Schlaes, *The Forgotten Man: A New History of the Great Depression* (New York: Harper Collins, 2007), 239–245.

19. The classic study of the early period in the history of American infrastructure is George R. Taylor, *The Transportation Revolution: 1815–1860*, Vol. 4: *Economic History of the United States* (New York: Harper & Row, 1951). For a modern examination of American infrastructural history see Henry Petroski, *The Road Taken: The History and Future of America's Infrastructure* (London: Bloomsbury, 2016).

20. On the origins and success of the TVA see David Lilienthal, *TVA: Democracy on the March* (Westport, CT: Greenwood Press, 1977 [1944]). The non-infrastructure aspects of the TVA have come in for trenchant criticism. See the classic study by Philip Selznick, *TVA and the Grass Roots: A Study in the Sociology of Formal Organization* (Berkeley: University of California Press, 1949).

21. Northwest Power and Conservation Council, "Grand Coulee Dam: History and Purpose," https://www.nwcouncil.org/reports/columbia-river-history/grandcouleehistory (accessed August 6, 2023).

22. *Electrifying Rural America*, Federal Reserve Bank of Richmond Economic Focus, https://richmondfed.org/publications/research/econ_focus/2020/q1/economic_history (accessed July 6, 2023); Tennessee Valley Authority, *TVA at a Glance*, https://www.tva.com /about-tva/tva-at-a-glance (accessed July 6, 2023); Lilienthal, *TVA*; Bureau of Reclamation, *Grand Coulee Dam: Statistics and Facts*, https://www.usbr.gov/pn/grandcoulee/pubs/fact sheet.pdf (accessed July 6, 2023); and NRECA, *The Electric Cooperative Story*, https://www .eletric.coop/our-organization/history (accessed July 6, 2023).

23. Clark C. Spence, "Early Uses of Electricity in Agriculture," *Technology and Culture* 3, no. 2 (Spring 1962): 153–154.

24. For a detailed discussion of the act, and the National Industrial Recovery Administration that it created, see Ellis Hawley, *The New Deal and the Problem of Monopoly* (Princeton, NJ: Princeton University Press, 1966).

25. A.L.A. Schechter Poultry Corporation v. United States, 295 U.S. 495 (1935). Amity Schlaes has a lively and informative discussion of this case in *The Forgotten Man*, 239–245.

26. Alvin Hansen, "Economic Progress and Declining Population Growth," *American Economic Review* 29, no. 1 (March 1939): 1–15.

27. Although it did bear some uncomfortable resemblances to fascism. Rexford Tugwell expressed admiration for what he perceived to be Benito Mussolini's similar efforts in Italy to merge the corporate and the governmental order, and Mussolini returned the favor, speaking admiringly about how the Americans were copying his ideas. James Q. Witman, "Of Corporatism, Fascism, and the First New Deal," *Journal of Comparative Law* 39, no. 4 (Autumn 1991): 747–778.

28. The most important constitutional case challenging the early New Deal was A. L. A. Schechter Poultry Corp. v. United States (295 US 495, 1935). This decision struck down the National Industrial Recovery Act, the centerpiece of the Roosevelt administration's plan to combat the Depression.

29. As we discussed in chapter 2, during the 1930s both American and foreign tariff policies severely distorted the international grain market, including the market for American farm products. This made propping up farm prices with mandatory crop reductions a tempting alternative. See Alfred E. Eckes Jr., *Opening America's Market: U.S. Foreign Trade Policy since 1776* (Chapel Hill: University of North Carolina Press, 1995), 100–103.

30. United States v. Butler, 297 U.S. 1, 1936.

31. For an extended consideration of the court-packing controversy see William E. Leuchtenburg, *The Supreme Court Reborn: The Constitutional Revolution in the Age of Roosevelt* (New York: Oxford University Press, 1995).

32. Wickard v. Filburn, 317 U.S. 111, 1936 (https://supreme.justia.com/cases/federal/us /317/111/).

33. United States v. Lopez, 514 U.S. 549 (1995).

34. Sidney Milkis, *The President and the Parties* (New York: Oxford University Press, 1993).

35. Franklin D. Roosevelt, "Fireside Chat 7: On the Works Relief Program and Social Security Act," Miller Center, University of Virginia. See also *The Fireside Chats of Franklin Delano Roosevelt* (Madrid: Hardpress Publishing, 2016).

36. Statista.com, "Share of Old Age Population (65 years and older) in the Total U.S. Population from 1950 to 2050," January 20, 2021; Social Security Administration, https:// www.ssa.gov/history/lifeexpect.html (accessed July 6, 2023). See also William Saletan, "Bygone Age: Old age Is Changing. So Should Social Security," *Slate*, March 18, 2006, https:// slate.com/technology/2006/03/old-age-is-changing-so-should-social-security.html.

37. Committee for a Responsible Federal Budget, *Analysis of the 2020 Social Security Trustees' Report*, April 22, 2020 crfb.org.

38. NLRA, 209 U.S.C. §§ 151–169; see also National Labor Relations Act, nlrb.gov; and Harry A. Mills, *From the Wagner Act to Taft-Hartley: A Study of National Labor Policy and Labor Relations* (Chicago: University of Chicago Press, 1999 [1950]).

39. Carolyn Puckett, "Administering Social Security: Challenges Yesterday and Today," *Social Security Bulletin* 70, no. 3 (2010), https://www.ssa.gov/policy/docs/ssb/v70n3 /v70n3p27.html.

40. Wilson, "American Politics, Then and Now." See also Mary Ann Glendon, *Rights Talk: The Impoverishment of Political Discourse* (Detroit: Free Press, 1993).

41. F. A. Hayek, "The Use of Knowledge in Society," *American Economic Review* 35, no. 4 (September 1945): 519–530. See also Hawley, *The New Deal and Monopoly.* On the various theoretical and practical obstacles to planning in general and government planning in particular see Bertrand de Jouvenel, *The Art of Conjecture* (New York: Basic Books, 1967).

42. "1966 Elections—A Major Republican Comeback," *CQ Almanac,* 1966, https://li brary.cqpress.com/cqalmanac/document.php?id=cqal66–1299950.

43. On Kennedy administration policies and politics as precursors to the Great Society see especially Robert Caro, *The Passage of Power: The Years of Lyndon Johnson,* vol. 4 (New York: Vintage Books, 2012.) On the Great Society itself see James T. Patterson, *Grand Expectations: The United States, 1945–1974* (New York: Oxford University Press, 1996); and Doris Kearns Goodwin, *Lyndon Johnson and the American Dream* (New York: St. Martin's Press, 1975). See also the splendid essays in Sidney Milkis and James Mileur, eds., *The Great Society and the High Tide of Liberalism* (Amherst: University of Massachusetts Press, 2005). For a revisionist view see Schlaes, *Great Society.*

44. US Department of Labor, "Eras of the New Frontier and the Great Society, 1961–1969," https://www.dol.gov/general/aboutdol/history/dolchp06a (accessed July 6, 2023). See also John Dickerson, "Kennedycare: Fifty Years before Obamacare, JFK Had His Own Health Care Debacle," *Slate,* November 2013, https://slate.com/news-and-politics/2013/11 /john-f-kennedys-health-care-failure-jfk-and-barack-obamas-tough-fights-to-reform -health-care.html.

45. Daniel Patrick Moynihan, *Maximum Feasible Misunderstanding: Community Action in the War on Poverty* (New York: Free Press, 1969).

46. Representative of this genre were Robert Nisbet's *The Quest for Community* (Oxford: Oxford University Press, 1953); and Paul Goodman's *Growing Up Absurd* (New York: Random House, 1960).

47. Moynihan, *Maximum Feasible Misunderstanding,* ch. 3. The *Port Huron Statement* is available at https://www.americanyawp.com/reader/27-the-sixties/the-port-huron-state ment-1962/ Manifestos/SDS_Port_Huron.html (accessed July 23, 2023).

48. Public attention to the widespread existence of poverty was galvanized by Michael Harrington, *The Other America: Poverty in America* (New York: Simon & Schuster, 1962).

49. Caro, *The Passage of Power.* The seminal work on civil rights and the Great Society is Hugh Davis Graham, *The Civil Rights Era: Origins and Development of National Policy, 1960–1972* (New York: Oxford University Press, 1990).

50. Christopher Caldwell, *The Age of Entitlement: America since the Sixties* (New York: Simon & Schuster, 2020), 22.

51. Caldwell, *Age of Enlightenment.*

52. Civil Rights Act of 1964, Section 701G.

53. Lyndon B. Johnson, Commencement Address at the University of Michigan, May 22, 1964, Miller Center, UVA, https://millercenter.org/the-presidency/presidential-speeches /may-22–1964-remarks-university-michigan (accessed July 6, 2023).

54. George Washington, Annual Message to Congress, 1790, https://www.mountvernon
.org/education/primary-sources/state-of-the-union-address (accessed July 6, 2023).

55. Northwest Ordinance (1787), https://www.archives.gov/milestone-documents
/northwest-ordinance (accessed July 6, 2023).

56. Jason Barnosky, "The Violent Years: Responses to Juvenile Crime in the 1950s," *Polity*
38, no. 3 (July 2006): 314–344.

57. LBJ, Commencement address, University of Michigan.

58. See, for example, Erik Fromm, *Escape from Freedom* (New York: Henry Holt, 1941);
and Sloan Wilson, *The Man in the Grey Flannel Suit* (New York: Pocket Books, 1956).

59. *Port Huron Statement.*

60. President Lyndon B. Johnson, "To Fulfill These Rights: Commencement Address
at Howard University," June 4, 1965, https://teachingamericanhistory.org/document/com
mencement-address-at-howard-university-to-fulfill-these-rights/ (accessed July 6, 2023).

61. US Department of Labor, Office of Contract Compliance, Executive Order 11246,
https://www.dol.gov/agencies/ofccp/executive-order-11246/regulations (accessed July 6,
2023).

62. *The Negro Family: The Case for National Action* (commonly known as the Moyni-
han Report), Office of Policy Planning and Research, United States Department of Labor,
March 1965, https://www.dol.gov/general/aboutdol/history/webid-moynihan (accessed
July 6, 2023).

63. The Social Security Amendments of 1965, Sec. 1843. Pub. L. 89–97, 79 Stat. 286, enacted July 30, 1965.

64. Elementary and Secondary School Act of 1965, https://www.federalregister.gov/do
cuments/2016/11/29/2016–27985/elementary-and-secondary-education-act-of-1965-as
-amended-by-the-every-student-succeeds-act—accountabilty and state plans (accessed
July 6, 2023).

65. Congressional Research Service, "Federal Grants to State and Local Governments:
A Historical Perspective on Contemporary Issues," https://fas.org/sgp/crs/misc/R40638.pdf
(accessed July 6, 2023).

66. Congressional Research Service, "Federal Grants," 21.

67. Martha J. Bailey and Nicolas J. Duquette, "How Johnson Fought the War on Poverty:
The Economics and Politics of Funding at the Office of Economic Opportunity," *Journal of
Economic History* 74, no. 2 (June 2014): 351–388. See also Schlaes, *Great Society.*

68. Lillian Rubin, "Maximum Feasible Participation: The Origins, Implications, and
Present Status," *Annals of the American Academy of Political and Social Science*, September 1969, https://journals.sagepub.com/doi/10.1177/000271626938500103 (accessed July 6,
2023).

69. Donald H. Haider, "Governors and Mayors View the Poverty Program," *Current
History* 61, no. 363 (November 1971): 273–278, 302–303. See also "Mayor Daley on the Community Action Program," UVA Miller Center, December 24, 1965.

70. Social Security Amendments of 1965.

71. On the different meanings of Affirmative Action see Urofsky, *The Affirmative Action
Puzzle.*

72. On the unabashed persistence of quotas despite court decisions see "Quotas Are a Quick Fix, but Companies Must Dig Deeper," *World Economic Forum*, January 2020. See also Akhil Amar and Neal Kumar Katyal, *Bakke's Fate*, UCLA Law Review 43 (1996), 1745.

73. However, Richard Sander and Stuart Taylor trenchantly argue that, on the whole, affirmative action has done more harm than good. See *Mismatch: How Affirmative Action Hurts Students It's Intended to Help, and Why Universities Won't Admit It* (New York: Basic Books, 2012).

74. Kurt Vonnegut, "Harrison Bergeron," in Steve Hallworth, ed., *Norton Anthology of Literature* (New York: Norton, 1968). Randall Kennedy makes an impressive argument in favor of affirmative action, in *For Discrimination: Race, Affirmative Action, and the Law* (New York, Pantheon Books, 2013).

75. NPR, "Majority of White Americans Say They Believe Whites Face Discrimination," October 24, 2017, https://www.npr.org/2017/10/24/559604836/majority-of-white-americans -think-theyre-discriminated-against.

76. James Pethokoukis, "Tallying the Costs and Benefits of LBJ's Great Society," *AEIdeas*, April 4, 2016, https://www.aei.org/economics/public-economics/tallying-the-costs -and-benefits-of-lbjs-great-society/0.

77. Congressional Research Service, "Medicare Insolvency Projections," updated May 29, 2020, https://fas.org/sgp/crs/misc/RS20946.pdf.

78. Kaiser Foundation, "Federal and State Share of Medicaid Spending, FY 2020."

79. Georgetown Health Policy Institute, "Medicaid and State Budgets: Check- ing the Facts (Yet Again)," February 28, 2019, https://ccf.georgetown.edu/2019/02/28 /medicaid-and-state-budgets-checking-the-facts-yet-again/.

80. "Free money" is also one reason for the inflation of health-care costs. In this way it is exactly like the pattern seen in home prices and the cost of a college degree, both of which escalated sharply after Congress made borrowing easier.

81. See Sidney Milkis, *Theodore Roosevelt, the Progressive Party, and the Transformation of American Democracy* (Lawrence: University Press of Kansas, 2009).

82. Humphrey, of course, was a famous reformer during his pre–White House career, but this counted little with the demonstrators in 1968. For firsthand accounts of the conven- tion see John Schulz, *No One Was Killed: The Democrat National Convention 1968* (Chicago: University of Chicago Press, 1998); and Normal Mailer, *Miami and the Siege of Chicago: An Informal History of the Republican and Democratic Conventions of 1968* (New York: World Publishing, 1968).

83. *The McGovern-Fraser Commission Report* (1971), available online at the Teaching American History website, https://teachingamericanhistory.org/document/mandate-for -reform-on-party-structure-and-delegate-selection/ (accessed July 6, 2023). Congressional Quarterly Press has also published an edition of the report edited by Randall Atkins, which contains the report in addition to primary documents associated with it. Randall Atkins, *The McGovern-Fraser Commission Report* (Washington: CQ Press, 1971).

84. Richard Hofstadter, *The Idea of a Party System* (Berkeley: University of California Press, 1970).

85. For impressive defenses of the old-fashioned party system see James Ceaser,

Presidential Selection (Princeton, NJ: Princeton University Press, 1979); Hofstadter, *The Idea of a Party System*; and Wilson C. McWilliams, "Political Parties as Civic Associations," in Patrick Deneen and Susan McWilliams, eds., *Redeeming Democracy in America* (Lawrence: University Press of Kansas, 2011). See also Byron Shafer and Regina Wagner, *The Long War Over Party Structure: Democratic Representation and Policy Responsiveness in American Politics* (Cambridge: Cambridge University Press, 2019).

86. Tevi Troy, "Evolution of Party Conventions," *National Affairs*, no. 49 (Fall 2021), https://www.nationalaffairs.com/publications/detail/the-evolution-of-party-conventions.

87. Shafer and Wagner, *The Long War Over Party Structure*.

88. Milton Rakove, *Don't Make No Wave, Don't Back No Losers: An Insider's Analysis of the Daley Machine* (Bloomington: Indiana University Press, 1976).

89. See Byron E. Shafer, *Quiet Revolution: The Struggle for the Democratic Party and the Shaping of Post-Reform Politics* (New York: Russell Sage Foundation, 1983).

90. Michael J. Malbin, *The Election after Reform: Money, Politics, and the Bipartisan Campaign Reform Act* (Lanham, MD: Rowman & Littlefield, 2006); and David B. Magleby and Anthony Corrado, *Financing the 2008 Election: Assessing Reform* (Washington, DC: Brookings Institution Press, 2011).

91. Open Secrets, "Total Cost of Election (1998–2020)," https://www.opensecrets.org/elections-overview/cost-of-election?cycle=2020&display=T&infl=N (accessed July 6, 2023).

92. Shafer and Wagner, *The Long War Over Party Structure*.

93. Moynihan, *Maximum Feasible Misunderstanding*.

94. Heritage Foundation, *The War on Poverty after 50 Years*, September 2014, https://www.heritage.org/poverty-and-inequality/report/the-war-poverty-after-50-years (accessed July 6, 2023).

95. "The Great Society at 50," *Washington Post*, https://www.washingtonpost.com/wp-srv/special/national/great-society-at-50/. See also "War on Poverty at 50—Despite Trillions Spent, Poverty Won," CATO Institute, https://www.cato.org/commentary/war-poverty-50-despite-trillions-spent-poverty-won (accessed July 6, 2023). The CATO Institute's figures are slightly different, but its conclusion is just as bleak: "Over the last 50 years, the government spent more than $16 trillion to fight poverty. Yet today, 15 percent of Americans still live in poverty. That's scarcely better than the 19 percent living in poverty at the time of Johnson's speech. Nearly 22 percent of children live in poverty today. In 1964, it was 23 percent."

96. U.S. Government Spending: US Education Spending History from 1900, http://www.usgovernmentspending.com/education_spending (accessed July 6, 2023).

97. This was the assertion in an address Bill Gates gave before the nation's governors in December 2011. Gates pointed out that while spending from all sources on public education has continued to rise, test results have remained flat. "Flip the Curve: Student Achievement vs. School Budgets," *HuffPost Latest News*, https://www.huffpost.com/entry/bill-gates-school-performance_b_829771.

98. Diane Ravitch and Tom Loveless, "Broken Promises: What the Federal Government Can Do to Improve American Education," *Brookings Review*. 18, no. 2 (March 1, 2000): 18–21.

99. Sean Reardon et al., "Is Separate Still Unequal? New Evidence on School Segregation and Racial Academic Achievement Gaps," *Stanford Center for Education Policy Analysis* (2022). See also Michael Metrilli and Brandon Wright, "America's Mediocre Test Scores," *Education Next*, 2019, https://www.educationnext.org/americas-mediocre-test-scores-education-poverty-crisis/.

100. Despite the similarities in nomenclature, Suzanne Mettler makes a very different and provocative argument in *The Submerged State: How Invisible Government Policies Undermine American Democracy* (Chicago: Chicago University Press, 2011).

101. Christopher DeMuth, "The Bucks Start Here: The Administrative State Doesn't Go Broke by Accident," *Claremont Review of Books* 13, no. 3 (Summer 2013).

102. Mark and Nicole Crain, *The Cost of Federal Regulation to the U.S. Economy: Manufacturing and Small Business. A Report of the National Association of Manufacturers*, September 10, 2014, https://www.nam.org/wp-content/uploads/2019/05/Federal-Regulation-Full-Study.pdf. See also Clyde Wayne Crews Jr., "Trump Administration Releases Updated Regulatory Cost-Benefit Report," *Forbes*, March 6, 2018, https://www.forbes.com/sites/waynecrews/2018/03/06/trump-administration-releases-updated-regulatory-cost-benefit-report/#6d993f9b5de5.

103. General Accountability Office, *America's Fiscal Future*, https://www.gao.gov/americas_fiscal_future? (accessed July 6, 2023); Federal Reserve Bank of St. Louis, *Federal Debt Held by the Public as a Percentage of GDP*, https://fred.stlouisfed.org/series/FYGFGDQ188S (accessed July 6, 2023).

104. DeMuth, "The Bucks Start Here."

105. Avik Roy, "Bitcoin and the Fiscal Reckoning," *National Affairs*, no. 49 (Fall 2021): 71–86.

106. Roy, "Bitcoin."

107. See also Tami Luhby, Katie Lobosco, and Kate Sullivan, "Here's What's in Biden's Infrastructure Proposal," CNN, April 21, 2021, https://www.cnn.com/2021/03/31/politics/infrastructure-proposal-biden-explainer/index.html (accessed July 6, 2023).

108. Geoff Colvin, "How Much Infrastructure Is in Biden's Infrastructure Proposal?," *Fortune*, April 6, 2021, https://fortune.com/2021/04/06/biden-infrastructure-plan-what-is-in-it-policy-proposal/.

109. James Capretta, "The Financial Hole for Social Security and Medicare Is Even Deeper Than the Experts Say." Market Watch, June 15, 2018, https://www.marketwatch.com/story/the-financial-hole-for-social-security-and-medicare-is-even-deeper-than-the-experts-say-2018-06-15.

110. Shep Melnick, "The Odd Evolution of the Civil Rights State," *Harvard Journal of Law and Public Policy* 37, no. 1 (2014): 114–134.

111. Melnick, "Odd Evolution," 125.

112. Melnick, "Odd Evolution," 125.

113. Melnick, "Odd Evolution," 126.

114. Melnick, "Odd Evolution," 126–127.

115. Melnick, "Odd Evolution," 127–131.

116. Melnick, "Odd Evolution," 96.

117. Environmental Protection Agency, "Criteria Air Pollutants," https://www.epa.gov/criteria-air-pollutants (accessed July 6, 2023).

118. Environmental Protection Agency, "EPA Denies Petition to Regulate Greenhouse Gas Emissions from Motor Vehicles," August 28, 2003.

119. Massachusetts v. Environmental Protection Agency, 549 U.S. 497 (2006), https://www.oyez.org/cases/2006/05–1120 (accessed July 6, 2023).

120. "Obama Unveils Historic Rules to Reduce Coal Pollution by 30%," *Guardian*, June 2, 2014, https://www.theguardian.com/environment/2014/jun/02/obama-rules-coal-climate-change. See also Columbia Law School, Columbia Climate School, Sabin Center for Climate Change Regulation Database, *New Source Performance Standards for GHG Emissions from Electric Generating Units*, https://climate.law.columbia.edu/content/regulation-database-new-source-performance-standards-ghg-emissions-electric-generating (accessed July 6, 2023).

121. The decision was based on Section 7411 of the Clean Air Act, which gives the EPA the power to determine the "best system of emission reduction" for buildings that emit air pollutants. That provision, the Trump administration contended, only allows the EPA to implement measures that apply to the physical premises of a power plant, rather than the kind of industry-wide measures included in the CPP. See Amy Howe, "Supreme Court Curtails EPA's Authority to Fight Climate Change," *Scotus Blog*, June 30, 2022, https://www.scotusblog.com/2022/06/supreme-court-curtails-epas-authority-to-fight-climate-change/.

122. The Trump administration crafted a less draconian plan, but it was vacated by the Federal Appeals Court for the District of Columbia. See Steven Mufson, "Federal Court Scraps Trump Administration's Power Plant Rule," *Washington Post*, January 19, 2021, https://www.wsj.com/articles/appeals-court-vacates-federal-rules-on-greenhouse-gas-emissions-at-power-plants-11611073318.

123. West Virginia et al. v. Environmental Protection Agency et al. Certiorari to the United States Court of Appeals for the District of Columbia, Circuit No. 20–1530. Argued February 28, 2022, and decided June 30, 2022.

124. Howe, "Supreme Court Curtails EPA's Authority."

125. Environmental Protection Agency, https://www.epa.gov/laws-regulations/summary-clean-water-act (accessed July 6, 2023).

126. Environmental Protection Agency, "Navigable Waters," https://www.epa.gov/wotus/about-waters-united-states (accessed July 6, 2023).

127. *Vox*, February 28, 2017, https://www.vox.com/energy-and-environment/2017/2/28/14761236/wotus-waters-united-states-rule-trump; EPonline, January 21, 2020, https://eponline.com/Articles/2020/01/21/The-Clean-Water-Regulations-of-2015-are-No-Longer-Thanks-to-the-EPA.aspx?Page=4.

128. For a study of this controversy that is highly critical of the efforts to construct the dam, see Zygmund J. B. Plater, *The Snail Darter and the Dam* (New Haven, CT: Yale University Press, 2014).

129. Robert Gordon, *Take It Back: Extending the Endangered Species Act's "Take" Prohibition to All Threatened Animals Is Bad for Conservation*, Heritage Foundation Regulatory

Report, https://www.heritage.org/government-regulation/report/take-it-back-extending
-the-endangered-species-acts-take-prohibition (accessed July 6, 2023).

130. Jonathan H. Adler, "Bad for Your Land, Bad for the Critters," *Wall Street Journal*, December 31, 2003, https://www.wsj.com/articles/SB107283504618484600.

131. Gordon, *Take It Back*.

132. For a fuller discussion of this phenomenon, see Helen Andrews, "The Law That Ate the Constitution," *Claremont Review of Books* 20, no. 1 (Winter 2019–2020).

133. Milkis, *The President and the Parties*.

134. "Trump Declares a National Emergency, and Provokes a Constitutional Clash," *New York Times*, February 15, 2019, https://www.nytimes.com/2019/02/15/us/politics/nation al-emergency-trump.html.

135. Philip A. Wallach, "An Opportune Moment for Regulatory Reform," Center for Effective Public Management at Brookings, https://www.brookings.edu/wp-content/up loads/2016/06/Opportune-Moment-for-Regulatory-Reform_Wallach.pdf (accessed July 6, 2023); Phillip A. Wallach, "Losing Hold of Reins: How Republicans' Attempts to Cut Back on Regulation Has Impeded Congress's Ability to Assert Itself," *Brookings*, May 2, 2019, https://www.brookings.edu/research/losing-hold-of-the-reins/.

136. Michael Kammen, *A Machine That Would Go of Itself: The Constitution in American Culture* (New York: Knopf, 1986).

CHAPTER 5: THINKING CONSTITUTIONALLY

1. Hamilton argued at the Constitutional Convention that an elected executive would have, "as the object of his ambition . . . to prolong his power, . . . to evade or refuse a degradation from his place. An Executive for life has not this motive for forgetting his fidelity, and will therefore be a safer depository of power." James Madison, *Notes of Debates in the Federal Convention of 1787* (New York: W. W. Norton, 1987), 137.

2. Wendell Cox, "America Is More Small-Town Than We Think," *New Geography*, September 10, 2008, https://www.Newgeography.Com/Content/00242-America-More-Small -Town-We-Think. Roughly 76 percent of the approximately 19,500 incorporated municipalities have fewer than five thousand people. *America: A Nation of Small Towns*, US Census Bureau, May 21, 2020, https://www.census.gov/library/stories/2020/05/america-a-nation-of -small-towns.html.

3. Alexander Hamilton, John Jay, and James Madison, *The Federalist: A Commentary on the Constitution of the United States*, ed. Robert Scigliano (New York: Modern Library, 2000). See also David Epstein's fine explication of "honorable determination" in *The Political Theory of the Federalist* (Chicago: University of Chicago Press, 1984), 119–120.

4. "The institutions of a township are to freedom what primary schools are to science; they put it within reach of the people; they make them taste its peaceful employ and habituate them to making use of it." Alexis de Tocqueville, *Democracy in America*, trans. Harvey C. Mansfield Jr. and Delba Winthrop (Chicago: University of Chicago Press, 2000), 57.

5. US Census Bureau, *Living Longer: Historical and Projected Life Expectancy in the United States*, 1960 to 2060, https://www.census.gov/content/dam/Census/library/publications/2020/demo/p25–1145.pdf (accessed July 6, 2023).

6. Since 1980 the wage gap between men and women has declined by 20 percent; for women between the ages of 25–34 the gap has declined to 7 percent. Although no progress was recorded in 2020, the trend line is unambiguously clear. Amanda Barroso and Anna Brown, "Gender Pay Gap in U.S. Held Steady in 2020," Pew Research Center, May 25, 2021, https://www.pewresearch.org/fact-tank/2021/05/25/gender-pay-gap-facts/.

7. Because many research reports and media discussions focus on the gap between white and Black measures of progress, they underplay the remarkable absolute progress Blacks have made. A good example of this one-sided reporting is the Pew Center's *Demographic Trends and Economic Well-Being*, which documents major and relatively rapid improvements in African American high school and college graduation rates and median income. Yet the tone remains dour and pessimistic because in these instances the gap between whites and Blacks has not lessened; https://www.pewresearch.org/social-trends/2016/06/27/1-demographic-trends-and-economic-well-being/ (accessed July 6, 2023). For similar across-the-aboard positive findings when measured in absolute rather than relative terms see Janelle Jones, John Schmitt, and Valerie Wilson, *50 Years after The Kerner Commission: African Americans Are Better Off in Many Ways but Are Still Disadvantaged by Racial Inequality*, Economic Policy Institute, February 26, 2018, https://www.epi.org/publication/50-years-after-the-kerner-commission.

8. Between 1970 and 2019, the combined emissions of the six disease-causing "criteria" pollutants that form the heart of the Clean Air Act (PM2.5 and PM10, SO2, NOx, VOCs, CO, and Pb) dropped by 77 percent and the rate of progress remained steady throughout this time frame even as economic growth rose throughout this period. Environmental Protection Agency, Air Trends Report: Economic Growth with Cleaner Air, 2020, https://gispub.epa.gov/air/trendsreport/2020/#growth. Water quality has also steadily and dramatically improved over the past fifty years. General Accountability Office, Water Quality and Protection, 2021, https://www.gao.gov/water-quality-and-protection. Of course, not all measurable conditions are improving. In some metropolitan areas housing has become terribly scarce, but that problem is the result of excessive zoning rules and constrictive environmental regulation, not the Constitution. Climate change is a serious matter—although the often-hysterical treatment it receives in much of the media is nothing short of apocalypse abuse. These scare stories are based on far-fetched scenarios, which are themselves based on false assumptions. Thus, their authors deprive themselves of a sober basis upon which to consider what combination of emissions reductions and mitigation efforts would be most prudent. If indeed the overall impact of climate change amelioration is to reduce worldwide GNP, that negative outcome must be measured against the benefits accruing to a more stable climate—especially since economic disruptions are likely to effect the global poor more quickly, and more seriously, than anyone living in the most developed economies. Likewise, critics and activists fail to consider the benefits that warming brings, including opening up northern regions to longer growing seasons, reduced deaths from exposure to frigid temperatures, and improved arctic navigation. Of course, such utilitarian calculations would

be immoral if the earth's very future were in danger, as so many headlines scream. But as theoretical physicist Steven E. Koonin—who served as the chief scientist of the Department of Energy under President Obama—bluntly states, the problem of climate change is "the apocalypse that ain't." Steven E. Koonin, *Unsettled: What Climate Science Tells Us and Why It Matters* (New York: Penguin Random House, 2021). See also Oren Cass, "Overheated: How Flawed Analyses Over-Estimate the Costs of Climate Change," Manhattan Institute, March 11, 2018, https://www.manhattan-institute.org/html/overheated-how-flawed-analyses-over estimate-costs-climate-change-10986.html; and Oren Cass, "How to Worry about Climate Change" *National Affairs*, Winter 2017, https://www.nationalaffairs.com/publications/detail /how-to-worry-about-climate-change. For a critique of the various scenarios from which alarmists derive their headlines see Zeke Hausfather and Glen P. Peters, "Emissions—the 'Business as Usual' Story Is Misleading." *Nature*, January 2020, https://www.nature.com /articles/d41586-020-00177-3#author-1. See also Matthew G. Burgess, Justin Ritchie, John Shapland, and Roger Pielke Jr., "IPCC Baseline Scenarios Have Over-Projected CO2 Emissions and Economic Growth," Environmental Research Letters

9. US Census Bureau, Historical Reported Voting Rates, https://www.census.gov/li brary/visualizations/time-series/demo/voting-historical-time-series.html (accessed August 4, 2023).

10. Anita C. Kumar, "Biden Begins Selling His \$4T Spending Plans," *Politico*, April 2021, https://www.politico.com/news/2021/04/29/biden-4-trillion-spending-plan-485055; *Build Back Better: Joe Biden's Jobs and Economic Recovery Plan for Working Families*, https://joe biden.com/build-back-better/ (accessed August 4, 2023).

11. Committee for a Responsible Federal Budget, "CBO Scores the Build Back Better Act," December 17, 2021, https://www.crfb.org/blogs/cbo-scores-build-back-better.act.

12. Remember that the hallmark act of the New Deal, Social Security, passed with a resounding bipartisan majority. Likewise, LBJ obtained passage of the 1964 Civil Rights Act only after painstaking negotiations with the Republican Minority Leader, Everett Dirksen.

13. Committee for a Responsible Federal Budget, "What's in the Inflation Reduction Act?," July 28, 2022, https://www.crfb.org/blogs/whats-inflaction-reduction-act.

14. The White House, Executive Order on Preventing and Combating Discrimination on the Basis of Gender Identity or Sexual Orientation, January 20 2022, https://www.whitehouse .gov/briefing-room/presidential-actions/2021/01/20/executive-order-preventing-and-combat ing-discrimination-on-basis-of-gender-identity-or-sexual-orientation/.

15. US Department of Education, Proposed Changes to Title IX Regulations, June 23, 2022, https://www.ed.gov/news/press-releases/us-department-education-releases-proposed -changes-title-ix-regulations-invites-public-comment.

16. For a penetrating discussion of the problem of mutability see Martha Derthick, "On the Mutability of American Laws," in Benjamin Wittes and Pietro Nivola, eds., *What Would Madison Do?* (Washington, DC: Brookings Institution, 2015), 129–147.

17. Tocqueville, *Democracy in America*, 52–53.

18. *GDP Per Capita*, Worldometer, https://www.worldometers.info/gdp/gdp-per-capita (accessed August 4, 2023).

19. See Sally Satel, "What Is Happening to My Profession?," *Quilette*, November 30, 2021, https://quillette.com/2021/11/30/what-is-happening-to-my-profession/.

20. The *Oxford English Dictionary* gives, as one of the definitions of "forebearance," "abstinence from enforcing what is due," and uses as an example "forgiving a debt."

21. Carroll Doherty and Jocelyn Kiley, "Key Facts About Partisanship and Political Animosity in America," June 22, 2016, https://www.pewresearch.org/fact-tank/2016/06/22/key-facts-partisanship/.

22. CATO Institute, https://www.cato.org/survey-reports/poll-62-americans-say-they-have-political-views-theyre-afraid-share (accessed August 4, 2023).

Bibliography

Aberbach, Joel, and Joel Rockman. "Mandates or Mandarins? Control and Discretion in the Modern Administrative State." *Public Administration Review* 48, 2 (March-April 1988): 606–612.

Ackroyd, Peter. *Civil War: The History of England*, vol. 3. London: Pan Macmillan, 2014.

Agresto, John, ed. *Liberty and Equality under the Constitution*. Washington, DC: American Historical Association, 1983.

———. *Rediscovering America*. Los Angeles: Asahina & Wallace, 2015.

Aldrich, John H. *Why Parties? A Second Look*. Chicago: University of Chicago Press, 2011.

Alexander, Barbara J. "Failed Cooperation under the NRA." *Journal of Economic History* 57, no. 2 (June 1997): 327.

Allen, David, and James Howell, eds. *Scientific Groupthink: Greed, Pathological Altruism, Ideology, Competition, and Culture*. Cham, Switzerland: Springer Nature, 2020.

Amar, Akhil. *The Bill of Rights: Creation and Reconstruction*. New Haven, CT: Yale University Press, 1998.

———. "Philadelphia Revisited: Amending the Constitution Outside Article V." *University of Chicago Law Review* 55, no. 4 (Fall 1988).

Anderson, Benedict. *Imagined Communities: Reflections on the Origin and Spread of Nationalism*, rev. ed. London: Verso, 2006.

Anderson, Fred. *Crucible of War: The Seven Years' War and the Fate of Empire in British North America, 1754–1766*. New York: Vintage, 2001.

Anonymous (Miles Taylor). *A Warning*. New York: Twelve, 2019.

Arcenas, Claire Rydell. *America's Philosopher: John Locke in American Intellectual Life*. Chicago: University of Chicago Press, 2022.

Aristotle. *Politics*. Translated by Ernest Barker. Oxford: Oxford University Press, 1995.

Atkins, Randall. *The McGovern-Fraser Commission Report*. Washington: CQ Press, 1971.

Atkinson, Rick. *The British Are Coming: The War for America*. New York: Holt Paperbacks, 2020.

Bailey, Jeremy. "Should We Venerate That Which We Cannot Love? James Madison on Constitutional Imperfection." *Political Research Quarterly* 65, no. 4 (December 2011): 732–744.

Bailey, Martha J., and Nicolas J. Duquette. "How Johnson Fought the War on Poverty: The Economics and Politics of Funding at the Office of Economic Opportunity." *Journal of Economic History* 74, no. 2 (June 2014): 351–388.

Baldwin, Peter. *The Narcissism of Minor Differences: How America and Europe Are Alike*. New York: Oxford University Press, 2009.

Barnosky, Jason. "The Violent Years: Responses to Juvenile Crime in the 1950s." *Polity* 38, no. 3 (July 2006): 314–344.

Barro, Robert. *Inequality, Growth and Investment*. Cambridge, MA: NBER Working Paper 7038, National Bureau of Economic Research, 1999.

Bauer, Raymond, Ithiel de Sola Pool, and Anthony Lewis Dexter. *American Business and Public Policy: The Politics of Foreign Trade*, 2nd ed. London: Routledge, 1963.

Beeman, Richard, et al. *Beyond Confederation: Origins of the Constitution and American National Identity*. Chapel Hill: University of North Carolina Press, 1987.

Beer, Samuel H. *British Politics in the Collectivist Age*. New York: Knopf, 1965.

———. *To Make a Nation: The Rediscovery of American Federalism*, 3rd ed. Cambridge, MA: Harvard University Press, 1997.

Bellah, Robert N. *The Broken Covenant: American Civil Religion in a Time of Trial*. New York: Seabury Press, 1975.

Bellamy, Edward. *Looking Backward: 2000–1887*. Las Vegas: Digibooks, 2021 [1881].

Bennett, Richard E. *We'll Find the Place: The Mormon Exodus, 1846–1848*. Norman: University of Oklahoma Press, 2009.

Bergmann, Barbara R. *In Defense of Affirmative Action*. New York: Basic Books, 1996.

Bessette, Joseph, ed. *Toward a More Perfect Union: Writings of Herbert J. Storing*. Washington, DC: AEI Press, 1995.

Boushey, Heather. *Unbound: How Inequality Constricts Our Economy and What We Can Do About It*. Cambridge, MA: Harvard University Press, 2019.

Caro, Robert. *The Passage of Power: The Years of Lyndon Johnson*, vol. 4. New York: Vintage Books, 2012.

Caldwell, Christopher. *The Age of Entitlement: America since the Sixties*. New York: Simon & Schuster, 2020.

Calvert, Greg, and Carol Neiman, eds. *The New Left*. Ann Arbor, MI: Radical Education Project, 1969.

Ceaser, James W. *Designing a Polity: America's Constitution in Theory and Practice*. Lanham, MD: Rowman & Littlefield, 2011.

———. *Presidential Selection: Theory and Development*. Princeton, NJ: Princeton University Press, 1979.

———. "Progressivism and the Doctrine of Natural Rights." *Social Philosophy and Policy* 29, no. 2 (2012): 177–195.

Chambers, William Nisbet. *Political Parties in a New Nation: The American Experience*. New York: Oxford University Press, 1963.

Charles, Joseph. *Origins of the American Party System*. New York: Harper & Row, 1961.

Chernow, Ron. *Washington: A Life*. New York: Penguin Press, 2010.

Chomsky, Noam, and Marv Waterstone. *Consequences of Capitalism: Manufacturing Discontent and Resistance*. Chicago: Haymarket Books, 2021.

Coates, Ta-Nehisi. "The Case for Reparations." *Atlantic*, June 2014, 5, 54ff.

Coby, John Patrick. "The Proportional Representation Debate at the Constitutional Convention: Why the Nationalists Lost." *American Political Thought* 7 (Spring 2018): 216–242.

Cohen, Mitchell, and Dennis Hale, *The New Student Left: An Anthology* (Boston: Beacon Press, 1966).

Connelly, William, Jr., John Pitney Jr., and Gary Schmitt. *Is Congress Broken?* Washington DC: Brookings Institution, 2017.

Cook, Brian. *The Fourth Branch: Reconstructing the Administrative State for the Commercial Republic.* Lawrence: University Press of Kansas, 2021.

Crenshaw, Kimberlé, Neil T. Gotanda, Gary Peller, and Kendall Thomas, eds. *Critical Race Theory: The Key Writings That Formed the Movement.* New York: New Press, 1996.

Croly, Herbert. *The Promise of American Life.* New York: MacMillan, 1910.

Cunningham, Noble, Jr. *The Jeffersonian Republicans: The Formation of Party Organization.* Chapel Hill: University of North Carolina Press, 1957.

Dahl, Robert. *How Democratic Is the American Constitution?* New Haven, CT: Yale University Press, 2001.

DeMuth, Christopher. "The Bucks Start Here." *Claremont Review of Books* 13, no 3 (Summer 2013).

Deneen, Patrick J. *Why Liberalism Failed.* New Haven, CT: Yale University Press, 2018.

Dexter, Anthony Lewis. *The Sociology and Politics of Congress.* Chicago: Rand McNally & Co., 1969.

Diamond, Martin. *As Far as Republican Principles Will Admit: Essays by Martin Diamond.* Edited by William Schambra. Washington, DC: American Enterprise Institute, 1992.

Dinan, John. *The American State Constitutional Tradition.* Lawrence: University Press of Kansas, 2006.

Dolbeare, Kenneth, and Michael S. Cummings, eds. *American Political Thought.* Washington, DC: CQ Press, 2010.

Douglass, Frederick. *Frederick Douglass Papers: Series One—Speeches, Debates, and Interviews.* New Haven, CT: Yale University Press, 1979.

———. *Narrative of the Life of Frederick Douglass, An American Slave.* New York: Penguin Classics, 2014.

———. "What to the Slave Is the Fourth of July?" In *Classics of American Political and Constitutional Thought*, vol. 1, 1012–1020, ed. Scott J. Hammond, Kevin R. Hardwick, and Howard L. Lubert. Indianapolis: Hackett, 2007.

Eberstadt, Nicholas. "The Future of the Work Ethic." *Claremont Review of Books* 19, no. 4 (Fall 2019).

Eckes, Alfred E., Jr. *Opening America's Market: U.S. Foreign Trade Policy since 1776.* Chapel Hill: University of North Carolina Press, 1995.

Edling, Max. *Perfecting the Union: National and State Authority in the U.S. Constitution.* New York: Oxford University Press, 2021.

Elkins, Stanley, and Eric McKitrick. *The Age of Federalism: The Early American Republic, 1788–1800.* New York: Oxford University Press, 1993.

Ellis, Richard J., ed. *Founding the American Presidency.* Lanham, MD: Rowman & Littlefield, 1999.

Epstein, David. *The Political Theory of the Federalist.* Chicago: University of Chicago Press, 1984.

Feldman, Stephen. *Pack the Court!: A Defense of Supreme Court Expansion.* Philadelphia: Temple University Press, 2021.

Ferling, John. *Adams vs. Jefferson: The Tumultuous Election of 1800.* Oxford: Oxford University Press, 2004.

Fishkin, Joseph, and William E. Forbath. *The Anti-Oligarchy Constitution: Reconstructing the Economic Foundations of American Democracy.* Cambridge, MA: Harvard University Press, 2022.

Foner, Eric *The Second Founding: How the Civil War and Reconstruction Remade the Constitution.* New York: W. W. Norton, 2019.

Freehling, William W. *The Road to Disunion: Secessionists at Bay, 1776–1854.* Oxford: Oxford University Press, 1990.

Furet, Francois. *The French Revolution: 1770–1814.* Oxford: Oxford University Press, 1996.

Glendon, Mary Ann. *Rights Talk: The Impoverishment of Political Discourse.* New York: Free Press, 1991.

Goldwin, Robert A., and William A. Schambra, eds. *How Capitalistic Is the Constitution?* Washington, DC: American Enterprise Institute, 1982.

Goodwin, Doris Kearns. *Lyndon Johnson and the American Dream.* New York: St. Martins' Press, 1975.

Gotanda, Neil T., Gary Pelle, and Kendall Thomas, eds. *Critical Race Theory: The Key Writings That Formed the Movement.* New York: New Press, 1996.

Graber, Mark. "Is Dysfunction an Illusion? Belling the Partisan Cats: Preliminary Thoughts on Identifying and Mending a Dysfunction Constitutional Order." *Boston University Law Review* 94, 3 (May 2014): 611–648.

Graham, Hugh Davis. *The Civil Rights Era: Origins and Development of National Policy, 1960–1972.* New York: Oxford University Press, 1990.

Greene, Jack P. *The Intellectual Construction of America: Exceptionalism and Identity from 1492 to 1800.* Chapel Hill: University of North Carolina Press, 1997.

———. *Interpreting Colonial America.* Charlottesville: University of Virginia Press, 1996.

Greenfield, Lisa. *Nationalism: Five Roads to Modernity.* Cambridge, MA: Harvard University Press, 1992.

Greer, Donald. *Incidence of Terror.* Cambridge, MA: Harvard University Press, 1966 [1935].

Griffin, Stephen. *Broken Trust.* Lawrence: University Press of Kansas, 2015.

Haider, Donald H. "Governors and Mayors View the Poverty Program." *Current History* 61, no. 363 (November 1971): 273–278, 302–303.

Hale, Dennis, *The Jury in America: Triumph and Decline.* Lawrence: University Press of Kansas, 2016.

———. "Mr. Dooley on Hate," *Commonweal,* December 22, 1972, 279–280.

Hamby, Alonzo. "The New Deal: Avenues for Reconsideration." *Polity* 31, no. 4 (Summer 1999): 665–681.

Hamilton, Alexander, John Jay, and James Madison. *The Federalist: A Commentary on the Constitution of the United States.* Edited by Robert Scigliano. New York: Modern Library, 2000.

Hammond, Scott J., Kevin R. Hardwick, and Howard L. Lubert, eds. *Classics of American Political and Constitutional Thought.* Indianapolis: Hackett, 2007.

Hannah-Jones, Nikole, Jake Silverstein, Caitlin Roper, and Ilena Silverman. *The 1619 Project: A New Origin Story.* New York: New York Times Co., 2021.

Hansen, Alvin. "Economic Progress and Declining Population Growth." *American Economic Review* 29, 1 (March 1939): 1–15.

Harrington, Michael. *The Other America: Poverty in America.* New York: Simon & Schuster, 1962.

Harris, Richard A., and Sidney M. Milkis. *Remaking American Politics.* Boulder, CO: Westview Press, 1989.

Hartz, Louis. *The Liberal Tradition in America: An Interpretation of American Political Thought.* New York: Harcourt, Brace, 1955.

Hawley, Ellis. *The New Deal and the Problem of Monopoly.* Princeton, NJ: Princeton University Press, 1966.

Hayek, F. A. "The Use of Knowledge in Society." *American Economic Review* 35, no. 4 (September 1945): 519–530.

Hennessy, Susan, and Benjamin Wittes. *Unmaking the Presidency: Donald Trump's War on the World's Most Powerful Office.* New York: Farrar, Straus & Giroux, 2020.

Himmelfarb, Gertrude. *The Roads to Enlightenment.* New York: Vintage, 2005.

Hobbes, Thomas. *Leviathan.* Edited by Edwin Curley. Indianapolis: Hackett, 1994.

Hofstadter, Richard. *The Idea of a Party System: The Rise of Legitimate Opposition in the United States, 1780–1840.* Berkeley: University of California Press, 1970.

Howard, Christopher. *The Hidden Welfare State: Tax Expenditures and Social Policy in the United States.* Princeton, NJ: Princeton University Press, 1997.

———. *The Welfare State Nobody Knows: Debunking Myths about U.S. Social Policy.* Princeton, NJ: Princeton University Press, 2007.

Howell, William, and Terry Moe. *Relic.* New York: Basic Books, 2016.

Huntington, Samuel P. "Political Modernization: America vs. Europe." *World Politics* 18, 3 (April 1966): 378–414.

Huq, Aziz. "Removal as a Political Question." *Stanford Law Review* 65, no. 1 (2013): 1–76.

Jaffa, Harry. *The Crisis of the House Divided: An Interpretation of the Issues in the Lincoln-Douglas Debates.* Chicago: University of Chicago Press, 2009.

Janis, Irving. *Victims of Groupthink: A Psychological Study of Policy Decisions and Fiascoes,* 2nd ed. Boston: Wadsworth, 1983.

Jefferson, Thomas. *The Papers of Thomas Jefferson,* vol. 15. Princeton, NJ: Princeton University Press, 1958.

Jones, A. H. M. *Athenian Democracy.* Baltimore: Johns Hopkins University Press, 1957.

Jones, Bryan D., Sean M. Theriault, and Michelle Whyman. *The Great Broadening: How the Vast Expansion of the Policymaking Agenda Transformed American Politics.* Chicago: Chicago University Press, 2019.

Jouvenel, Bertrand de. *The Art of Conjecture.* New York: Basic Books, 1967.

———. "The Chairman's Problem." *American Political Science Review* 55, 2 (June 1961): 368–372.

———. *The Ethics of Redistribution.* Indianapolis: Liberty Fund, 1990.

———. *On Power: Its Nature and the History of Its Growth.* Boston: Beacon Press, 1962.

———. *The Pure Theory of Politics.* New Haven, CT: Yale University Press, 1963.

———. *Sovereignty: An Inquiry into the Political Good.* Carmel, IN: Liberty Fund, 1998.

———. "Utopia for Practical Purposes," *Daedalus* 94 (Spring 1965): 437–453.

Kammen, Michael. *A Machine That Would Go of Itself: The Constitution in American Culture.* New York: Knopf, 1986.

Kelman, Steven. "Limited Government: An Incoherent Concept." *Journal of Public Policy and Management* 3, no. 1 (Autumn 1983).

Kendi, Ibram X. *Stamped from the Beginning: The Definitive History of Racist Ideas in America.* New York: Nation Books, 2016.

Kennedy, David. *Freedom from Fear: The American People in Depression and War, 1929–1945.* Oxford: Oxford University Press, 1999.

Kennedy, Randall. *For Discrimination: Race, Affirmative Action, and the Law.* New York, Pantheon Books, 2013.

Kessler, Anke. "Communication in Federal Politics: Universalism, Policy Uniformity, and the Optimal Allocation of Fiscal Authority." *Journal of Political Economy* 122, no. 4 (August 2014).

Kettl, Donald. *The Divided States of America: Why Federalism Doesn't Work.* Princeton, NJ: Princeton University Press, 2020.

Key, V. O. *Southern Politics in State and Nation.* Knoxville: University of Tennessee Press, 1949.

———, with Milton C. Cumming Jr. *The Responsible Electorate.* Cambridge, MA: Harvard University Press, 1966.

King, Anthony. *The British Constitution.* Oxford: Oxford University Press, 2007.

Kohn, Hans. *Nationalism: Its Meaning and History.* Princeton, NJ: Princeton University Press 1955.

Koonin, Steven. *Unsettled: What Climate Science Tells Us, What It Doesn't, and Why It Matters.* New York: Penguin Random House, 2021.

Kuznets, Simon. "Economic Growth and Inequality." *American Economic Review* 45, 1 (March 1955): 1–28.

Landy, Marc. "Mega-Disasters and Federalism." *Public Administration Review* 68, no. 1 (December 2008): 186–198.

Landy, Marc, and Sidney M. Milkis. *Presidential Greatness.* Lawrence: University Press of Kansas, 2000.

Landy, Marc, Marc Roberts, and Steve Thomas. *The Environmental Protection Agency: Asking the Wrong Questions.* Oxford: Oxford University Press, 1994.

Laslett, Peter. *The World We Have Lost.* Oxfordshire, UK: Routledge, 1965.

Lazare, Daniel. *The Frozen Republic: How the Constitution Is Paralyzing Democracy.* New York: Houghton Mifflin, 1996.

Lerner, Ralph. *The Thinking Revolutionary: Principle and Practice in the New Republic.* Ithaca, NY: Cornell University Press, 1987.

Leuchtenburg, William. *Franklin D. Roosevelt and the New Deal: 1932–1940.* New York: Harper & Row, 1963.

———. *The Supreme Court Reborn: The Constitutional Revolution in the Age of Roosevelt.* New York: Oxford University Press, 1995.

Levin, Martin, and Barbara Ferman. "The Political Hand: Policy Implementation and

Youth Employment Programs." *Journal of Policy Analysis and Management* 5, no. 2 (1986): 311–325.

Levinson, Sanford. *Framed: America's Fifty-One Constitutions and the Crisis of Governance.* New York: Oxford University Press, 2012.

———. *Our Undemocratic Constitution.* New York: Oxford University Press, 2006.

Levinson, Sanford, and Cynthia Levinson. *The Framers, Their Fights, and the Flaws That Affect Us Today.* Atlanta: Peachtree Publishers, 2017.

Lilienthal, David. *TVA: Democracy on the March.* Westport, CT: Greenwood Press, 1977 [1944].

Lincoln, Abraham. *Lincoln: Speeches, Letters, Miscellaneous Writings, the Lincoln-Douglas Debates.* New York: Library of America, 1989.

Locke, John. *An Essay Concerning Human Understanding.* New York: Everyman's Library, 1961.

———. *The Second Treatise of Government.* Edited by C. B. Macpherson. Indianapolis: Hackett, 1980.

Main, Thomas, ed. *Is the Constitution Obsolete?* Durham, NC: Carolina Academic Press, 2014.

McCoy, Drew R. *The Elusive Republic.* New York: W. W. Norton, 1980.

McGinnis, John O., and Michael B. Rappaport. "Supermajority Rules as a Constitutional Solution." *William and Mary Law Review* 40, no. 2 (February 1998-1999): 395–469.

McWilliams, Wilson C. *The Idea of Fraternity in America.* Berkeley: University of California Press, 1973.

———. "Parties as Civic Associations." In Susan McWilliams and Patrick Dineen, eds., *Redeeming Democracy in America.* Lawrence: University Press of Kansas, 2011.

Madison, James. *Notes on Debates in the Federal Convention of 1787.* New York: W. W. Norton, 1987.

Magleby, David B., and Anthony Corrado. *Financing the 2008 Election: Assessing Reform.* Washington, DC: Brookings Institution, 2011.

Maier, Pauline. *Ratification: The People Debate the Constitution, 1787–1788.* New York: Simon & Schuster, 2010.

Mailer, Norman. *Miami and the Siege of Chicago: An Informal History of the Republican and Democratic Conventions of 1968.* New York: World Publishing Co., 1968.

Malbin, Michael J. *The Election after Reform: Money, Politics, and the Bipartisan Campaign Reform Act.* Lanham, MD: Rowman & Littlefield, 2006.

Mansfield, Harvey C., Jr. *America's Constitutional Soul.* Baltimore: Johns Hopkins University Press, 1991.

———. *Taming the Prince: The Ambivalence of Modern Executive Power.* New York: Free Press, 1989.

Meed, Douglas V. *The Mexican War: 1846–1848.* Oxfordshire, UK: Routledge, 2005.

Melnick, R. Shep. "The Odd Evolution of the Civil Rights State." *Harvard Journal of Law and Public Policy* 37, 1 (2014): 113–134.

Mettler, Suzanne. *The Submerged State: How Invisible Government Policies Undermine American Democracy.* Chicago: Chicago University Press, 2011.

Milkis, Sidney. *Political Parties and Constitutional Government.* Baltimore: Johns Hopkins University Press, 1999.

———. *The President and the Parties.* New York: Oxford University Press, 1993.

———. *Theodore Roosevelt, the Progressive Party, and the Transformation of American Democracy.* Lawrence: University Press of Kansas, 2009.

Milkis, Sidney, and James Mileur, eds. *The Great Society and the High Tide of Liberalism.* Amherst, MA: University of Massachusetts Press, 2005.

Miller, William Lee. *Arguing about Slavery: The Great Battle in the United States Congress.* New York: Knopf, 1995.

Mills, Harry A. *From the Wagner Act to Taft-Hartley: A Study of National Labor Policy and Labor Relations.* Chicago: University of Chicago Press, 1999 [1950].

Millis, Harry A., and Emily Clark Brown. *From the Wagner Act to Taft-Hartley: A Study of National Labor Policy and Labor Relations.* Chicago: University of Chicago Press, 1950.

Montesquieu, Charles de. *Spirit of the Laws.* Cambridge: Cambridge University Press, 2002.

Moynihan, Daniel Patrick. *Maximum Feasible Misunderstanding: Community Action in the War on Poverty.* New York: Free Press, 1969.

———. *The Negro Family: The Case for National Action* (commonly known as the Moynihan Report). Office of Policy Planning and Research, United States Department of Labor, March 1965.

Mucciaroni, Garry, and Paul J. Quirk. "Deliberative Choices: Debating Public Policy in Congress." *Political Science Quarterly* 122, 1 (March 2007): 152–154.

Nordhaus, William. *A Question of Balance: Weighing the Options on Global Warming Policies.* New Haven, CT: Yale University Press, 2008.

O'Neil, Patrick H., Karl Fields, and Don Share. *Comparative Politics,* 7th ed. New York: W. W. Norton, 2021.

O'Neill, William L. *The New Left: A History.* Hoboken, NJ: Wiley-Blackwell, 2001.

Osborn, Ronald. "William Lloyd Garrison and the United States Constitution: The Political Evolution of an American Radical." *Journal of Law and Religion* 24, no. 1 (2008/2009): 65–88.

Ostrander, Gilman M. "Emerson, Thoreau, and John Brown." *Mississippi Valley Historical Review* 39, no. 4 (March 1953): 713–726.

Packer, George. *Last Best Hope.* New York: Macmillan, 2021.

Paine, Thomas. *Common Sense, The Rights of Man, and Other Essential Writings of Thomas Paine.* New York: New American Library, 1969.

Pangle, Lorraine Smith, and Thomas L. Pangle. *The Learning of Liberty: The Educational Ideas of the American Founders.* Lawrence: University Press of Kansas, 1995.

Pangle, Thomas. *The Spirit of Modern Republicanism: The Moral Vision of the American Founders and the Philosophy of John Locke.* Chicago: University of Chicago Press, 1990.

Patterson, James T. *Grand Expectations: The United States, 1945–1974.* New York: Oxford University Press, 1996.

Peterson, Merrill D. *Adams and Jefferson: A Revolutionary Dialogue.* Atlanta: University of Georgia Press, 1976.

Petroski, Henry. *The Road Taken: The History and Future of America's Infrastructure.* London: Bloomsbury, 2016.

Phillips, John A., and Charles Wetherell. "The Great Reform Act of 1832 and the Political Modernization of England." *American Historical Review* 100 (April 1995): 411–436.

Piott, Steven L. *Giving Voters a Choice: The Origins of the Statewide Initiative and Referendum in the United States.* Colombia: University of Missouri Press, 2003.

Pitkin, Hannah. *The Concept of Representation.* Berkeley: University of California Press, 1972.

Polanyi, Karl. *The Great Transformation.* New York: Farrar, 1944.

Port Huron Statement of the Students for a Democratic Society (SDS). https://www.americanyawp.com/reader/27-the-sixties/the-port-huron-statement-1962/.

Potter, David. *People of Plenty: Economic Abundance and the American Character.* Chicago: University of Chicago Press, 1954.

Pressman, Jeffrey, and Aaron Wildavsky. *Policy Implementation,* 3rd ed. Berkeley: University of California Press, 1984.

Rakove, Jack N. "James Madison and the Bill of Rights: A Broader Context," *Presidential Studies Quarterly* 22, no. 4 (Fall 1992): 667–677.

Rakove, Milton. *Don't Make No Wave, Don't Back No Losers: An Insider's Analysis of the Daley Machine.* Bloomington: Indiana University Press, 1976.

———. *We Don't Want Nobody Nobody Sent: An Oral History of the Daley Years.* Bloomington: Indiana University Press, 1979.

Ratcliffe, Donald. "The Right to Vote and the Rise of Democracy, 1787–1828." *Journal of the Early Republic* 33, no. 2 (Summer 2013): 219–254.

Reich, Robert. *The System: Who Rigged It and How to Fix It.* New York: Vintage, 2021.

Remini, Robert. *The Life of Andrew Jackson.* New York: Harpers, 1988.

Riordan, William L. *Plunkitt of Tammany Hall: A Series of Very Plain Talks on Very Practical Politics.* New York: Bedford Books/St. Martin's Press, 1993 [1905].

Robb, Graham. *The Discovery of France: A Historical Geography.* New York: W. W. Norton, 2008.

Rohr, John. *To Run a Constitution: The Legitimacy of the Administrative State.* Lawrence: University Press of Kansas, 1986.

Sander, Richard, and Stuart Taylor. *Mismatch: How Affirmative Action Hurts Students It's Intended to Help, and Why Universities Won't Admit It.* New York: Basic Books, 2012.

Schlaes, Amity. *The Forgotten Man: A New History of the Great Depression.* New York: Harper Collins, 2007.

———. *Great Society: A New History.* New York: Harper Collins, 2019.

Schlesinger, Arthur, Jr. *The Coming of the New Deal.* Boston: Houghton Mifflin, 1958.

———. *The Imperial Presidency.* Boston: Houghton Mifflin, 1973.

———. *The Politics of Upheaval.* Boston: Houghton Mifflin, 1960.

Schulz, John. *No One Was Killed: The Democrat National Convention 1968.* Chicago: University of Chicago Press, 1998.

Schwartz, Nancy. *The Blue Guitar: Political Representation and Community.* Chicago: University of Chicago Press, 1988.

Selznick, Philip. *TVA and the Grass Roots: A Study in the Sociology of Formal Organization*. Berkeley: University of California Press, 1949.

Shafer, Byron E. *Quiet Revolution: The Struggle for the Democratic Party and the Shaping of Post-Reform Politics*. New York: Russell Sage Foundation, 1983.

Shafer, Byron E., and Regina Wagner. *The Long War Over Party Structure: Democratic Representation and Policy Responsiveness in American Politics*. Cambridge: Cambridge University Press, 2019.

Silbey, Joel. *The Partisan Imperative: The Dynamics of American Politics before the Civil War*. Oxford: Oxford University Press, 1987.

Stamp, Kenneth M. *America in 1857: A Nation on the Brink*. Oxford: Oxford University Press, 1990.

Stauffer, Devin. *Hobbes' Kingdom of Light*. Chicago: University of Chicago Press, 2018.

Stiglitz, Joseph. "Inequality and Economic Growth." *Political Quarterly* 86, S1 (December 2015): 134–155.

Stoner, James. *Common Law Liberty: Rethinking American Constitutionalism*. Lawrence: University Press of Kansas, 2003.

Storing, Herbert. *What the Anti-Federalists Were For*. Chicago: University of Chicago Press, 1981.

Sundquist, James. *Dynamics of the Party System*. Washington, DC: Brookings Institution, 1973.

Sunstein, Cass, and Adrian Vermeule. *Law and Leviathan: Redeeming the Administrative State*. Cambridge, MA: Belknap Press of Harvard University Press, 2020.

Taine, Hippolyte A. *The Origins of Contemporary France*, vol. 2, *The French Revolution*. Gloucester, MA: Peter Smith, 1962 [1876]).

Taylor, George R. *The Transportation Revolution 1815–1860*. London: Routledge, 1951.

Teaford, Jon C. *The Municipal Revolution in America: 1650–1825*. Chicago: University of Chicago Press, 1975.

Theriault, Sean M. *Party Polarization in Congress: The War over Two Social Contracts*. Cambridge: Cambridge University Press, 2019.

Thoreau, Henry David. "Disobedience to Civil Government" and "Slavery in Massachusetts." In *Classics of American Political and Constitutional Thought*, vol. 1, ed. Scott J. Hammond, Kevin R. Hardwick, and Howard L. Lubert, 932–940, 1024–1030. Indianapolis: Hackett, 2007.

Tocqueville, Alexis de. *Democracy in America*. Translated by Harvey C. Mansfield Jr. and Delba Winthrop. Chicago: University of Chicago Press, 2000.

———. *The Old Regime and the French Revolution*. Translated by Stuart Gilbert. New York: Anchor Books, 1955.

Toulmin, Stephen. *Cosmopolis: The Hidden Agenda of Modernity*. Chicago: University of Chicago Press, 1992.

Tussman, Joseph. *Obligation and the Body Politic*. New York: Oxford University Press, 1960.

Urofsky, Melvin. *The Affirmative Action Puzzle: A Living History from Reconstruction to Today*. New York: Pantheon Books, 2020.

Waldo, Dwight. *The Administrative State: A Study of the Political Theory of American Public Administration.* London: Routledge, 1948.

Waldstreicher, David. *Slavery's Constitution: From Revolution to Ratification.* New York: Hill & Wang, 2009.

White, Leonard. *The Jacksonians: A Study in Administrative History, 1829–1861.* New York: Free Press.

Wilentz, Sean. *No Property in Man.* Cambridge, MA: Harvard University Press, 2018.

Will, George. *The Conservative Sensibility.* New York: Hatchett Books, 2019.

Wilson, James Q. *American Politics, Then and Now.* Washington, DC: AEI Press, 2010.

———. *Bureaucracy: What Government Agencies Do and Why They Do It.* New York: Basic Books, 1991.

Wilson, Woodrow. *Congressional Government.* Camp Road, UK Wentworth Press, 2016.

———. *The New Freedom.* New York: Doubleday, Page, 1913.

Witman, James Q. "Of Corporatism, Fascism, and the First New Deal." *Journal of Comparative Law* 39, no. 4 (Autumn 1991): 747–778.

Wittes, Benjamin, and Pietro Nivola, eds. *What Would Madison Do?* Washington, DC: Brookings Institution, 2015.

Wolf, Jacob. "Harmonizing Heaven and Earth: Democratization and Individualism in American Religion." PhD thesis, Boston College, 2020.

Wood, B. Dan, Soren Jordan, and David Hopkins. *Red Fighting Blue: How Geography and Electoral Rules Polarize American Politics.* Cambridge, MA: Cambridge University Press, 2017.

Wood, Gordon. *Creation of the American Republic, 1776–1787.* Chapel Hill: University of North Carolina Press, 1969.

———. *Empire of Liberty: A History of the Early Republic, 1789–1815.* New York: Oxford University Press, 2009.

Yarborough, Jean. *American Virtues: Thomas Jefferson on the Character of a Free People.* Lawrence: University Press of Kansas, 1998.

Zuckert, Michael. "James Madison's Consistency on the Bill of Rights." *National Affairs* 51 (Spring 2022): 154–164.

Index

Printed in the USA
CPSIA information can be obtained
at www.ICGtesting.com
CBHW021407190424
7210CB00007B/69/J

9 780700 636235